EVOLVING THE
HUMAN RACE
~ GAME ~

A Spiritual and Soul-Centered Perspective

To Joelee,
May you live with
Joy. With Heart,
Prof. Cliff
Carroy U. Ferguson
5/19/18

In *Evolving The Human Race Game: A Spiritual and Soul-Centered Perspective,* Carroy "Cuf" Ferguson invites us to deepen not only our thought process but also our experience of what it means to be human, and an evolving human in an evolving world. If we are all mirrors to one another, what we love and fear in another becomes an invitation to embrace those qualities in ourselves. Cuf Ferguson suggests that if we look underneath the more superficial, ego-based, cultural, sociological and psychological models of race (and/or the other), which focus on separateness, to a deeper spiritual and soul-centered model, we can integrate the disenfranchised parts of ourselves personally and collectively, and be co-creators in the larger evolutionary process of life.

Linda Marks
Founder of the Institute for Emotional-
Kinesthetic Psychotherapy
Author of *Living with Vision: Reclaiming the Power of the Heart* and *Healing the War Between the Genders: The Power of the Soul-Centered Relationship*
Board Co-Chair of Boys to Men New England

This is not just another book about race relations. It is about a quantum shift in our consciousness and understanding of who we are as souls. Carroy "Cuf" Ferguson's basic premise is that as souls, we each experience multiple incarnations (lifetimes) within a variety of racial (and cultural) patterns in order to personally experience and integrate different archetypal energies (soul qualities) uniquely expressed through what he calls one's *current racial form.* This perspective allows us to see our racial identity and the racial identity of those we encounter as being only relative to what we each have chosen to learn in this incarnation. And if we can go one step further, and allow for the possibility that in another incarnation our racial identities may well be reversed, it becomes difficult to maintain our tendency to stereotype any race that appears different from our own as "other".

At this time of such political and cultural and ideological polarization throughout the world, Cuf Ferguson offers us a radically different map of reality that not only lays the ground for *evolving the human race game*, but also opens us to a deeper dimension of peace and compassion for ourselves and for our fellow journeyers along the way. For those who seek transformation at the deepest level, this is a very engaging, an exciting, an intriguing, and a genuinely worthy read.

Leland "Chip" Baggett
Author of *Waking Up Together: An Interactive Practice for Couples (www.wakinguptogether.net)* and *So Where's The Dawn*
Past President and Past Co-President of the Association for Humanistic Psychology
Past President of the North Carolina Mental Health Counselors Association
Private Psychotherapy Practitioner

This is a transformative time in our history and it is imperative that we learn to act from the highest, most developed consciousness that we are capable of. This is the "spirit and soul-centered perspective" that Carroy "Cuf" Ferguson presents in such a rich and comprehensive way in his book *Evolving The Human Race Game: A Spiritual and Soul-Centered Perspective*. In order to heal the divisions in our culture, especially as they relate to the "human race game," we need to evolve to a more inclusive way of being in the world and Cuf Ferguson has presented us with a way of moving from our limited ego-centric stance towards a more world-centric view through spirit and soul work from many diverse perspectives. The reader can find many gems in this book that will help them in becoming "Bridgers" as Cuf Ferguson has said. The need for this paradigm shift is all too apparent and Cuf Ferguson's voice has added a very unique perspective and a highly important element into this important process.

Ray Greenleaf
Retired Chair of the Transpersonal Psychology
Department, John F. Kennedy University
Founding Member of the Ken Wilber Integral Institute
Board Member of the Association for
Transpersonal Psychology
Licensed Marriage and Family Therapist

EVOLVING THE HUMAN RACE GAME

A Spiritual and Soul-Centered Perspective

CARROY U. FERGUSON, PhD

TATE PUBLISHING
AND ENTERPRISES, LLC

Published by Tate Publishing & Enterprises, LLC
127 E. Trade Center Terrace | Mustang, Oklahoma 73064 USA
1.888.361.9473 | www.tatepublishing.com

Tate Publishing is committed to excellence in the publishing industry. The company reflects the philosophy established by the founders, based on Psalm 68:11,
"The Lord gave the word and great was the company of those who published it."

Published in the United States of America
ISBN: 978-1-62902-905-4
1. Self-Help / General
2. Self-Help / Spiritual
14.05.02

DEDICATION

As we parent, we guide and share as best we can. In turn, our children "gift" us with invaluable life experiences. This book, therefore, is dedicated to my loving daughter, Carenna E. Ferguson, who has given me many "life gifts" as her father, including the "gift" of becoming a grandfather to my beautiful and wonderful granddaughter, Maya.

CONTENTS

PREFACE

The content of this book "feels" as if it came from a deeper part of me, beyond my ego or personality. Rationally, I can tell myself that I sat down at a computer and wrote whatever occurred to me, or that I wrote things down when I "felt" a burst of inspiration while doing other things. Rationally, I can tell myself that this is a similar process that any author goes through when constructing a book. Some, therefore, may simply view this process as a creative use of my intuition and imagination in relation to my rational mind.

And yet, this does not fully capture the full essence of the experience. My truth is that I felt guided by a "Higher Source" to produce the words in the text. My truth is that I felt that I was involved in a co-creative process with my Higher Self to produce this book. How the production of the content of this book is characterized, however, is not as significant as the intent of the material itself to serve as a stimulus for looking anew at who we are as human beings. I first started writing this book in 2000, and interestingly the ending (or stopping point) of the book was written before the beginning of the book.

There are now two versions of this book—an original co-creative version and a refocused integrative version. This is the refocused integrative version of the book. The original co-creative version uses the term "we" when speaking to "you," the reader, and refers to me as "author." And yet, I also feel that "we" is more and refers to more than just the "I" that I know and am consciously aware of and what I think of as my connection with my Higher Self. I say this because when "I" allow "we" to speak, often I have little awareness of what "we" will say and I experience wisdom that transcends my day-to-day focus in my reality.

As "author," therefore, I also sought to include researched references or clarifying comments, where possible, to confirm, ground, or footnote what "we" were saying. I included these references or clarifying comments in the body of the text, in parentheses, as I found myself wondering if there was any substantive literature or comment on the material that "we" were talking about.

This refocused integrative version of the book incorporates more of my editorial voice in the text. In this re-focused integrative version, the term "we" is simply used as it is typically used to refer to a collective experience, as in being members of the same larger group. My voice as a primary author of the book is also reflected in the refocused integrative version of the book. In this regard, the narrative voice of "I" is used as primary author, while acknowledging the integrative influence of my Higher Self.

I realize that what I have just written may sound a little convoluted. However, the description represents an approximation of my inner experience in terms of how I experience an expansive aspect of myself, and how the original co-creative book was produced or emerged, and how this refocused integrative version of the book was produced.

If someone were to ask me about my personality, I would probably describe myself as a "gentle" personality, sometimes prone to putting others' needs ahead of my own. My background in this life, among many other things, includes growing up in the segregated South. I attended all-black schools until the age of eighteen where I graduated first in class. Interestingly, the person who graduated second in my class was Charles F. Bolden, Jr., one of the few black astronauts, who was nominated by President

Obama and confirmed by the US Senate to serve as NASA Administrator (He began his duties on July 17, 2009). I attended an all-male, predominantly white undergraduate college on an academic scholarship, where I majored in psychology and graduated with honors. I attended a graduate program at a progressive university in the Northeast with a focus on community and clinical psychology, where I received an MA and PhD in psychology.

In the process of my life journey, I became a human relations trainer and organization development consultant; a supervisor and program manager; a cofounder of two organizations to address cross-cultural and human understanding matters; a clinical practitioner (therapist) for over thirty years; a researcher and author on various topics related to relationships, consciousness, and other matters; president of a national and international professional psychology association; and a tenured professor and college administrator (acting dean) at a Northeastern university.

I mention these personal and professional roles as they represent one line of expression of part of the journey of my personality. Yet, throughout my entire professional experience, I was and continue to be aware that I was and am merely playing roles, while "being" myself—the same person and ever-expanding consciousness as in my personal life. Indeed, one of my mantras was and is: "I, being myself, help others be themselves somehow."

As a person of African American descent, I was and am also aware that my presentation of self may not always fit others' projections about who they think I am. And so, stereotypes often melt through honest and open dialogue. This can often be a powerful source of learning for others and myself. Learning and growth is a life-long process.

My interest in consciousness and soul-centered phenomena stems from a couple of expanded states of consciousness that I experienced, but had no words at the time to explain them. I was in my twenties at the time, attending graduate school. Maslow's "peak experience" concept came closest to an explanation and was a very helpful construct. Yet, there appeared to be something missing.

I then attended an Association of Black Psychologists conference in Boston, Massachusetts, where I encountered a woman who gave a presentation on the "inner world" and the "power of beliefs." After the presentation, I approached her and she asked if she could do a "reading" for me. Since I had never had a "reading" and was curious, I agreed. She said some interesting things, of which I was skeptical, and then she recommended a book that I might find useful. Interestingly, I "heard" the name of the book as *Self Speaks*.

When I went in search of the book, I could not find it anywhere in the psychology sections of bookstores. I gave up looking. Then, shortly thereafter, I was in another bookstore and was about to leave when I asked one of the clerks about this title. He said, "Oh, you must mean *Seth Speaks*. It's not in the psychology section. It's in the occult section. It's a channeled book and has become very popular." I was taken aback at first, but decided to purchase the book anyway.

I was unfamiliar with "channeling" at the time and so I first had to overcome my personality's fear and skepticism about how the book was produced. I decided to simply focus on the content of the book, and I found the "material" intriguing and fascinating. It gave me "words" for the earlier expansive experiences that I had.

Later, I began to read all of Jane Roberts' (the channeller for Seth) books and the *Seth Material*. I also read a number of other esoteric books, as well as other professional psychology books, to provide balance. I felt no need to share any of this with anyone, as this was part of my own personal journey. Others, however, who were on a similar path, nevertheless did begin to show up in my life. And so, my self did begin to speak. Indeed, I became a university teacher, "a professor."

Meanwhile, I also became active in two professional pioneering organizations. Each organization was a rich arena for networking and sharing ideas related to consciousness and soul-centered phenomena. The two organizations were the Association of Black Psychologists (ABPsi) and the Association for Humanistic Psychology (AHP).

With ABPsi, I was elected chairperson of a Northeastern metropolitan chapter of the organization and served in this role for several years. With AHP, I was elected to the national board of the organization and subsequently became president of AHP in July of 2006, a position that I held solely for an unprecedented four terms, and as of this writing in 2013 continue to occupy as a co-president. I, therefore, became the first African American and first person of color to hold the position of AHP President since the founding of AHP in 1962.

In attending conventions of both groups, there were two recurring observations. First, during similar time periods, both groups began to speak about consciousness and how reality is created according to the nature of one's beliefs. Second, the two groups did not engage in any official collaborative dialogue. While both groups gave great value to the human condition and the "concept of inclusion," they, however, did not "speak" to each other. With these two groups, therefore, the unrecognized potential existed, and continues to exist, for "multiracial" collaboration and sharing. As president and co-president of AHP, the "possibility" to open up and nurture such a collaborative dialogue is enhanced for the future.

AHP nurtured the birth of Humanistic Psychology, often referred to as a "Third Force" movement in psychology. It came into being in response to the mechanistic beliefs of behaviorism (the "First Force" movement) and the biological reductionism and determinism of classical psychoanalysis (the "Second Force" movement). Humanistic Psychology, therefore, was and is a contemporary manifestation on an ongoing historic creative tension in the field of psychology to affirm the inherent value and dignity of human beings.

Some of the luminary founders of Humanistic Psychology and AHP include Abraham Maslow, Carl Rogers, Rollo May, Clark Moustakas, Charlotte Buhler, Gordon Allport, James F. T. Bugental, Gardner Murphy, Henry Murray, Jacques Barzum, Rene Dubos, and Floyd Matson. These founders and AHP gave birth to what is called The Human Potential Movement. The now commonly-held notion that we live in an interdependent world is an outgrowth of The Human Potential Movement.

Past Presidents of AHP include eminent humanistic figures in the field such as James F. T. Bugental, Sidney M. Jourad, Charlotte Buhler, Jack R. Gibb, Stanley Krippner, Eleanor Criswell, Jean Houston, George Leonard, Virginia Satir, Lawrence LaShan, John Vasconcellos, Frances Vaughan, Maureen O'Hara, Arthur Warmoth, and J. Bruce Francis. With my historic election in 2006, I found myself joining a long list of prominent thinkers, scholars, authors, and cultural creators who have sought to bring to consciousness the value and dignity of the human being in the field of psychology.

The Association of Black Psychologists was founded in San Francisco in 1968 by a number of black psychologists from various regions of the United States. Guided by the principle of self-determination, these psychologists sought to actively change the discourse regarding social problems affecting the larger black community and other segments of the population whose needs society has not fulfilled. Past presidents of ABPsi include prominent black psychologists like Charles W. Thomas, Robert Green, Henry Tomes, Robert L. Williams, Reginald L. Jones, Thomas O. Hilliard, Ruth E. G. King, Maisha Bennett, Halford H. Fairchild, Na'im Akbar, and Wade Nobles.

In my view, AHP and ABPsi have been two pioneering organizations that, in their own way, planted and continue to plant seeds for the transformation of consciousness and a spiritual and soul-centered perspective on life. I have mentioned them because each has played a role in providing me with a platform for sharing and "being" myself.

Using a spiritual and soul-centered perspective, this book is but another step in my sharing and "being" myself. Hopefully, it can stimulate readers to create constructive dialogue as human beings, including intra-racial, interracial, and broader human dialogue. Hopefully, it can stimulate sharing at both the individual and group levels. It is my hope that readers will find some of the ideas useful.

It is also my hope that readers will apply any useful ideas that they encounter to a process for evolving the human race game in specific and general terms—a game that has been very destructively played over the years, but can be played constructively if each person is allowed to be themselves, their truer selves. The book, therefore, is intended to invite readers to take meaningful and courageous first steps to evolve the human race game in specific and general terms through evolving their own consciousness.

In general, the content of the book provides a spiritual and soul-centered framework for evolving one's consciousness as it relates to the human race game in specific and general terms. Thus, Chapters 1 through 6 progressively invite readers to "become aware" of the limited consciousness currently used in playing the human race game in specific and general terms. Chapters 7 through 14 then progressively invite readers to *awake* to the possibility of being conscious creators or co-creators in evolving the human race game in specific and general terms.

Interspersed throughout the text are exercises to assist readers in examining self-limiting, race-linked beliefs, and beliefs about "the Other." Interspersed also are conceptual tools to assist readers in expanding their consciousness in this regard. Both ego-driven race games (lower self race games) and essence-oriented race games (higher self race games) are discussed. Transformative dynamics and steps are also identified in a discussion on what is called the Transformational Race Game.

The book further looks at emerging visions, patterns, tools, and opportunities for evolving the human race game in specific and general terms. The book, therefore, walks readers through a process for understanding the nature of the human race game in specific and general terms and provides some tools for evolving it.

AN INTRODUCTION
TO EVOLVING THE
HUMAN RACE GAME

I will be exploring an age-old drama. It is an important drama that has always and will continue to be with us as a human species. It is a drama that is often misunderstood or misinterpreted, but is one that impacts all phases of the human experience. It has a specific higher purpose, which is unique to each person, and a generic higher purpose. From a spiritual and soul-centered perspective, one general purpose of the drama is to help each person to evolve or to expand his/her consciousness. In this context, I suggest that its true intent is to help each person learn or recognize the true nature of the self as a multidimensional or multileveled being. What is this drama? It is the drama, as can be currently understood in linear terms, which I will call the human race game in specific and general terms.

I intentionally use the phraseology human race game as it has multiple meanings in both specific and general terms. The phrase "human race game" implies that, as this age-old drama is explored, each person's consciousness may shift to: (1) emphasize the general nature of a game "acted out" externally by various members of the human race, (2) focus specifically on race as a unique human phenomenon of the human experience, (3) focus on general and common human race experiences, or (4) have both race-specific and general human race emphases. From a spiritual and soul-centered perspective, it can be argued that each individual on the face of this planet chose to incarnate as a particular race in this lifetime, as the phenomenon is currently understood, for her/his own reasons and to participate in the human race game in specific and general terms for purposes of learning and growing. Each person, therefore, will encounter various lessons as he plays the human race game in specific and general terms.

The human race game in specific and general terms can be defined as an ongoing drama related to one's projections regarding the self, not self, and the phenomenon of race—that is, the racial group or groups that one perceives and with which one identifies. As such, it is an ever-evolving game that each person has so far "unconsciously" co-created at individual and collective levels. In this context, it mirrors the evolution of human consciousness at both individual and collective levels.

In many ways, this book may be viewed as representing the state of affairs of a collective inner dialogue about the nature of the human race game in specific and general terms. The essence of the book was intuitively received and is presented as I got impressions, thoughts, and feelings, sometimes in the wee hours of the night, and perused various written materials. Where possible, therefore, intuitions were grounded by research and the literature. Often in moments of inspiration it is all one can do to gather a pen and paper and record the material that floods the mind. Thus the book represents an ever-emerging process at the present moment, even as these words are recorded.

Given that I identify myself as African American, I periodically use my unique lens on the human race game as a metaphor for evolving human consciousness. It is important, however, to recognize that my lens is only one lens, and that the material can be applied and is intended to relate to the many human lenses with which each person may identify and has human experiences.

In addition to race, other lenses typically include the following: gender, class, religious or spiritual orientation, culture, ethnicity, tribes or other self-described group affiliations, and nationality. To some extent, each person will complete this book in her/his own way as he/she writes new scripts for her/his "conscious experience" in regard to the human race game in both specific and general terms.

The essence of the book speaks of a new framework for redefining the nature of the self. It is, as indicated, a spiritual and soul-centered framework. Such a framework calls upon each person to speculate about "what if," as they embrace and incorporate an age-old idea into thinking about the human race game and the self in specific and general terms. That idea is, "what if" a person is more than they "think" they are. Such an idea ultimately leads to stretching the concept of self to learn more about the nature of human consciousness, the nature of the unconscious, the nature of self-creation, and the exploration of an ancient concept that is called reincarnation.

What happens to the concept of self if the ideas of race, the nature of consciousness, the nature of the unconscious, self-creation, and reincarnation are married? A person would begin to encounter a new framework, along with all of its implications, for viewing the self. It would be a new framework that is more expansive, inclusive, intuitive (or inner-directed), and spiritual. The reference to spiritual here is different from the religious dogmas with which most readers are familiar. I am referring to a soul-centered perspective beyond dogma, inclusive and yet also beyond the level of ego and personality in terms of consciousness and energy.

As readers seek to entertain or to embrace this new framework, there may be some material that various people simply are unable to relate to. So, one may feel the urge to fill in gaps by pursuing other written materials. Each person should allow their self, or rather the self they think they know, to be guided to various resource materials, teachers, and guides. Indeed, it is assumed that readers of this book have been intuitively guided to become a more "conscious person" in evolving the human race game in both specific and general terms.

THE PURPOSE AND INTENT OF A SPIRITUAL AND SOUL-CENTERED HUMAN RACE GAME PERSPECTIVE

The purpose of the book, therefore, is multifold:

- To challenge each person to expand one's current concept of self in regard to the human race game in specific and general terms

- To offer an alternative framework for viewing the connection between the human race game and consciousness in specific and general terms

- To reveal basic elements about what can be called the mirror effect and the nature of the human race game as a game of projection in specific and general terms

- To identify how each person currently plays the human race game in specific and general terms in accord with what might be called the lower self (the domain of ego and personality, or one's lower consciousness)

- To look at how each person may play the human race game in specific and general terms in accord with the higher self (one's higher purpose or higher focus, or one's higher consciousness)

- To assist each person in becoming a "conscious person" in regard to evolving the human race game in specific and general terms

It is assumed that readers of this book have already gained some degree of awareness about their self. It is further assumed that readers have already begun to question old belief structures in regard to how individually and collectively one currently plays the human race game in both specific and general terms. It is also assumed that readers are seeking answers or have a fine curiosity about how things work. And, it is assumed that readers also at some level want to make the world better for humanity.

This book may or may not provide specific answers for readers. What it will do, however, is to provide a new perspective and invite each reader to consciously look deeper inside their self for answers that are already there. Implied here is that a person needs only desire to look with honesty and openness and to intuitively receive what is there without judgment. Readers will need to uncover their internalized ideas related to: the nature of light and dark, the nature of life and death, the nature of consciousness and the unconscious, the nature of God and Satan, and the nature of the waking state and the dreaming state. I suggest that a person's best guide will be their intuition and each person's friend and companion will be their higher self.

Becoming a conscious person in regard to the human race game in both specific and general terms opens a person to the possibility of exploring various aspects of their self, in both one-dimensional and multidimensional terms. Although the current physical world is called a three-dimensional world (height, width, depth), in actuality a person's five physically-focused senses (seeing, hearing, touching, smelling, and tasting) currently provide the person with a "one-dimensional linear experience" of physicality, which has continuity in terms of height, width, and depth in time and space. In multidimensional terms, a person may experience these senses and others in other varied ways.

Therefore, becoming a conscious person challenges a person to look at the self with old and new eyes. It invites a person to become a conscious creator or conscious co-creator of their own reality and a partner in self-creation with their higher self. Some readers already know and understand this process and call it reality creation. And yet, while there is talk of reality creation as humanity's next evolutionary step, there is reluctance to make a direct link involving the process of reality creation, human relations, race relations, and the human race game in specific and general terms.

As I received intuitive thoughts in writing this book, I was aware that I was and am engaged in my own process of what I call *uncovery*, and that each person is also engaged in their own process of uncovery as they play the human race game in specific and general terms. I was also aware that I *chose* to be a black person in this life for my own reasons. And, I understand what my "blackness" means to me, which may or may not have a similar meaning for other people who have chosen to be black in this life.

Some readers who have just read the last few statements above may consciously or unconsciously understand what was just written. Other readers may be puzzled or curious, or may dismiss the entire book because of these statements. Additionally, there may be those who may dismiss me as someone who is off-the-wall, unscientific, or unprofessional, or as one of those "New Age" people talking in circles again, for how can anyone "prove" these statements or the experience?

There also may be those who simply see me as a black person "struggling to know himself" or see me as a spiritual person "discussing an aspect of himself." Since I work in a professional arena as a university professor/administrator and a clinical practitioner/psychologist, such a perspective may be seen as risky business for me or, for the more "progressive-minded" in these arenas, the perspective may be seen as innovative and challenging. Whatever one's reactions and formulations, it is important to begin to understand that they are being generated and screened by one's beliefs and that the human race game in specific and general terms is very much linked to the nature of one's beliefs.

For example, if a person's belief in science is used as the final yardstick against which to determine and measure reality or what is "real," then the realities related to the human race game in specific and general terms can only be "proven" to a reader by using scientific data and studies. I am not suggesting here that such studies are meaningless, for indeed very significant studies have been carried out and continue to be carried out that pertain to the human race game in specific and general terms.

What is being suggested, however, is that a person's reactions to, interpretations of, and acceptance of data, scientific or otherwise, flow from and are in accord with their beliefs and what the person considers to be "true." It is also a person's beliefs that will shape how open or closed the person is to their own process of uncovery regarding the nature of the human race game and how the person plays it in specific and general terms.

Humanity now stands at the threshold of evolving into "New Human Beings," human beings who act *consciously* to create and co-create reality, rather than human beings who react *unconsciously* to a perceived reality. In this context, never before has it been more important for each person to become more "conscious" about the nature of the *human race game* in specific and general terms. Never before has it been more important for each person to become more "conscious" about how s/he as an individual plays her/his *human race game* in the "Now" in specific and general terms. And, never before has it been more important for each person to become more conscious about how to play the human race game in specific and general terms, individually and collectively, in such a way that is more in line with their higher purpose or higher focus.

The human race game in specific and general terms is a global phenomenon that is directly connected to the souls and minds of each person who has chosen to share his or her perspective and energies during this and other periods of existence. It is assumed here that some part of each reader of this book has or is beginning to recognize how "unconscious" they may have been about the nature of the human race game in specific and general terms.

And, it is assumed that this part of the person wants themselves to become more "conscious" about how "they" play the human race game in specific and general terms.

The intent of this book is to stimulate thought, not to give prescribed and prepackaged answers. Indeed, each person's truest answers regarding the nature of the human race game in specific and general terms, and their own unique relation to it, lie within the person and this they must uncover themselves. The book, however, does offer a new perspective and a new framework—a spiritual and soul-centered framework—to assist each person as they engage in their unique process of uncovery.

What One Should Expect to Encounter in the Material

Readers will be introduced to an alternative model of human nature. Readers will be encouraged to begin to recognize that how they think of the self now is not the only way to think of the self. Readers will also become aware of a spiritual and soul-centered component to the human race game in specific and general terms. Readers will be asked to entertain the idea of having a lower self (ego and personality) and a higher self (higher personal essence) and soul-source that are aware of how they are currently playing the human race game in specific and general terms. And readers will be asked to entertain the idea that their higher self and soul-source may want them to begin to examine how they in their present physical form are playing the human race game in specific and general terms, and to affirm their current, ongoing uncovery process in this regard.

The material is intended to explain how each person is currently creating their reality in regard to the human race game in specific and general terms as they operate in what might be called three life spaces—a personal life space, a societal life space, and a global life space. Here, readers will be reminded of some core beliefs at play and how these beliefs are serving to limit their perception and understanding of the human race game in specific and general terms.

Readers will be presented with the current framework regarding race, color, and consciousness. Readers will be asked to consider that the way they think about what may be called their current racial form is connected to three lower self states of consciousness or limiting states of consciousness.

The terms lower self consciousness and higher self consciousness in this context are meant to communicate relative degrees of expanded consciousness in regard to the conscious self and not better or worse per se. The terms simply refer to the higher or lower vibrational levels, that is, the higher or lower vibrational frequencies at which a person may be "focusing" their consciousness, for whatever reasons.

In other terms, the lower self may be thought of as the outer self, while the higher self may be thought of as the inner self. In these terms, then, the relative degree of expanded consciousness is in regard to the openness a person may or may not experience between the outer self and the inner self.

Some of the material is meant to help build "bridges of vibrational energy" across what a person may currently think of as "racial lines" and taken-for-granted human demarcations in the human race game in specific and general terms. The material in this regard is related to what I call the Path of the Bridger. It is a path that expands consciousness through exploring the authentic essence of soul qualities known as acceptance, inclusion, harmony, and love.

This path involves a person with the issue of relationships and consciousness, that is, personal and group relationships and personal and group consciousness, including race consciousness, race relations, human consciousness, and human relations in specific and general terms. One intention of this path, among many others, is to create space and time that involves opportunities to express the qualities of acceptance, inclusion, harmony, and love as the self explores areas of communality and uniqueness. In this context, it will be suggested that these and other soul qualities have an archetypal nature to them.

Readers will be encouraged, therefore, to explore deeply the basic elements of human relationships and to look closely at how mistrust, miscommunication, and fear cloud perceptions in clearly seeing the humanity of another person or groups of other people. Readers will also be reminded of some of the basic elements and principles that are helpful in building positive and constructive human relationships. And readers will be encouraged to look into their own life spaces (personal, societal, and global) and their inner psychic space to see if these constructive elements and principles are at play in regard to how they are currently playing the human race game in specific and general terms. What readers discover as they do this will be the mirror effect.

The mirror effect will be explained, along with some illustrations. As an introduction to the mirror effect, I suggest that each reader use their intuition and answer the following personal questions: What is being "reflected back" to you in regard to the human race game in specific and general terms in your life spaces, and how does this correlate with your inner psychic space? What kind of human race game are you playing in specific and general terms?

Readers may find it challenging to entertain a new framework—a spiritual and soul-centered framework—for looking at the self and the meaning of "race" in terms of the human race game in specific and general terms. Examining the meaning of the phenomenon called "race" in this new framework evokes creative imagination, individually and collectively.

Readers will be entertaining, exploring, and beginning to incorporate notions about race or their current racial form, while also examining ideas about the nature of consciousness, the nature of the unconscious, self-creation, reality-creation, and reincarnation. As this is done, readers will begin to uncover unique, higher vibrational energies, or what might be called archetypal energies as a part of their soul or unique authentic essence. And readers will begin to understand how, by blocking the expression of these archetypal energies, they distort the true intent of the human race game in specific and general terms.

Some of the material will take readers a step further in suggesting that there are some things that their higher self wants them to learn while in their current racial form. Some possible lessons are identified. But, in the final analysis, however, only the individual can uncover the nature of the lessons that they have chosen for their outer self. As each person uses their life spaces as arenas for learning one's lessons in regard to the human race game in specific and general terms, some guidelines, emerging visions, patterns, and opportunities as well as cognitive tools are suggested that can be used.

Playing the human race game in specific and general terms from the perspective of and in alignment with the higher self in general invites possibilities for more joyful life experiences rather than painful life experiences. In this regard, the choice is up to each person—learn how to grow with joy or continue to grow with pain as one plays the human race game in specific and general terms. I recommend the former approach.

Finally, since the human race game is an ongoing game in specific and general terms, it is important to uncover one's higher focus or higher purpose for it and to find the most constructive ways to play it. Information and exercises are provided in this material to assist each person in their uncovery process so that they can play the human race game in specific and general terms as it was intended. Here, one's intuition will be tapped. In this light, each person will be allowing the self to affirm and to embrace all of who they are.

How each person plays the human race game in specific and general terms is connected to a large extent to how the person views the self. How a person views the self is largely connected to models the person carries in their conscious or rational mind, often culturally entrenched, about what is one's nature as a human being. For this reason, I will begin the exploratory discussion by examining in a very general way some alternative models of human nature, as currently used to view the self.

I will then present a new alternative model of human nature for consideration as a cognitive tool. My hope is that each person will have a pleasant and rewarding journey as they play the human race game in specific and general terms!

ALTERNATIVE MODELS OF HUMAN NATURE FOR EVOLVING THE HUMAN RACE GAME

Throughout history, as it is understood, humanity or human consciousness has devised numerous models to describe the nature of the self and the characteristics of human nature. These models become the context within which humanity, at individual and collective levels, learns how to view the self at particular points in time and space. The models serve as cognitive tools for how to explain human behavior and the human drama to the self. In addition, humanity, at individual and collective levels, also uses these models to create an infinite number of human dramas or games.

These games serve as arenas and opportunities to learn more about the self individually and collectively. However, in playing the games, the individuals that are involved often do not tell the self or the individuals forget that they are the creators and co-creators of these games, and they act as if events and things are simply happening to them. They are not conscious of their own creations. Yet, it is the models that spell out the parameters for the games, give rise to a variety of dramatic roles, and serve as contexts within which to view the self as individuals enact these roles.

To some extent, the models coincide with how humanity, at individual and collective levels, is describing human evolution to the self at a given point in history. The models reflect or "mirror" what and how humanity, at individual and collective levels, is thinking or feeling about who we are as human beings. Often, however, individuals can forget they are using a model. Individuals can get lost in the drama. Individuals may over-identify with their roles. Their perceptions within the drama can get distorted. Individuals may lose sight of the drama's true intention. Or individuals may misinterpret the creative energy and creative impulse behind the drama. Individuals forget that they have created the models and the illusions, and they act as if the dramatic role itself is their unique authentic essence. Individuals then may experience or create fear and confusion for the self and act accordingly.

This is the state of affairs in regard to many human dramas related to the human race game in both specific and general terms. Humanity, at individual and collective levels, has used a variety of models to create and enact many self-limiting human dramas in regard to the human race game in specific and general terms, and individuals have been lost more often than not in unknowingly enacting dramatic roles based on fear and confusion. At individual and collective levels, many also have forgotten the connection between the human race game in specific and general terms and the process of evolving as human beings or expanding each person's consciousness.

The human race game in specific and general terms is a global game. It is largely experienced, however, as a personal game that more often than not extends outwardly as a local, national, or international phenomenon. The extent to which a person perceives the self as having local, national, or international connections is the extent to which the person carries a personal sense of the human race game in specific and general terms into these various arenas. In this regard, then, the human race game in specific and general terms can be viewed as largely a game that is a function of what is called the "ego" and its creations.

The ego is the most externally focused portion of the conscious mind. The conscious mind is often referred to also as the rational mind or intellect. The ego's creations are the models individuals create as personalities and hold in the conscious mind about who they are and are not.

Let's briefly look at some of the models humanity has used to describe the process of evolving as human beings, the nature of the self, and self-creation.

THE HUMAN RACE GAME AND CURRENT MODELS OF HUMAN NATURE OR MODELS ABOUT THE SELF

If a model is devised which says that each person has an unconscious part of the self where they put everything they consider to be unsavory, chaotic, or simply too problematic for the person to deal with consciously, one has created a model that implies a person must fear aspects of the self. If the person then uses what is called the ego part of the self to protect the self against all of that yucky unconscious stuff, particularly all that lusty, sexual stuff and that violent, aggressive stuff, now they can pat their self, or the self they think they know, on the back for being a consciously "civilized" and "good" person. If the person should do anything "bad," it is simply because somehow some of that unconscious stuff found a way to escape. Or, it is because those "bad people out there" evoked their righteous actions. The person then does not have to fully accept responsibility for their actions. And, the person gets to pretend that they are unaware of how they created their own reality. Currently, Western culture is highly influenced by this model of the self and human nature. It is called the Freudian or Neo-Freudian model.

And so it is that the human race game in specific and general terms from a Western perspective is also intimately related to this model of the self and human nature. In other-oriented or racial terms, the "bad people," or those who are perceived to be "alien, foreign, or different" to the self, become the other or those from an "other race" who are viewed through a distorted lens. The distorted lens blinds the perceiver from seeing a higher purpose of the human race game in specific and general terms. The distortion often occurs when there is a perception of personal or societal stress. In this context, the person projects out onto the other, or the "bad, racially different other," their fears in regard to their view of "stuff" in their unconscious.

To a large extent, the "bad other," or those who are "alien, foreign, or different" to the self in the human race game, represent in specific and general terms the feared unconscious portions of the self. Some call these feared unconscious portions of the self the shadow aspects of the self. When a person uncovers that they have been playing the human race game in specific and general terms within this framework, the task is to learn how to embrace and to own the so-called shadow aspects of the self so that they no longer project them out onto the other, or those who they view as belonging to a different race or different other.

In non-Western cultures, similar models of the self are used with different names or lenses to cast shadow aspects of the self onto a "bad other" or an "alien, foreign, or different other." In some other cultures, for example, ethnic or tribal over-identification has fueled the nature of the human race game in specific and general terms, often with violent outbursts justified by using dogmatic religious or political ideas, ideals, or beliefs. Here, an emphasis is placed on getting rid of, containing, or "cleansing" the culture of the "bad, alien, or different other" from the field of play. Here, elements of a cultural orientation are confused with thoughts about the phenomenon known as "race." The ethnic or tribal conflicts in Sudan (Darfur), Rwanda, Bosnia, Yugoslavia,

Israel and Palestine, Indonesia, Sri Lanka, Lebanon, Russia, Iraq, and Syria are examples of this confused state of affairs.

In yet other models, if one "objectifies" everything, including the nature of the human being, and views the self as simply a physical entity that acts and reacts to other external or physical "objects" in the world, one does not have to be concerned with the self having some unsavory, unconscious part. The "bad or alien other" simply becomes those independent or separate from the self who seek to control and manipulate either as bully or victim. In terms of the human race game in specific and general terms, these models thus allow a person to view "the bad or alien other" or the "bad, racially different other" as those who either monitor how "they" provide the outer self with what the person or they think the outer self needs, or withhold from the outer self what the person or they consider to be essential for the outer self's survival and growth. These kinds of models have been referred to as behaviorist and neo-behaviorist models, and as economically-driven models (e.g., Marxist and neo-Marxists models or capitalist and neo-capitalist models) when applied at a cultural level.

In other terms, a person's view of the self and human nature constitute and reflect or "mirror" the nature of their beliefs. These beliefs flow from current models that largely view the self as separated into a mind and a body and, in some instances, a spirit. The mind is relegated to the field of psychology and its various clinical models; the body is relegated to the field of medicine and the scientific and medical models; and the spirit is relegated to religion and its various theological models. In this context, it is often difficult to maintain a view of the self as a whole entity with interdependent aspects, that is, the outer self appears as a self with independent, unrelated, and non-interacting one-dimensional parts rather than a self with interdependent and multidimensional aspects.

As a person thinks about who they are, then, or how a person defines the self, or what a person believes to be true about the self, the outer self as a particular race or mixture of races comes into play as a method of helping the person to view the self clearly in time and space. In doing so, a person makes distinctions between (or form beliefs about) self and not-self. In turn, the person attempts to use external or physical or perceptual cues and criteria to assist him or her in making distinctions, based on the phenomenon of "race" or what can be referred to as their current racial form.

Sometimes, rather than viewing and valuing the beauty in the diversity that emerges, a person's vision in the game of distinction may become unclear or cloudy. Out of fear and insecurity, particularly during moments of perceived stress, the person may begin to view, or form beliefs about, the distinctions as reasons to defend and protect the self rather than as opportunities to learn and grow. If, however, a person pushes and tests the external cues and criteria scientifically and objectively, they will always find exceptions. The person may then create alternative explanations which may perpetuate the fear and insecurity. The upshot is that, in this game of distinctions, and specifically racial distinctions, many distortions and self-limiting concepts have emerged throughout linear history, as it is understood. The distortions and self-limiting concepts reflect or mirror humanity's struggle to explore and to understand different aspects of itself, as each self uses its various racial forms to express growth-filled soul qualities and meaning.

As a species, humanity is still exploring and have yet to find models of human nature that help to better understand the nature of the human race game. Most scientists today, however, have concluded that the use of external criteria leaves a lot to be desired for defining and making attributions about a person's race. Despite this, many people continue to persist in using external or physical criteria to reinforce the idea that what is perceived as one's own race and someone else's race is something that is externally derived. Many believe that their own race and another's race has some "meaning" beyond what is created in their own Mind. The same thing could also be said in relation to one's so-called ethnicity, or the other human lenses I earlier identified (i.e., gender, class, religious or spiritual orientation, culture, tribes or other self-described group affiliations, and nationality) (see p. 21). It is important, therefore, for each person to be open to exploring their own creations and their own meanings. It is also important to understand that the creation of the physical racial form is part of the process of self-creation. This, however, has nothing to do with one so-called race being better than, or having qualities superior to, another race. Such self-limiting beliefs are a person's own creations.

How a person currently thinks about the self, therefore, is not the only way to think about the self. A person's conceptions of the self and human nature are based in large part on beliefs and ideas that have been acquired by acquiescing to a view of the self through the lens of a model or models that are part of a particular societal and cultural context. The model(s) in the societal and cultural context, for the most part, reflect or mirror a consensus about how to describe the self and human nature in time and space, as it is understood. A societal or cultural model, however, simply represents one of many ways to view the self.

THE HUMAN RACE GAME AND ALTERNATIVE MODELS OF HUMAN NATURE: A PARADIGM SHIFT AND A "NEW" SPIRITUAL AND SOUL-CENTERED MODEL OF HUMAN NATURE

Some alternative models do exist and are being explored in US society, in Western cultures, and in the world. They are related to the evolutionary idea of viewing the human being as a vibrational being, body and reality of consciousness-energy. They are also related to the evolutionary idea of each person becoming a conscious creator or co-creator of reality, who can understand the nature of consciousness, the principles of self-creation, and the proper use of creative energy. The essence of these alternative models is that each person has four interdependent, vibrational bodies and realities or multidimensional aspects of the self: (1) a physical body and its vibrational reality (i.e., the visible appearance of one's current racial form), (2) an emotional body and its vibrational reality, (3) a mental body and its vibrational reality, and (4) a spiritual body and its vibrational reality.

The alternative models seek to affirm that each person lives in two interdependent vibrational worlds—a multidimensional material world and a multidimensional spiritual world. In relation to this vibrational interdependence, the alternative models also seek to affirm in consciousness-energy terms that the material world is caused by the spiritual world, as each person works with universal energy laws knowingly and unknowingly. The alternative models have emerged from what has been called in Western cultures a paradigm shift. The paradigm shift may be represented simplistically by the following diagram:

Figure 1.   Representation of the "Old Paradigm" and the Shift to a "New Paradigm."

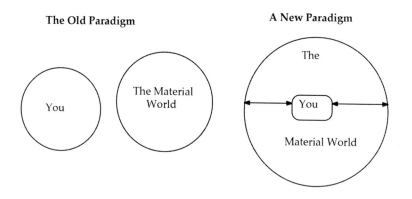

Many in Western cultures and in the world continue to use the old paradigm as a guide for how to view reality. Briefly, in the old paradigm, the outer self and human consciousness (you) are perceived as independent and apart from the material world. The belief is that the human mind can know this material world "objectively." And, it is often thought and felt that if one can know something, one therefore can control it. This is a mechanistic view of the self and the vibrational material world, stemming from philosophers of the seventeenth century, as linear time is understood.

The new paradigm, so to speak, places each person and human consciousness (you) in a vibrationally active and relatively open energy interchange with the material world. And there are a number of emerging versions of this new paradigm. In this emerging context, the vibrational relationship between each person as consciousness-energy and the material world is interdependent. Individually and collectively, each person and their consciousness give rise to the creation of material form, and physical form in turn impacts consciousness. Underlying the nature of this interdependence are Creative Energy Principles governing the exchange, transmutation, and transformation of energy. This implies a need for a spiritual and soul-centered model for how to view the self and the vibrational world in relation to the human race game in specific and general terms.

The diagram below represents one such model (see Figure 2). It presents one view of the self and aspects of a multidimensional reality or multileveled consciousness. However, it is not intended to be the only way to view reality. Rather, it is intended to be one representation of an emerging view of reality, or the vibrational world, that may assist each person in evolving the human race game in specific and general terms.

Figure 2. *A Spiritual and Soul-centered Model of Human Nature for Evolving the Human Race Game*

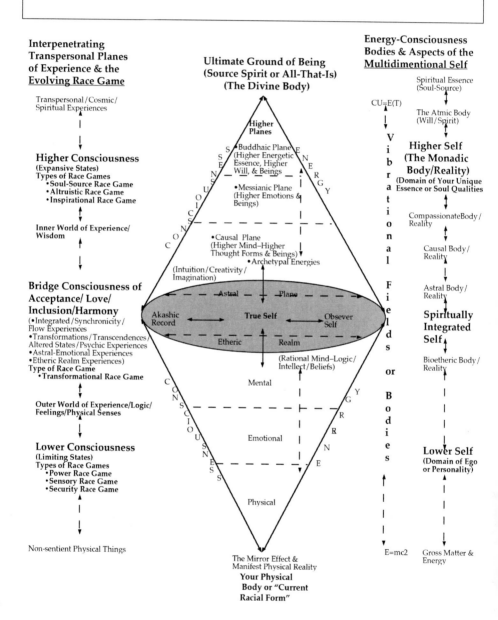

Interpenetrating Transpersonal Planes of Experience & the Evolving Race Game

Transpersonal/Cosmic/ Spiritual Experiences

Higher Consciousness
(Expansive States)
Types of Race Games
• Soul-Source Race Game
• Altruistic Race Game
• Inspirational Race Game

Inner World of Experience/ Wisdom

Bridge Consciousness of Acceptance/ Love/ Inclusion/Harmony
(•Integrated/Synchronicity/ Flow Experiences
•Transformations/Transcendences/ Altered States/Psychic Experiences
•Astral-Emotional Experiences
•Etheric Realm Experiences)
Type of Race Game
• Transformational Race Game

Outer World of Experience/Logic/ Feelings/Physical Senses

Lower Consciousness
(Limiting States)
Types of Race Games
• Power Race Game
• Sensory Race Game
• Security Race Game

Non-sentient Physical Things

Ultimate Ground of Being (Source Spirit or All-That-Is) (The Divine Body)

Higher Planes

• Buddhaic Plane (Higher Energetic Essence, Higher Will, & Beings

• Messianic Plane (Higher Emotions & Beings)

• Causal Plane (Higher Mind–Higher Thought Forms & Beings)
• Archetypal Energies
(Intuition/Creativity/ Imagination)

Astral — Plane
Akashic Record   True Self   Observer Self
Etheric   Realm
(Rational Mind–Logic/ Intellect/Beliefs)

Mental

Emotional

Physical

The Mirror Effect & Manifest Physical Reality
Your Physical Body or "Current Racial Form"

SOURCE SPIRIT OR ENERGY

CONSCIOUSNESS

Energy-Consciousness Bodies & Aspects of the Multidimentional Self

Spiritual Essence (Soul-Source)

$CU=E(T)$

The Atmic Body (Will/Spirit)

Higher Self (The Monadic Body/Reality)
(Domain of Your Unique Essence or Soul Qualities

Compassionate Body/ Reality

Causal Body/ Reality

Astral Body/ Reality

Spiritually Integrated Self

Bioetheric Body/ Reality

Lower Self
(Domain of Ego or Personality)

$E=mc2$ Gross Matter & Energy

Vibrational Fields or Bodies

Using this spiritual and soul-centered model, imagine consciousness as aware-ized vibrational energy that knows its whole or greater self and uses the electromagnetic properties of thought, and at other levels of emotion, to create "form." Imagine that these electromagnetic properties form various vibrational fields or bodies and realities of consciousness-energy. The slower the vibration or frequency of energy, the denser that the properties of the fields or body and reality become. In the physical realm with which humanity is familiar, the physical body and the properties of the material world (gross matter and energy; non-sentient physical things), thus vibrate at a very low or slower frequency, providing for the appearance of solidity (manifest physical reality).

A most notable and brilliant personality known as Einstein, therefore, in a highly intuitive state of consciousness, discerned that energy equaled mass times the square of the speed of light ($E=MC^2$), and vice versa (i.e., the square of the speed of light times mass equals energy). The principles came to him in the form of kinesthetic sensations in his muscles. This led to his theory of relativity, which has fascinated the minds of many scientists and scholars.

At a spiritual and soul-centered level, a consciousness unit (CU) may be said to equal directed or focused aware-ized energy (E^{fa}) as a function of thought (T), that is $CU=E^{fa}(T)$, and vice versa. That consciousness unit (which I will also call soul or soul-source) contains all of the properties of the creative impulse of source energy/spirit or All-That-Is. Using directed thought, therefore, to speed up or slow down the vibrational levels of energy (frequencies), various interdependent bodies and realities of consciousness-energy (spiritual, mental, emotional, and physical) and planes of experience and being-ness are formed at various times and in various spaces, as the time-space continuum is understood. The process can be a continuous one in linear time and space, as it is understood, as the CU explores its uniqueness and expands its sense of an ever-emerging self.

In this model, beyond the time-space continuum, the spiritual and soul-centered planes of experience and being-ness generally include what others and I will call the Buddhaic Plane, the Messianic Plane, and the Causal Plane. In the broadest of terms, these higher planes constitute what some have called the celestial planes, and they connect the CU, or the soul-source, to source energy/spirit or All-That-Is. There are, however, other ways that these spiritual planes have been presented or described. I present them in this form simply to invite readers to entertain the idea that each person as a CU has a spiritual body and reality that may have different forms in relation to these higher planes, as well as having a physical body in relation to the physical plane.

In other terms, the astral plane, while also spiritual in nature, can be said to be closer to the physical plane in terms of the frequency of the energy of the vibrational field. Among other functions of this vibrational field, the astral plane is often an arena where one may and can practice probable realities and explore what it would be like to actualize or materialize particular thoughts and emotions before a person manifests them physically. Each person does this by using directed thought and the vehicle that some know as the astral body. While a person can become more conscious about this process (e.g., Rick Stack's *Out-Of-Body Adventures*, 1988), it currently remains largely an unconscious, or more precisely a subconscious or unknown, process for many.

In the spiritual and soul-centered realms (or inner planes, subtle planes, celestial planes, angelic realm, or higher planes), as different terms have been used to describe these realms, the CU may be referred to as the higher self or higher consciousness. Higher consciousness resonates with and mirrors what can be called soul-source with its divine body and reality, or that part of the self that simultaneously connects each person mentally, emotionally, and energetically with source energy/spirit, the ultimate ground of being, or All-That-Is. More specifically, as a self-aware whole entity at the soul level, the CU as the higher self can be said to have what can be called a Monadic body and reality, whereby seeming polarities are experienced as the spirit of unity consciousness. The soul, in a manner of speaking, therefore, is that which gives spirit and unity to the higher self or higher consciousness.

In this model, the higher self is the domain of a person's unique and higher personal essence, their authentic spiritual essence, or the domain of what can be called the person's soul qualities. It is the domain of a person's inner vibrational world of experience and wisdom, which gives rise to and is where each person also experiences their being-ness. In this context, one's soul qualities flow from or are in alignment with what can be called Archetypal Energies.

Archetypal energies are universal governing energy principles and qualities vibrating within the cosmos and are at work deep within individual lives and psyches. They transcend historical, geographical, and cultural boundaries. In other terms, one's soul qualities are archetypal energies. From an energy vibrational point of view, archetypal energies may be viewed as ever-emerging, ever-creative, and ever-evolving soul qualities, flowing from source energy/spirit or All-That-Is, that playfully urge, support, and sustain the joyful expansion of consciousness. A person tends to experience them as creative urges to move one towards what might be called one's optimal self and optimal realities. I will use easily recognized terms to evoke a common sense of these archetypal energies. Wisdom as a soul quality is one of those archetypal energies, for example.

However, for those who are more scientifically oriented, I suggest that they scientifically research and study various cultures. As a person does so, they will find the various archetypal energies that I will identify and discuss in detail later. In various cultures, archetypal energies have been given various labels and various expressions in one form or another. I will be discussing later, therefore, twenty-five archetypal energies, as they each relate to one's search for the meaning of the human experience, the phenomenon of race, and the creation of various types of human race games. For purposes of the discussion at this point, I will simply note that there are seven generic types of race-linked human games related to archetypal energies, as these higher vibrational energies seek form and expression. Three types can be called higher self race games: (1) the Inspirational Race Game, (2) the Altruistic Race Game, and (3) the Soul-Source Race Game.

The three higher self race games, which I will discuss later, are to some extent connected to three variations or states of vibrational realities of the higher self or higher consciousness. These three variations or states of vibrational realities include: (1) the Higher Mind (or Superconscious Mind) with what can be called the causal body and its vibrational reality, (2) the Higher Emotions with what can be called the compassionate body and its vibrational reality, and (3) the Higher Will and Energy with what can be called the atmic body and its vibrational reality. The three higher self race games are thus related to these three higher or more expanded states of consciousness. The three spiritual bodies and realities identified are three spiritual forms and realities of the soul or Monadic body and its reality, given unique identity, focus, and expression as the higher self at these expanded levels of consciousness. And so it is that as the physical body and consciousness grow and change in time and space, so do the spiritual body (soul) and consciousness grow and expand in various states of being.

Higher consciousness thus encompasses three higher cognitions that it uses to manifest energetically and consciously authentic essence or soul qualities, as the self as CU seeks to find ways to give unique physical expression for various archetypal energies. From an energy vibrational point of view, the higher cognitions allow the self to tap into the creative energies of the higher planes. The three higher cognitions are: (1) the cognition of one's higher mind tapping into and mirroring the vibrational energies from the causal plane, (2) the cognition of one's higher emotions tapping into and mirroring the vibrational energies from the messianic plane, and (3) the cognition of one's higher will/energy tapping into and mirroring the vibrational energies from the buddhaic plane.

The higher self has been called by many names in various human cultures. Some of these names are: Soul, Atman, the Inner Self, the Causal Self or Causal Body, the One, the Spiritual One or Spiritual Self, the God within, the Essence Self or Essence, the Christ within, the Compassionate Self, the Angel, the Divine Perceiver, the Watcher, the Interpreter, the Observer, the Flame of Spirit, the Light Body. Thus, the labeling scheme I am using in this spiritual and soul-centered model is simply for descriptive purposes and is somewhat arbitrary. It is not so important, however, what the higher self and its aspects are called as it is to understand that the higher self contains all of the possibilities of one's ever-emerging, ever-creative, and ever-evolving nature. The higher self, therefore, is not a static, personal essence. It is a living, responsive presence of vibrational being-ness, a consciousness of great love, wisdom, and intelligence.

In the physical or denser realms, the physical plane, the CU in this spiritual and soul-centered model may be referred to as the lower self or lower consciousness. This is the domain of what is called the ego with a physical body or a person's current racial form. The lower self operates in the outer vibrational world of experience (see Jacquelyn Small's *Transformers: The Artists of Self-Creation*, 1994), taking on a variety of roles in numerous dramas and contexts. The lower self may also be called the personality, as a person uniquely embraces and identifies with many of these roles, including the role that the person calls their racial identity.

The lower self or personality thus has physical, emotional, and mental aspects. In the physical realm, a person also tends to experience these vibrational aspects of the lower self or personality as separate from the vibrational universe as a whole. That is, the person tends to view the self as having their own body or current racial form, an identity with feelings, and a consciousness with a rational or conscious mind. In the model, it is one of the initial ways that source energy/spirit, or All-That-Is, creates games through which they learn more about their aspects and dimensions (or ever emerging multidimensional nature)—the primary motivating force. In this context and in relation to this model, lower self race games, which I will also discuss later, may be referred to as follows: (1) the Security Race Game, (2) the Sensory Race Game, and (3) the Power Race Game.

The human race game, therefore, is part of an evolving and exploratory self-creation process, although many people may have distorted its purpose. The distortions have emerged from an over-identification with aspects of the lower self to the exclusion of authentic essence, with the accompanying fear that this engenders. The human race game is not meant to be played with fear as a motivating force. The outcome of such dramas is the creation of distortions and growth with pain. I will discuss some of these distortions in more detail later. The lower self is thus in a process of becoming, learning more about aspects of the self as the self becomes more and more itself on the physical plane.

Behind all living things in the physical realm, however, is what has been called bio-etheric bodies or life energies. Bio-etheric bodies are like energetic, vibrating templates for living forms with consciousness. They are partially reflected in what is known as the auras of the physical body or the phantom images that have been seen in what is known as Kirlian photography and more recently in what has come to be known as aura imaging photography. Bio-etheric bodies, however, do not come from matter as it is currently understood. Rather, in this model, living matter vibrationally conforms to them and, to an extent, is sustained by them.

In accord with this model, during the incarnation process, as alluded to earlier, authentic spiritual essence slows its vibrational intensity through stages so as to be able to integrate with the developing physical vehicle without burning it up. In other words, authentic spiritual essence through stages molds around itself these bands of energy that are aligned with the buddhaic, messianic, and causal Planes. These stages are the subtle bodies, the bio-etheric bodies, the bands of energies that surround and interpenetrate the physical. It is through accessing, understanding, and finding ways to physically integrate and express the essence of these higher energies that a person also begins the process of uncovering their authentic spiritual essence. A person's authentic spiritual essence, therefore, is unique to that person alone, while not being static and unchanging in its nature. When uncovering one's authentic spiritual essence on the physical plane, then, a person simply becomes more and more of their truer self. For purposes of this discussion, I will use the terms "truer self," "true self," and "authentic spiritual essence" somewhat interchangeably to connote an ever-evolving, multidimensional self-creation process.

In other terms, many are aware of the *Chakras*, the seven or more energy vortexes or centers of energy that operate in and around the physical body, and *chi* energy or *prana* energy as other components of bio-etheric bodies. It is through these seven or more chakra centers or vibrational energy foci and their expansion and extension, sometimes into other realms, that each person (the outer self) uniquely experiences the universe energetically, emotionally, intellectually, and instinctively. This individualized experience constitutes a person's personal energy system. It is through the vortexes of the personal energy system, the chakras, that a person taps into the flow of universal energy.

Other names have also been used for the chakra centers or vibrational energies related to bio-etheric bodies. Some authors, for example, have referred to the opening, expansion, and extension of these energy centers as awakening one's "light bodies," or the auras of the higher self (e.g., Roman-Orin and Packer-

DaBen's work, orinanddaben.com, 1986 through the present; Rother and the Group's work, Lightworker.com, 1996 through the present). While this description may be more or less accurate, I will refrain for the moment from using the term light bodies since the terms light and dark currently carry rather specific connotative meanings in some cultures and are currently misapplied in relation to the race-linked human games. For purposes at this point, therefore, I simply want to emphasize that it is in relation to what might be called racially-linked energy blocks associated with the chakras that lower self race games are fueled. When I discuss lower self race games later, I will also explore the nature of these racially-linked energy blocks.

As implied in this model, at other levels of physicality are other etheric beings and vibrational energies, which have more of a connection to plant and animal life. Although the etheric realm will not be a focus of this discussion, I mention it here only to give a broader sense of the vibrational world that each person inhabits, as well as to provide a glimpse into expanded aspects of the self as represented in this spiritual and soul-centered model.

As many know, the emotional body or emotional reality, as it is currently understood, is where a person vibrationally experiences desires, feelings, and emotional attitudes as physical sensations. The emotional body provides a person with a vibrational feeling-tone about their world. It is the aspect of the self that a person uses to connect with others in their world. Each person uses their five senses to provide themselves with sensory feelings about the self and others in their world. The emotional body often provides the impetus for communication and lends intensity to a person's beliefs. The rational or conscious mind (the intellect) and its beliefs, therefore, largely influence the emotional body. That is, a person's feelings largely follow the vibrational flow of the person's reasoning.

In this spiritual and soul-centered model, however, the emotional body also extends to other inner or higher vibrational realms of experience beyond the physical senses, as they are currently understood. This extension is into what some know as the astral plane and in more expanded states into the messianic plane. A person may get a sense of the emotional energy of these inner or higher vibrational planes through the opening of the heart center during deep relaxation or meditative experiences, again employing one's imagination and intuition. Many esoteric schools of thought, of which some are aware, have described these inner or higher vibrational planes of experience in one form or another (e.g., Vedic scriptures; Buddha teachings; classical Hindu teachings; theosophical teachings; Rosicrucian teachings; Kriya Yoga teachings). And so, I will suggest that readers do further research into this matter or simply refresh their memories in accord with their beliefs and interests.

For purposes here, the importance of mentioning the higher or more expanded emotional aspects of the self is to illustrate that, from an energy vibrational point of view, who a person knows the self to be emotionally is far greater than what the person may currently think. Implied in this model, the astral plane, for example, is where a person's consciousness goes at night, in a manner of speaking, when the person is asleep. In a broader sense of this spiritual and soul-centered model, the astral plane is also where a person's consciousness goes in between lifetimes and where a person's consciousness goes when physical plane lessons are learned. In this model, what has been called the astral or subtle body, or the subtle reality as a consciousness-energy experience, is what is at play here, whereby each person as a CU (the person with their astral body) is focused on emotional lessons (e.g., see R. Bruce & C. E. Lingren's *Astral Dynamics: A New Approach to Out-of-Body Experiences*, 1999 & R. Bruce's *Astral Dynamics: The Complete Book of Out-of Body Experiences*, 2009; R. Bartlett's *Matrix Energetics: The Science and Art of Transformation*, 2009; C. Dale's *The Subtle Body: An Encyclopedia of Your Energetic Anatomy*, 2009).

The mental body or mental reality is the seat of the mind. The mind is the container of beliefs, which structure what a person thinks is their all-powerful reality. The mind, however, can be said to have three aspects to it: (1) the Conscious or Rational Mind (the intellect), that creates form, content, and context as a person uses beliefs or reasoning to make sense of what they know as the outer self and their reality, (2) the Subconscious Mind, which stores all data a person has encountered directly and indirectly, no matter how minute, and guards the content of the inner realities that influences, but does not control, who the person is, and (3) the Superconscious Mind, which guards the content or information of a person's other realities or the person's past, future, and parallel lifetimes. Some readers know about other realities from reading about them in various esoteric materials, from engaging in what has been called past-life regressions, or from hearing about what scientists now call possible parallel universes (see Fred Alan Wolf's *Parallel Universes*, 1990; D. Deutsch's *The Fabric of Reality: The Science of Parallel Universes and Its Implications*, 1998 & *The Beginning of Infinity: Explanations That Transform the World*, 2011; B. Greene's *The Elegant Universe: Superstrings, Hidden Dimensions, and the Quest for the Ultimate Theory*, 2003; S. Kaehr's *Beyond Reality: Evidence of Parallel Universes*, 2010; M. Kaku's *Parallel Worlds: A Journey Through Creation, Higher Dimensions, and the Future of the Cosmos*, 2006, and *Physics of the Impossible: A Scientific Exploration into the World of Phasers, Force Fields, Teleportation, and Time Travel*, 2009). The subconscious mind and the superconscious mind, therefore, may be thought of as lower and higher levels of what may be called the unconscious mind or higher mind.

The ego is the most outwardly focused part of the rational or conscious mind and personality structure. The ego has and uses free will to accept, modify, and reject various beliefs in accord with a person's unique life spaces, cultures, and environments.

Many of the core beliefs, however, that the person currently uses to structure the human race game are unconscious or transparent to the outer self. In most instances, these core beliefs operate in the person's subconscious mind to influence the person's perception of human relations and race relations. However, they can be made more conscious as the person moves closer to an understanding of their truer self.

Using the vibrational mental tools of imagination, logic, and intuition to explore aspects of the self and the nature of beliefs, a person can uncover many limiting beliefs related to the human race game. The person can also learn how to remove those beliefs that are creating less than desirable human and racial circumstances. Further, the person can open up possibilities for experiencing higher ideas from the superconscious mind in regard to individual and collective racial forms, and the human race game. As a person evolves their beliefs and inner images about the self and racial forms, they will also be evolving the human race game.

In this model, the truer self or truer consciousness is an ever-emerging expression of the spiritually integrated self. The truer self also represents the consciously evolving self, an aspect of which relates to the context of the human race game and the person's current racial form. The truer self recognizes and legitimizes the higher and lower aspects of the self, vibrationally creating an integrated bridge consciousness that is motivated by the archetypal energies—acceptance, love, inclusion, and harmony.

The truer self in this model thus creates, or more precisely, is a bridge between the rational, or conscious, and unconscious aspects of the mind. That is, it creates a vibratory bridge between the subconscious or lower unconscious mind and the superconscious or higher unconscious mind, between the intellect and intuition. In that sense, the truer self in this model emerges as a bridge or an integrated self with transformed aspects of the higher and lower selves.

The truer self in this model also recognizes the interdependent nature of the vibrational world each person inhabits and the
interpenetrating nature of various lower and higher vibrational
planes of experience. The truer self in this model recognizes
how consciousness-energy creates forms and experiences,
and flows up and down and in and out of these various lower
and higher vibrational planes. As a person learns and grows
in accord with various earth lessons, the truer self can use an
aspect of itself, the observer self, to remain detached from the
ego or the personality's melodramas in order to help the person
maneuver comfortably through a myriad of ebbs and flows of
energy transformations, transmutations, and changes. In this
context and in relation to the human race game, the truer self
emerges and evolves through playing what can be called the
Transformational Race Game.

From an energy vibrational point of view in this model, the
truer self further has the ability to tap into what some know as the
Akashic Records in order to help clarify the person's higher foci
for this lifetime. Some authors have described the akashic records
as the storehouse for all experience in the universe (e.g., Roman-
Orin, *Spiritual Growth: Being Your Higher Self*, 1992; Christeaan,
Van Hulle, & Clark's *Michael: The Basic Teachings*, 1988; Linda
Howe's *How to Read the Akashic Records: Accessing the Archive of
the Soul and Its Journey*, 2010). In other terms, the well-known
personality and psychologist, Carl Jung (*The Archetypes and the
Collective Unconscious*, 1981), has described aspects of the akashic
records as the "collective unconscious."

In this model, the akashic records is not an energy vibrational
plane where a person experiences their being-ness, but rather is
an energy vibrational plane to go to for information or reference
(see Kevin Todeschi's *Edgar Cayce on the Akashic Records: The Book
of Life*, 1998; Ervin Lasio's *The Akashic Experience: Science and
the Cosmic Memory Field*, 2009; Cheryl Trine's *The New Akashic
Records: Knowing, Healing & Spiritual Practice*, 2010). Using one's

imagination and intuition, which are tools of the mental body on the physical plane, the truer self, from an energy vibrational point of view in this model, expands one's consciousness enough so that information from the akashic plane can be "sensed."

In this model, from an energy vibrational point of view, the truer self also has the ability to tap into the astral plane in regard to various emotional lessons that may be impinging on a person's current experiences. In other terms in this model, some of the spiritual dispatches to the truer self may come to the person vibrationally in the form of intuitions, dreams, synchronicity experiences, altered states, psychic experiences, flow experiences, etheric realm experiences, sensing the energy around or between one's self and another person, or in the symbolism behind what I am calling the "mirror effect." In this model, the truer self understands that meaning is contained in the symbolic messages of a person's creations, as the language of spirit is archetypal.

The truer self, as the spiritually integrated self in this model, thus constructs a vibrational bridge between the rational mind and the higher mind, using logic, intuition, and imagination. It does so as the person creatively evolves a consciousness that mirrors acceptance, inclusion, harmony, and love in their life spaces. The truer self in this model also has the ability to be a conscious creator or co-creator of reality. A person's higher good, therefore, is manifested through the truer self as the person seeks to uncover more about the self and to expand their consciousness. On the physical plane, then, and in other terms, the truer self in this model may be considered the "soul in physical clothes."

Through what has become known as the new physics and the science of quantum reality, some researchers and thinkers in Western cultures and in the world have found value and validity for alternative models of human nature, such as the one presented here. Even those who might prefer to view the self through the lens of a more literal materialistic perspective or a mechanistic model (such as the scientific model or a Marxist or capitalist interpretation of the self) can find direction and meaning in such alternative models. One can do so by focusing on how material or economic forms of energy are exchanged.

Each person's current racial form in quantum reality, for example, can be viewed, from an energy vibrational point of view in this model, as having its own unique energy markers in the material world. Likewise, from an energy vibrational point of view in this model, money as "objectified material energy" (paper, metal, and electronic currents) can be viewed as a means of exchanging valued energy with conscious intent for the purpose of creating and manifesting what one wants individually and collectively.

In this context, it can be argued in this model that metaphysics and the scientific model have begun to dialogue to create a new framework of understanding reality. Energy may then be viewed as the primary underlying, vibrating reality and matter as its derivative state. Consciousness may be viewed as the source of manifestation of a spectrum of lower and higher vibrational realities, and not simply a mirror of a "consensus reality." Reality may be viewed as consciousness-energy, whereby consciousness is considered the inside of energy and energy the outside of consciousness. In this framework, consciousness and energy share each other's properties but are not reducible to each other. Rather, each is a reflection of the other. A person's current racial form, consequently, is composed vibrationally of physical, emotional, mental, and spiritual bodies and realities of energy and is thus a reflection of the person's evolving consciousness.

In this context, from a spiritual and soul-centered perspective, no race or racial form in this model is more evolved than another, as the self or souls may assume a variety of racial forms and have assumed the current racial forms for their own reasons. In this model, each person is therefore consciousness, looking out and exploring the self and giving the self an identity by what they can objectify through the illusion of identifying with what they find. The self is on the inside looking out, suspecting that there may be something more. The self is also what is reflected back and more. In this model, people are souls with a physical body—one's current racial form.

In this model, as people look out onto the outer vibrational world of experience, using their various racial forms individually and collectively, that part of the person that they know as the ego tries to make sense of or give meaning to what the person thinks they perceive. Those ego perceptions and meanings are in regard to: the person's physical or current racial form; the physical or current racial form of others; color; the familiar and unfamiliar patterns of thoughts, emotions, and behaviors of the self and others (i.e., cultures); and the myriad of human and racial dramas at personal, societal, and global levels. These dramas, as I have suggested, are intimately connected to a person's search for the meaning of the human experience, the phenomenon of race, and deeper understanding of the self.

Many distortions related to the concept of the self, however, have emerged over time, as it is understood. As implied in this model, most people have forgotten that there is already meaning for the human race game beyond their illusions. They have forgotten that they use their current racial form as a vehicle to give unique self-expression for their life-nurturing soul qualities. They have forgotten that one of the intents of the human race game is to serve as a game for expanding a person's consciousness and for exploring the multidimensional nature of the self. Most people have forgotten that the games of the universe, including the human race game, can be and are intended to be joyful-learning experiences.

As implied in the soul-centered model, people do have free will, which must be used wisely. I will say more on the wise will later. In this regard, unfortunately, in individual and collective discussions about the meaning of the human race game and the search for self, many people have more often than not created distortions and less than joyful, often destructive, dramas in relation to playing the human race game.

THE SEARCH FOR "SELF" AND THE "MEANING" OF RACE THROUGH PLAYING THE HUMAN RACE GAME

Over the years, as linear time is understood, there have been numerous attempts to understand the meaning of the phenomenon of race in relation to the human experience. The phenomenon as currently understood is an unavoidable fact for the visually oriented human species. Yet, in all the attempts, there have been derived no definitive answers and perhaps no definitive answers will ever be derived using the current framework. For purposes of this exploratory discussion, however, let me briefly characterize the nature of this search for the meaning of the phenomenon of race in relation to the human experience as a search for self through playing the human race game. In this context, the individual and collective dialogues have centered on three basic disciplines of thought about the phenomenon of race in relation to the human experience, as they are understood: (1) race as a biological concept, (2) race as an anthropological and sociological concept, and (3) race as a psychological concept.

I am therefore suggesting a fourth area for discussion—race as a spiritual and soul-centered concept. Together, these four basic areas of dialogue may be connected to the paradigm shift

I alluded to earlier and the emerging newer models related to people's overall basic natures as human beings. As I suggested earlier, a number of current writers, researchers, and explorers of the nature of consciousness who have engaged the paradigm shift, have argued that human beings are fourfold vibrational beings in a vibrational environment (e.g., Ester & Jerry Hicks' *Ask and It Is Given*, 2005 & *The Amazing Power of Deliberate Intent: Living the Art of Allowing*, 2006; Christopher & Jeannine Jelm's *New Humans, New Earth: The Grand Celestial Plan for Personal and Planetary Transformation*, 2009 & *Transcendent Humans, Transcendent Earth*, 2012), or what I would call fourfold consciousness-energy beings, with a physical body, an emotional body, a mental body, and a spiritual and soul-centered body. For this reason, empirical research that I have conducted is also interwoven into the discussion below.

The four disciplines of thought represent various ways people have and can frame and play the human race game in specific and general terms as they search for self and the meaning of the phenomenon of race in relation to the human experience. Using the framework of the four disciplines of thought about the human experience, the collective focus on the meaning of race as a biological concept has been centered on the nature of people's physical bodies—people's visible racial forms. The collective focus of the meaning of race as an anthropological and sociological concept has been centered on the nature of people's emotions or the emotional body—that is, people's emotional relationships, or ways of emotionally connecting as individuals and groups culturally (ethnically; tribally) and societally. The collective focus on the meaning of race as a psychological concept has been centered on the nature of the mind or the mental body, that is, on what one thinks and believes to be true about the phenomenon of race (e.g., one's stereotypes, prejudices, interpretations of research data, etc.), or on what one believes to be true about one's own or another person's mind, body, and emotional life. I am suggesting a fourth focus—a spiritual and soul-centered concept of race.

In regard to the first three foci, there have been numerous distortions in people's individual and collective discussions. Most of the distortions emerge out of an over-identification by the ego aspect of a person's personality with one of the above concepts about the human experience and the phenomenon of race (as an aspect of the self) to the exclusion of others (a self-limiting attitude) and the fear that accompanies this over-identification. Distortions continue when a person allows fear to direct the focus of their consciousness in their individual and collective study of the self. Left out of the discussions so far has been consideration of spiritual and soul-centered aspects, except as it has related to religious dogma to justify actions and practices of discrimination and prejudices. Before I discuss the spiritual and soul-centered perspective, let's take a closer look at the three other concepts related to the phenomenon of race and some of the distortions that have taken place in the human experience, individually and collectively.

RACE AS A BIOLOGICAL CONCEPT

At the level of the physical body, a great deal of consciousness-energy has been expended, focusing on and making attributions about race as a biological concept in relation to the human experience in terms of the meaning of the physical body's size, shape, and color. When taken to the extreme, as some authors in the past have attempted to do (e.g., Morton's *Crania Americana*, 1839 & 2012), the logic may extend to viewing the many races as being separate species.

More recent scientific views, however, have concluded that using the criteria of physical features to define the meaning of race in relation to the human experience is a rather arbitrary exercise. For any physical feature that can be identified, someone who has been identified as belonging to a particular race can always be found who does not fit the mold. Some might continue to argue, nevertheless, that the people who do not fit the mold are simply exceptions to the rule. Yet, if the physical or biological perspective is pushed, it inevitably leads to trying to understand the physical body and the meaning of race at the microscopic level—at the level of atoms, genes, chromosomes, DNA, and perhaps even the quarks, neutrinos, and strings of quantum physics. So, let's push it a bit and see what distortions might arise.

At the microscopic level, the argument becomes that members of a particular race seem to have similar body types in terms of size, shape, and color and that this is due to DNA codes which tell the cells of the body how to grow in terms of size, shape, and color. Rather than celebrating how miraculous this process may be and the consequent beauty the body forms that may result from this process, the tendency has been to fear the differences and to distort the meaning of these physical differences. If one looks a little closer one will discover, however, that no two body forms are exactly the same and that each set of DNA code tells the cells to evolve a body form that has never existed before.

Scientifically, again according to belief structures, it is now known that each person's DNA is unique to that person, even though it was acquired from two parental figures. If each body form is unique, then how can race as a biological concept have any meaning since the phenomenon would be based on a unique criterion, uncommon to any other person who might be classified as belonging to that particular race? Even scientists, who do DNA testing in a field of study called genetic genealogy, have found difficulty in classifying a person's racial heritage. That is, DNA testing has often linked a person's current racial form to the genetic pools of racially-linked body forms other than the ones with which the person identifies.

At a quantum level, the physical or biological perspective becomes even more precarious. In accord with human experience, researchers would have to try to ascribe racial meaning to particles of an atom (or to subatomic particles) that exist in time and space for perhaps a billionth of a second or less, as it is understood. Another question that also would continue to elude researchers is how does the DNA know what to tell the cells? To say that there are certain chemical reactions from the DNA of the two parental donors or that the new and original DNA codes are that way by nature begs the question. If it is an accident of nature, then how does nature's accident know how to continue to happen in the same way that it does? How do these chemicals know what to do? Who or what programmed in the code?

But what about color, one might ask. It is also now known scientifically that the primary reason that people are able to see color is because of the light waves that are reflected from an object. This is another miraculous event to which some have somehow given distorted meaning in terms of evaluative judgments. For example, there is a common color code in American culture that involves those labeled "the black race" and "the white race." Here, one can find numerous distortions about the color of the body in terms of evaluative judgments that involve a white as good and pure and black as bad and impure color code. The evaluative judgments related to this "color code" are reinforced by the connotative meanings in the language, symbols, and imagery that permeate much of American culture (e.g., white lie; snow-white; blacklist; black cloud; black-and-white to characterize a sharp divide; black sheep; brides wear white; mourners dress in black).

In actuality, black and white, scientifically, are colorless; they have no hue in that sense. Further, scientifically, when the colors of the spectrum are actually brought together, you get light, not black or white. When light, on the other hand, encounters a prism, its primary colors of red, blue, and yellow are revealed—the combination of these primary colors of light constitute the nature of all other colors that we see. In other terms, the actual modal color of those labeled as part of the white race is not white but pinkish tan; the actual modal color of those labeled as part of the black race is not black but brown. And yet, the color code in American culture is extended to include other colors, such as "red" for Native Americans, "yellow" for Asian Americans, and "brown" for Spanish-speaking or Latin Americans.

The use of a color code and evaluative judgments in regard to the color of the body exists in many cultures. One extreme example existed in South Africa in the form of its apartheid system, recently dismantled in historic time, which was based solely on the color of the body. Such a system vividly illustrates what can happen systemically when the color code distortion is allowed to rule the focus of consciousness. A somewhat subtler example can be said to exist with two countries known as the Dominican Republic and Haiti, which now share a relatively small island with arbitrary demarcations of the land based in part on a color code. Both groups are considered "groups of color." However, other groups, such as the Spanish, the French, and Americans, influenced both groups. In the two cultures, therefore, "light-brown skin" and "dark-brown skin" carry rather specific connotative meanings and evaluative judgments.

Interestingly, the Dominican group, it can be argued, was derived from a mixture of body types. In terms of a color code, these body types would include being descendants of red Indians called the Tainos, white or brown Spanish invaders, and black Africans. Yet, in the Dominican Republic, Dominicans with Haitian descents and Haitian immigrants may experience discrimination based, in part, on a color code. The Haitian group, on the other hand, carries the influences of the white French, more linguistically than in terms of body type. They can be said to be descendants of black Africans in terms of a color code. One result has been a history of power struggles between the groups, in part fueled by the color code and labeling associated with economic concerns. Hidden behind the economic tensions are American values and their relation to the two groups of color in terms of a color code.

Labeling, however, is not the issue—the good-bad meanings that some people attach to the labels are. It is at the meaning level of the labeling process where the distortion takes place as those who do so fail to celebrate the miracle of the colors of the body. The social movement in the late 1960s in the United States by African Americans to give the term "black" a more positive meaning was an attempt to confront at an individual and societal level how people are creators of evaluative meanings in this regard. It only partially succeeded. Go a step further then and ask who "the seer" is. Is it a person's eyes that really see or the atoms that make up the person's eyes and brains? Who attributes meaning to what is seen? Can each person see and experience the authentic essence of another beyond the physical body? Can each person appreciate and celebrate the physical body as a unique expression of essence or of people's souls?

RACE AS AN ANTHROPOLOGICAL AND SOCIOLOGICAL CONCEPT

At the level of the emotional body, the primary emphasis on the phenomenon of race as an anthropological and sociological concept in relation to the human experience has been in terms of how race has been a vehicle for human beings to feel a sense of belonging. Here, human beings have sought to understand the meaning of race as it relates to a group identity. Unfortunately, distortions have also emerged here, guided principally by the emotion of fear—fear of the different, fear of the unfamiliar, fear of the new, and fear of death or annihilation. Fear and the desire to feel a sense of belonging are the two kinds of feeling states, then, that have guided much of the individual and collective discussions about the phenomenon of race in relation to the human experience at this level.

When a person over-identifies as a member of a particular group in their desire to belong, it is easy for the person to assume that they have nothing in common with those who have indicated that they identify with another group. Rather than embrace the different, the unfamiliar, or the new as opportunities to learn more about the self, the person may allow over-identification and fear to take root and the person may often retreat or attack. Recorded and oral history, as it is understood, is replete with example after example of humanity creating conflicts and wars in the name of maintaining someone's idealizations of sameness by fearing and attacking the different, unfamiliar, or new. Often the over-identification occurs as a person evolves a sense of racial or other group identity in the context of a culture. Let's take a closer look at how some distortions may emerge in regard to race and culture in a person's human experience.

At an emotional level, a person may confuse the meaning of race with misconceptions about culture (or beliefs about a cultural, ethnic, or tribal group). The person may assume, for example, that culture is static and that their racial identity is what gives culture its meaning and vice versa. The person may then use the concept of race to justify the maintenance of their culture and the meanings they have ascribed to their racial identity. The fallacy here is that culture is static. Culture is not static.

Culture is an ongoing problem-solving process in response to the human environment—physical, social, and spiritual—and may have little or nothing to do with racial heritage per se. In individual and collective discussions, however, people may assume that the two phenomena—race and culture—are somehow innately connected. Culture is assumed to be an outgrowth of a person's racial heritage and, in turn, the person assumes their racial identity is highly linked to their cultural environment. Yet, there are numerous examples in what is known as past- and present-day reality that vividly illustrates the distortion here.

Protestants and Catholics in Ireland share what is thought to be a common racial heritage, yet they are in conflict at a cultural level and have been for some time, as it is understood. People, past and present, in countries like Algeria, Burma (Myanmar), Burundi, Congo, Colombia, Sudan (Darfur), Bosnia, Yugoslavia, Kosovo, Rwanda, or Egypt similarly share what is thought to be common racial heritages respectively, yet they have divided themselves along what they consider relevant ethnic or tribal lines and also struggle at a cultural level. The same also could be said about the interchanges among ethnic groups in the present-day multicultural experiences in the United States, but to a lesser degree in terms of volatility (e.g., in the wake of 9/11, Islamic-related tensions emerged in a 2010 national debate about the location of an Islamic cultural center in New York).

In these contexts, people's fears associated with an over-identification with religious dogma or with distorted perceptions about ethnic symbolism underlie the cultural conflicts. Under these circumstances, race as an anthropological and sociological concept (or as a concept about a common racial heritage) appears to have little or no meaning as a unifying societal self-concept or as a meaningful concept in providing a coherent sense of societal group identity. Rather, the concept of race mistakenly has been applied to create the illusion of internal societal enemies (e.g., racial, ethnic, or tribal groups) against which a majority or minority group must struggle to maintain a sense of identity. Let's take a closer look at the generic experience in the United States.

Underlying the grand experiment that is called America or the United States has been an ongoing struggle regarding the meaning of race and culture. Yet, historically, as it is understood, there has never been a common racial heritage. At a spiritual and soul-centered level, the experiment, it can be argued, was and is to create a physical place on the planet whereby representatives of all races, as the phenomenon is presently understood, would be brought together to invent a multicultural society and an alternative perspective for humanity that would value each person. It would be a rich arena for exploring the multidimensional nature of human beings. Humanity would be able to more fully comprehend the nature of their multidimensional selves, mirrored externally. Race and culture were to be celebratory phenomena in regard to one's individual and collective evolution and one's individual and collective achievements.

At the ego (or personality) and emotional level, however, many people have made numerous mistakes or "miss takes" (missing the take on an experience; misperceptions) along the way and have created many distortions about race and culture. There are those in the world, however, who are beginning to value the concept of diversity, albeit sometimes on a surface level at this point in time. Too often a person's over-identifications with their emotions can cloud their view of the self. People are not their emotions. They have emotions and these largely follow the flow of their reasoning, or their mental or thought constructions.

Hence, many distortions have occurred as people have sought to understand and to value the self in relation to the constructs of time and what I will call the economy of energy. The issue of time here refers to the construction of a view of the self through historical lenses, as it is understood. From an energy vibrational point of view, economy of energy refers to the give-and-take of energy for the purpose of a creative enterprise.

The United States thus evolved as a future-oriented, fast-paced culture. In this context, people, unfortunately and without much awareness, began to view each other as objects to be manipulated for gain or in the name of progress. As a result, those who were allowed to act in control overlooked how economic forces were based on a valued exchange of energy. The concept of race, then, became a tool for manipulating people and controlling the exchange of energy, and a whole group of people—African Americans, in particular—were devalued as human beings. The underlying beliefs were a belief in scarcity and a belief in the lack of energy regarding the economy of energy.

Rather than the state of the economy being perceived as a vibrational, interdependent whole with an abundance of valuable, individualized energy for exchange, the majority group, so to speak, adopted a separating attitude to create the illusion of control. The majority group, therefore, misunderstood the source of energy, viewing it as external to themselves and others.

As a future-oriented culture, people also became too busy looking forward, often failing to appreciate the beauty of the present and often distorting the past to justify a present sense of self. In this context, the idea of race and culture as celebratory concepts was never allowed to fully emerge, as many people in the majority group over-identified with their reference group and became protective about a way of life.

Futuring is not innately a destructive cultural pattern, but it can lend itself to destructive imaginings when based on distortions about the past. When people fail to realize that the past is just as much of an invention as a probable future, the seed for distortion is born. At the personal level, then, it is important to recognize that each person uses highly selective memories, as they understand them, in their discussions about race and culture. At the societal or institutional level, the same can be said.

For example, out of fear, some people in so-called majority groups in some societies have attempted to invent self-concepts related to the concept of race by evoking and citing biblical scriptures or other religious scriptures out of context. This is a common practice in American culture for those over-identifying with a reference group and for those who somehow fear genetic annihilation.

Further, a person also may get a very different sense of the self from various historical perspectives, depending on the historical, anthropological, sociological, or cultural writer and the worldview being touted. For example, from what has been called a Eurocentric perspective, the personality known as Abraham Lincoln may be viewed as the Great Emancipator. He presumably developed a proclamation as President of the United States to free African American slaves as the country raged about race and culture via a civil war.

However, from what has been called an Afrocentric perspective, the personality known as Abraham Lincoln may be viewed as the Reluctant Emancipator (e.g., L. Bennett's "Was Lincoln a White Supremacist?", *Ebony*, 1968). He would be viewed as developing a proclamation only after he saw that he could do harm to the Southern forces by proclaiming free the millions of African American slaves who already had declared a strike, left the fields, and were across the Northern lines. Indeed, from the Afrocentric perspective, it would be emphasized that barely a year into the Civil War, Lincoln suggested an "emancipation with compensation" proposal, a proposal to buy slaves from slaveholders for $400 apiece with each Southern state, in return for the payment, being allowed to gradually emancipate slaves over a twenty-year period. The discussions at the emotional level, therefore, still leave a lot to be desired. The culprits again are over-identification and fear.

RACE AS A PSYCHOLOGICAL CONCEPT

What are people really afraid of, then? To answer this question, interestingly it is perhaps best to go to the next level of discussion about the meaning of race in relation to the human experience, the mental level—that is, race as a psychological concept. At the mental level, a person's emotions, vibrationally, follow the flow of their reasoning. That is, the person's emotions flow from what they reason to be true. When this question is honestly answered, then, from a Western and American perspective, I suggest that what many people may be afraid of is the deeper, inner aspects of the self. Why might this be the case?

One explanation is that for well over a century, cultural models have been used, models of reasoning, about the nature of the psyche that tell people that these deeper, inner aspects of the self are not to be trusted, are unsavory, and must be contained. This is a fundamental tenet of many mainstream Western and American psychological schools of thought, particularly the psychoanalytic and neo-psychoanalytic models, as I discussed earlier. It is through these lenses that both helpful constructs and distortions about race as a psychological concept have emerged.

In the above context, the dialogue about the meaning of race in relation to the human experience elevates to mental constructs about a racial identity. That is, at the mental level, "We are who we *think* we are," for the most part. An identity based on self-definitions as opposed to definitions by others is important at the mental level. However, it is also important to understand how a person can over-identify with their own mental constructions to the exclusion of other aspects of the self.

It is at the mental level that a person's beliefs about self, their racial identity, and their vibrational world are experienced as *real*. What the person may over-identify with, then, are their beliefs, as if they are all-encompassing truths and as if they are reality. Beliefs may create distortions if they imply basic limitations about who the person is, or who the person believes other people are, and if the person allows a Self-limiting belief to operate unexamined at a core level of the self to organize their experiences. The person may then experience the self as cut off from their authentic essence and the authentic essence of others. A core self-limiting belief such as "my group has *the truth* and no other group has it" may lead to this kind of distortion.

In individual and collective discussions about psychology, a great deal has been learned about how a person acquires various attitudes, including racial attitudes, stereotypes, and prejudices. Researchers have learned how racial attitudes are translated into discriminatory behaviors. Researchers have learned how people use a variety of self-defenses—such as denial, rationalization, and projection—to avoid looking closely at what they think and do. And, researchers have learned how people use these same self-defenses to create a sense of control over the inner aspects of the self. Yet, humanity appears to be no closer to understanding the meaning of race. The importance of having high self-esteem and a positive self-image is also well known. And yet, most people often do not realize that they are not their high self-esteem, nor their positive self-image. These too are the person's mental constructions about the self.

What appears to be missing is that many people may be out of touch with and out of alignment with their authentic essence. I am simply presenting a reminder here that it is a person's authentic essence that gives rise to both a high self-esteem and a positive self-image. Many mainstream psychological models, however, do not acknowledge an authentic essence or spiritual and soul-centered perspective of the self. Therefore, I want to build on what has been learned at the mental level about race as a psychological concept and to extend the individual and collective discussion about the meaning of race in relation to the human experience to include a spiritual and soul-centered perspective.

RACE AS A SPIRITUAL AND SOUL-CENTERED CONCEPT

As I suggested earlier and based on a literature review, a spiritual and soul-centered perspective places the discussion regarding the meaning of race in relation to the human experience into the realm of new emerging paradigms, a new worldview, and newer models about human nature, like the one that I presented. Paradigms are broad conceptual frameworks which help to explain why things are the way they are. Worldviews contain philosophical assumptions and metaphors about what is possible and what is not, or what types of things can be known and how they can be known. By most accounts, therefore, one of the older paradigms that has influenced much of how many people have thought about the self and the vibrational world is the Cartesian-Newtonian paradigm and the mechanistic-materialistic worldview, both of which date back to the seventeenth century personalities and philosophers Descartes and Newton.

In *Transformers: The Artists of Self-Creation* (1992), Small suggests that this old paradigm and worldview perspective are based on basic notions that separate human consciousness from the material world. The function of the separation was to create the illusion of having objectivity and control over the material world. The new emerging paradigms, on the other hand, discussed by numerous authors such as Fritjof Capra, Marilyn Ferguson, Robert Ornstein, James Redfield, Stanislav Grof, and Mark Woodhouse, describe an alternative vision of a globally interconnected world in which biological, psychological, social, environmental, and spiritual phenomena are all vibrationally interdependent. Some years ago, Woodhouse, in *Paradigm Wars* (1996), for example, suggested that the new emerging paradigms be discussed in terms of Systems Holism and the Perennial Philosophy.

Systems holists seek to bring together traditional holistic philosophies of science (e.g., Smuts' 1926 & 2010 *Holism and Evolution)* and contemporary systems theory (e.g., Immanuel Kant; Fritjof Capra). They work with paradigms that reflect the vibrational interdependence of three levels. The first vibrational level is the level of gross mass/energy (the domain of physics and chemistry, ranging from the four forces of electromagnetism, gravity, strong nuclear and weak nuclear forces to minerals and rocks). The second vibrational level is the level of living things (the domain of biology, ranging from one-celled organisms to humans). And, the third vibrational level is the realm of mind or consciousness (the domain of certain schools of psychology, philosophy, and religion). They emphasize higher and lower levels of organization. From this new worldview, quantum/relativistic physicists, for example, have discovered that matter or form is not solid and that life appears to be about vibrational relationship, fluctuation, and energy flow. Consciousness is also viewed as pre-causal to experience and matter and interdependent with the material world.

Perennialists, on the other hand, seek to bring together the experiences and traditions of both Eastern (e.g., *Upanishads*; Patanjali in *Yoga Sutras*; Sri Aurobindo in *The Life Divine*; Lama Govinda in *Foundations of Tibetan Buddhism*) and Western (e.g., Plato's *Republic*; Sufi mystic Rumi's *Mathnawi*; William James' *The Varieties of Religious Experience*; Houston Smith's *Beyond the Post-Modern Mind*; Aldous Huxley's *Perennial Philosophy*; Ken Wilber's *The Spectrum of Consciousness* and *Sex, Ecology, Spirituality*) mystics and spiritual leaders and their philosophical insights with the teachings of psychically gifted individuals (e.g., Jane Roberts; Gurdjieff; Alice Bailey; Pat Rodegast; Jach Pursel; Pythagoras; Emmanuel Swendenberg) or groups (e.g. Gnosticism; Kabbalism; the Theosophical Society; Rosicrucians; shamanic traditions from aboriginal to Native American). Both traditions stress the existence of consciousness and multileveled vibrational dimensions beyond the physical, a Godhead or ground source of being, spiritual evolution, and the interconnectedness of all things.

The emerging new paradigms and new worldview, as I have alluded, would suggest that in regard to the human race game, humanity has been looking for meaning where it cannot be found. That is, humanity has been looking externally for the meaning of the phenomenon of race in relation to the human experience. In other words, human beings have been over-identifying with the physical body, the emotional body (i.e., via a person's parents, their families, their religion, their externalized culture), or the mental body (i.e., via a person's externalized beliefs, their externalized principles and causes, their creative endeavors) to the exclusion of the spiritual body. As a result, many people have separated themselves—the ego or ego aspects of their personality—from the causal energy for their experiences and their authentic essence. From a spiritual and soul-centered perspective, causal energy flows from a person's higher consciousness, the domain of the spiritual and soul-centered body, which focuses, translates, and channels the person's authentic essence for experience through their lower consciousness, the domain of ego or personality.

As I suggested earlier, the new paradigms and new world-view have given birth to a number of newer models about human nature and consciousness. I have presented one such model (see Figure 2). As with this model, other emerging models also challenge the old paradigm (e.g., Grof's *The Holotropic Mind* and *The Cosmic Game*). Likewise, they too suggest that each person has a lower consciousness or lower self, the domain of ego or personality, and a higher consciousness or higher self, the domain of essence, soul, spirit, or inner self (e.g., Lazaris-Purcel's *The Sacred Journey-You and Your Higher Self*; Key's *Handbook to Higher Consciousness*; Hoodwin's *The Journey of Your Soul*; Roberts-Seth's *The Nature of Personal Reality*; Small's *Transformers*; Roman-Orin's *Spiritual Growth-Being Your Higher Self*).

Again, many other descriptive labels have been used to refer to the lower dimension (e.g., Physical self, Bio-energetic level, Bio-etheric level) and higher dimension (e.g., Causal Self, Spiritual Self, Soul, Essence). It is not so important what these aspects of the self are called, as it is to have models that seek to acknowledge the whole self and to explain the role of consciousness. The significance of these models, then, to the individual and collective discussion about the meaning of the phenomenon of race in relation to the human experience is that they raise important questions about how to view the self and the vibrational world.

To reiterate, most of the newer emerging models suggest that perhaps the more accurate way to view the self as human beings is as a consciousness-energy entity and that the stuff of reality is actually consciousness and energy experienced at various vibratory frequencies. The slower or lower the frequencies, the denser that substance and matter becomes; the faster or higher the frequencies, the less dense that substance and matter becomes.

Here, then, are two thoughts for consideration. Could it be that the realm of spirit is simply a higher vibratory level of the self and that consciousness and energy simply have different vibrational forms at this level? This is the framework of the spiritual and soul-centered model I presented (see Figure 2). Does the phenomenon of race have a meaning at this level?

As with the spiritual and soul-centered model I presented, Woodhouse (1996) and others (e.g., *A Course in Miracles*, 1996; Williamson's *The Gift of Change*, 2006; Tolle's *The Power of Now*, 2004, & *A New Earth*, 2008) similarly express or imply the following views:

1. Consciousness is a transcendental field presupposed by its objects, not simply an object or series of states within that field;

2. Consciousness is not just a mirror of consensus reality, but is the source of manifestation of a spectrum of realities;

3. Consciousness and energy are interconnected aspects of a Great Chain of Being and share each other's properties; and

4. Consciousness is the inner subjective aspect of energy (the inside of energy), and energy, whether in physical forms or in forms not currently recognized by physics, is the outward, objective aspect of consciousness (the outside of consciousness).

In this context, then, consciousness acts as the cookie cutter for the manifestation of energy—it gives purpose and meaning. Using this framework, the spiritual or soul-centered aspects of the self may be viewed as higher conscious forms of the self with much higher vibratory frequencies and abstract qualities, where meaning is formulated. Consciousness and meaning, therefore, precede manifestation. What happens now if we look for the meaning of the phenomenon of race in relation to the human experience at this level?

A Spiritual and Soul-Centered Perspective on the "Meaning" of Race in Relation to the Human Experience

From the level of the spiritual and soul-centered body and in accord with the spiritual and soul-centered model, I suggest that the meaning of the phenomenon of race in relation to the human experience flows from what I have called archetypal energies, each with ever-expanding vibrational qualities that seek unique expression through each person's psyches and life spaces. Archetypal energies are transcendent in nature, yet they operate deep within individual and collective psyches. When given unique expression and form, they tend to lead people toward their optimal selves and optimal realities. To evoke a common sense of these archetypal energies, I have used easily recognized terms and have labeled them as follows: Love, Beauty, Joy, Harmony, Enthusiasm, Trust, Hope, Courage, Acceptance, Inclusion, Flexibility, Abundance, Humor, Patience, Serenity, Compassion, Oneness, Understanding, Inspiration, Vision, Truth, Wisdom, Clarity, Peace, and Unity.

In resonance with the spiritual and soul-centered model of human nature, as well as similar kinds of models, these archetypal energies may be considered aspects of a person's authentic essence or what I have called the person's soul qualities. In this light, higher consciousness can be viewed as co-creating the person's racial forms and channeling these aspects of their authentic essence for authentic manifestation and experience through their lower consciousness. How the person gives physical form or physical expression to these archetypal energies, however, is up to that person in accord with their free will, but contained within them are some of the person's earth lessons.

The higher and lower domains are not separate, therefore, but energetically and vibrationally interdependent. As reflected in Figure 2, the dictum "As above, so below," which dates back

to ancient Egyptian mystery schools and the so-called mythi-
cal sage-god Hermes Trismegistus, provides a Perennial perspective here (see Everard's translated book, *The Divine Pymander of
Hermes Mercurius Trismegistus*, 2010). In this context, I suggest
that if humanity were to genuinely understand the meaning of the
phenomenon of race in relation to the human experience, people
would view the phenomenon with a spirit of celebration—that
is, people would view the meaning of the phenomenon of race in
relation to the human experience as providing each person with
earth lessons and physically-focused opportunities to learn more
about these soul qualities, particularly in regard to learning how
to grow with joy.

The phenomenon of race in relation to the human experience,
then, in whatever way a personality uniquely defines and experiences it, becomes primarily a game of projection. When played
in accord with the higher self, it becomes a meaningful game
only in the context of manifesting more and more of the person's authentic essence and sharing various perspectives about the
nature of the person's evolving consciousness and their evolving
and emerging truer self. As a game of projection, however, distortions have and continue to occur at the ego or personality level,
the lower self.

At the level of the lower self (the ego or personality), difficul-
ties occur primarily when there are energy blocks to the flow of
these archetypal energies. In part, energy blocks are created by
the ego or personality. When there are over-identifications and
self-limiting beliefs, ego fears get associated, resulting in energy
blocks. When energy blocks occur, a person's lower self consciousness tends to focus on the energy blocks. The result is that the person tends to create a variety of *control dramas*. These control dramas are fueled by a sense of separation from authentic essence and
the emerging truer self. In this context, the person tries to address
some perceived need that they tell the self they have to have in
order to create or to restore a sense of balance and wholeness.

Examples of control dramas (adapted from Woodhouse, 1996) where the meaning of the phenomenon of race in relation to the human experience may get distorted are:

1. *Intimidation*—the exercise of power in ways that push and invite the fear buttons in others;

2. *Interrogation*—the discovery and exploitation of another's flaws to produce and to invite guilt or anxiety;

3. *Aloofness*—a frequent cloak for denial which invites others to come to you; and

4. *Victimization*—an attitude associated with low self-esteem that prompts or invites others to give their energy to you.

A core subconscious self-limiting belief here is the belief in the lack of energy. The assumption is that others have to be controlled, overtly or subtly, in order to maintain or to restore a sufficient and steady supply of energy for the self.

Ultimately, however, control dramas do not work because the person can never get enough of whatever it is they think they need outside of the self to satisfy the ego or personality. In the process of enacting control dramas, often addictively, the person tends to lose sight of and to become even further alienated from their authentic essence. Most control dramas center on perceived needs for security, sensory or feeling stimulation, or power. It is in this context that the ego or personality may mistakenly use the phenomenon of race to justify control dramas in the person's personal life space, societal life space, or global life space and the person may become addictively stuck.

In regard to life spaces, the person then may find their lower self using the phenomenon of race as a projective device. The lower self repeats the same self-limiting patterns of thought and behavior by creating three kinds of illusions: (1) the illusion that somehow the person has power over others (the Lower Self Power Race Game); (2) the illusion that the person is protecting the self from the experience of insecurity (the Lower Self Security Race Game); or (3) the illusion that the person is protecting the self from frightening feelings and sensory perceptions (the Lower Self Sensory Race Game).

I will present and define the life spaces, the illusions, and lower self race games with a bit more detail later. In this context, the ego or personality would have defined itself as less than whole and as needing something outside of the self to somehow make itself whole. The new emerging paradigms, however, suggest that as consciousness-energy beings, each human being is already a whole person (their truer self), with interdependent and multidimensional aspects of the self—physically, emotionally, mentally, and spiritually.

A spiritual and soul-centered perspective regarding the meaning of the phenomenon of race in relation to the human experience thus connects or reconnects each person with their authentic essence. Meaning in the form of archetypal energies or soul qualities is derived from aspects of a person's authentic essence. In this light, each person uniquely experiences meaning as their higher self or higher consciousness channels these aspects of their authentic essence to their personality for authentic manifestation and experience, using their current racial form. The motivation is to learn more about the self, to grow, and to expand each person's consciousness.

If allowed, then, by the ego or personality, because one has free will, each person would view the meaning of the phenomenon of race in relation to the human experience as an opportunity to get in touch with their soul qualities and their evolving and emerging truer self. Some Perennial philosophies would also suggest that a person lives a number of lives in various racial forms, so to apply a good-bad value judgment toward any particular racial form would inevitably cut the person off (the current personality) from access to valuable information about various aspects of their soul and valuable information about their evolving soul and consciousness. Good-bad value judgments applied to one's own or another's racial form, then, would inevitably cut the person off from the experience of their soul qualities, and their evolving and emerging truer self.

One of the important soul lessons that may be derived from the meaning of the phenomenon of race in relation to the human experience is a lesson associated with the archetypal energy Wisdom, and its connection to the archetypal energies Truth, Compassion, Love and Oneness. In the literature, Roman-Orin (*Spiritual Growth: Being Your Higher Self*, 1992) suggests:

> *Wisdom* is the ability to be *conscious* of what is happening around you, to see the *Higher Truth*, and express your Self with *Compassion*. Feeling *Love* rather than judgment changes negative Energy into harmless Energy. The wise heart embraces others with a feeling of *Compassion* for whatever stage they are at in their Souls' evolution; it approaches them with a feeling of *Love* and *Oneness* rather than judgment.

There are a number of other lessons, however, which I will discuss later.

In a spiritual and soul-centered context, then, a person begins to see and to experience the self as a soul manifested vibrationally as a physical body, an emotional body, and a mental body, expressing their archetypal energies or aspects of their authentic essence. Learning to manifest and to express these archetypal energies, therefore, constitute the nature of a person's soul lessons on the planet. From a spiritual and soul-centered perspective, therefore, to understand the meaning of race in one's personal life space, societal life space, and global life space, a person only needs to ask the self: what aspects of authentic essence or soul qualities have been caused or allowed to be manifested in regard to the phenomenon of race in relation to the human experience? That is, what soul qualities have been allowed and have been blocked from experience, using one's current racial form? What have been one's own creations in regard to the human race game, and what is now being created?

ROLE OF THE "MIRROR EFFECT" IN EVOLVING THE HUMAN RACE GAME

People's creations are reflected back to them through what can be called the mirror effect. Many people have read about this effect in various esoteric literatures or have an intuitive sense about it, as they use their thoughts and emotions to make or allow things to happen in their world. People create visions or goals and use passion and emotion to fuel their actions in attempting to actualize their visions or goals. However, when they accomplish these tasks, often they do not connect their accomplishments to an inner source. They simply see the results. And so, from that point of view, the mirror effect is not something with which people are unfamiliar, although they may be unaware of its underlying processes and the energies related to it. It may be called by many names (e.g., Byrne's *The Secret*, 2006; Pinckley's *Reality Creation 101: Mastering Manifestation Through Awareness*, 2008).

Used wisely, the role of the mirror effect is to make conscious that which is unconscious (either from the subconscious or super-conscious), or to make conscious that which is out of a person's current awareness. In this context, it may be very important that each person use the mirror effect wisely to consciously evolve the human race game. Let's take a closer look at the mirror effect and how it may be consciously used to evolve the human race game.

THE "MIRROR EFFECT," CORE BELIEFS, AND THE THREE LIFE SPACES

All outward experiences begin with a thought, an idea, or a belief. However, at the level of the personality, as it is understood, many thoughts, ideas, or beliefs are acquired from others or from a mass set of beliefs that is called culture. Left unexamined in the mind, they can and often do subconsciously or superconsciously influence (not control) a person's perceptions, feelings, and actions. They also manifest in the outer world of experience as the person's subconscious and superconscious creations. The person may then wonder why things or circumstances are the way they are. The nature of what I am calling lower self race games, which will be discussed later, are largely connected to a variety of unexamined subconscious beliefs. They operate at a core level of the person's self in time and space. I have already alluded to a few of these beliefs, such as the belief in scarcity and the belief in a lack of energy.

To more fully understand what is going on, then, it is important to examine one's thoughts or ideas or beliefs first. From a spiritual or soul-centered perspective, a person's thoughts, ideas, and beliefs are vibrational. They act like energy magnets to attract relevant people, events, and circumstances into the person's life spaces. This happens in accord with, or rather in harmony with the person's intent and the vibrational intensity of the person's emotional energy.

The mirror effect, therefore, can be defined as the effect(s) manifested in a person's life spaces—personal, societal, and/or global—which has emerged or flows from the energy vibrationally attracted to the person's core beliefs (core ideas) about the self (mind, body, and spirit) and their world (physical and spiritual).

Core beliefs are transparent. They are so basic to the way a person orients their life that the person rarely stops to think about them. For the most part, they are subconscious and unexamined, and in some instances superconscious. Core beliefs are important, however, because they influence almost every action a person takes in their life. The mirror effect, then, is the externally reflected outcomes or conditions of inner-directed energy in accord with these core beliefs and in accord with the uses and misuses of what some authors have called Universal Energy Laws. Another way of saying this is that where a person lives inside energetically and vibrationally is reflected in their individual and collective experiences and relationships externally and is mirrored back to the person in their personal, societal, and global life spaces. I will review briefly the nature of Universal Energy Laws later.

Having defined the mirror effect in this way, some people will be tempted to confuse the mirror effect with the *blame game*. And given the current lack of clarity about the meaning of the human race game, the blame game becomes even more tempting as a perspective to embrace. In the blame game, the emphasis and energy is directed toward blaming a person's self, their own group, someone else, or another group in order to derive meaning for events or circumstances. This is not the purpose, intent, or the nature of the mirror effect. Do not confuse the two.

In the context of the mirror effect, meaning is derived from increased awareness and knowledge that a person acquires from their earth lessons. A person's earth lessons are about what is helping or hindering the person, individually and collectively, from being in touch with and giving "form" and "expression" to the qualities and visions of their higher consciousness. A person's earth lessons may also be about what is helping or hindering the person from allowing their higher qualities (i.e., archetypal energies) and visions to be manifested (or actualized) in practical ways in the person's personal, societal, and global life spaces. The mirror effect thus shows a person, through the symbolism of real and imagined effects, what is working and what is not working for the person, individually and collectively, at personal, societal, and global levels in the co-creation of optimal realities.

As human beings with conscious minds, each person simultaneously lives in three life spaces—a personal life space, a societal life space, and a global life space. Even though a person may think of these life spaces as external, and each person does have direct and indirect experiences in what I and other authors have called the Outer, Vibrational World of Experience, the three life spaces all exist in the mind as beliefs about the self and the person's vibrational world. These beliefs, culturally-derived and otherwise-derived, serve to structure the person's reality when they operate at a core level of the self.

Even though a person may share some common cultural or otherwise-derived beliefs with others, the three life spaces are unique to that person. That is, each person has uniquely integrated particular core beliefs in their own way. Again, many of these core beliefs operate unconsciously or transparently, but a person can become conscious of them. One way to become conscious of them, one's core beliefs, is to learn how to wisely use the mirror effect to understand the lessons (often symbolic in nature) that are being reflected in one's various life spaces. Each person, then, uniquely integrates and gives unique expression to their set of core beliefs.

Imagine three overlapping circles (see Figure 3). Each circle contains a person's core beliefs, ideas, thoughts, attitudes, feelings, decisions and choices (i.e., the person's programming), regarding information the person has consciously or unconsciously screened or scanned into the mind. One circle represents the person's personal life space; the second circle represents the person's societal life space; and the third circle represents the person's global life space. Each person and their conscious, or rational, mind are at the center where the three circles overlap. Each person engages in actions, expressions, and relationships in the Outer, Vibrational

World of Experience in accord with their conscious and sub-conscious programming. Each person also has superconscious programming from their higher consciousness which functions somewhat like an ever-emerging blueprint, as nothing is predes-tined in that sense. Each person uses their free will to form their life and to alter this blueprint in accord with their desires, assess-ments, talents, and skills.

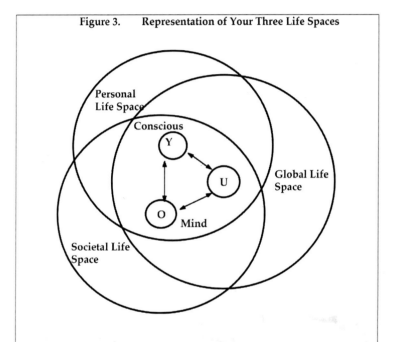

Figure 3.   Representation of Your Three Life Spaces

In the diagram, Y-O-U and your conscious mind are at the center of your three life spaces. In your personal life space, "Y" is the aspect of you that represents your personal life space programming, i.e., your beliefs, ideas, thoughts, attitudes, feelings, decisions, & choices screened into your mind from "direct face-to-face experiences" <u>with</u> people, events, objects, or places. In your societal life space, "O" is the aspect of you that represents your societal life space programming based on "other than face-to-face" or "indirect societal experiences" <u>about</u> people, events, objects, or places. In your global life space, "U" is the aspect of you that represents your global life space programming based on a sense of "universal second-hand information" or "indirect global experiences" <u>about</u> people, events, objects, or places.

In the metaphor above, personal life space experiences and relationships refer to direct, face-to-face experiences that a person has *with* people (enacting various personal, social, or institutional roles and scripts), events, objects, or places around which the person may have conscious, subconscious, or superconscious thoughts and feelings.

Societal life space experiences and relationships refer to indirect societal experiences that do not involve face-to-face contact, which a person has *about* people (enacting various personal, social, or institutional roles and scripts), events, objects, or places around which the person may have conscious or unconscious thoughts and feelings. These indirect societal experiences include, for example, encounters with books, the media, data, past or present second-hand information from others about the nature of society or societal issues and dynamics and public figures.

Global life space experiences and relationships refer to indirect global experiences that do not involve face-to-face contact, which a person has *about* people (enacting personal, social, or institutional roles and scripts), events, objects, institutions, or places around which the person may develop conscious or unconscious thoughts and feelings. The indirect global experiences include, for example, encounters with books, the media, data, past or present second-hand information from others about the nature of global or international issues and dynamics and international figures.

At an individual level, therefore, what exists at a societal or global level, for the most part, exists in the mind as indirect experiences for each person. If, however, a person is or has been fortunate enough to physically travel to other places in a society or in the world, or a person has or had face-to-face encounters with people enacting their various societal or global institutional roles and scripts in accord with their beliefs about shared codes, cultural scripts, and man-made laws, then whatever societal and global experiences a person encounters or has encountered face-to-face become part of their unique personal life space. That is, they exist in the mind as personal memory and beliefs (thoughts and feelings) about those societal and global experiences.

HOW THE "MIRROR EFFECT" RELATES TO EVOLVING THE HUMAN RACE GAME

So, how does all of this relate to evolving the human race game? I, in the spiritual and soul-centered model of human nature, as well as others, have suggested that a person's higher consciousness is the guardian of all the information and possibilities of change and growth related to the self and the person's conscious, subconscious, and superconscious experiences. The role of higher consciousness is to nurture each person in becoming more of who they are and more of source energy/spirit or All-That-Is. But, based on the person's thoughts and feelings as determined by their attitudes and beliefs, each person must choose and decide what form and context the information and possibilities will take. That is, each person must consciously choose when, how, and under what circumstances to receive the gifts from their higher consciousness.

In terms of the human race game, then, what are mirrored back to each person and are entertained at the level of the individual in the person's three life spaces are their choices, decisions, attitudes, and beliefs. Also mirrored back to each person is the personal, societal, and global forms and contexts that each person individually and collectively co-creates or focuses on (i.e., cause or allow into their experience by their conscious, subconscious, or unconscious programming, from an energy vibrational point of view). It is these forms and contexts that constitute what I have called the mirror effect. It is these forms and contexts which show each person where they are at individually and collectively in their process of evolving the human race game.

What then are the implications of the mirror effect and its connection to a person's higher consciousness in developing strategies for evolving the human race game? I will discuss three of the implications, although there are others. One of the implications is that a person's higher consciousness as guardian already contains information for mirroring the possibility of evolving the human race game. But each person, individually and collectively, must choose and decide what forms and contexts this possibility will take in their personal, societal, and global life spaces. Developing strategies in this regard, therefore, means that it is important for each person to be a conscious creator or co-creator of individual and collective visions for evolving the human race game.

It is important for each person to develop and to nurture beliefs and attitudes that will vibrationally attract personal, societal, and global events and circumstances for positively evolving the human race game. It is important for each person, in other words, to reprogram themselves with beliefs and attitudes that vibrationally invite and nurture racial harmony and other relational harmony in general. This requires, however, an understanding of Universal Energy Laws and how one's higher consciousness and personality can work together to utilize these laws. I will briefly discuss this issue shortly.

A second implication is that the mirror effect can be viewed as a tool and gift, provided by a person's higher consciousness, for assessing, at the personality level, race-related forms and contexts (and other relational forms and contexts) in the person's personal, societal, and global life spaces. That is, as a tool, it reflects to each person the individual and collective creative energy that each person has and has not applied toward evolving the human race game. In turn, each person can get a sense of where more creative energy can be strategically applied for evolving the human race game.

For example, as circumstances in many countries are looked at, race and ethnicity have preoccupied the nature of many conflicts because of a belief in scarcity or a belief in the lack of energy. Using the mirror effect, then, people know that a great deal more creative energy needs to be applied toward developing and implementing economic strategies for evolving the human race game. The upshot of this implication, therefore, is that it is important for each person to ask themselves: What direct or indirect experiences have I had with developing and nurturing strategies for evolving the human race game? The next step is to affirm or to create one's own strategic vision and then to continue to act and/ or to take new action in accord with that vision.

In using the mirror effect for such an assessment, it is important to recognize that all levels of activity are unique, significant, and have meaning. They contribute to becoming more of who one is and more of source energy/spirit or All-That-Is. For example, parents who raise their children to appreciate and to think positively about all aspects of who they are are making a significant contribution to evolving the human race game.

A person who spends a great deal of time reading, studying, engaging in personal growth activities, and talking with friends and acquaintances about issues pertaining to and for improving the human condition is contributing significantly to evolving the human race game. A person who joins a network which supports positive political and economic strategies related to race relations and human relations is contributing significantly to evolving the human race game. Likewise, political and social activists whose daily personal life space experiences involve numerous strategic meetings, actions directed toward rectifying what is not working for human care, and the dissemination of educational and positive ideas and visions for improving race relations and human relations are contributing significantly to evolving the human race game.

The point is that from the perspective of a person's higher consciousness, the possibility for evolving the human race game is, can be, and will be mirrored in a variety of forms and contexts. The person simply needs to make conscious, recognize, acknowledge, appreciate, legitimize, integrate, and consciously nurture and expand the nature and variety of these forms and contexts. Indeed, some souls are currently using the Internet for this very purpose. In doing so, they are mirroring what I will call the "Inner-net." I will have more to say later about the role of the Internet and the Inner-net as tools to assist in evolving the human race game.

The third implication is that contained in the possibility of evolving the human race game are numerous earth lessons related to how to formulate, take action, create, and co-create arenas and opportunities for the constructive expression of the authentic essence of who people are. At a practical level, what this means is that a person can learn a great deal about how they individually and collectively co-create and relate to various aspects of life in their personal, societal, and global life spaces. The person can also learn more about how to alter constructively and strategically those areas when they are not working for them individually and collectively.

To a large extent, many of the lessons related to evolving the human race game center on learning about what beliefs a person has formed in regard to their emotions, their relationships, and their sexuality. Some of the lessons are also centered on learning about the consequences of a person's beliefs in terms of how the person relates to their body, to their money, to their work and to their spirituality. Uncovering self-limiting beliefs in regard to these areas of one's life and how they may be limiting one's perception of one's own authentic essence and the authentic essence of others underlie the nature of these lessons.

It all adds up, ultimately, to evolving the human race game by becoming a conscious creator or co-creator. As each person transforms self-limiting beliefs and lets go of the fears that these self-limiting beliefs engender, each person is evolving the human race game. The role of the mirror effect here is to point the way for where and how the person may want to direct their energy. Are there, for example, people with different racial forms that are part of what the person might consider their support group circle? Are these close relationships or acquaintances? If there are no close relationships and the person has preferred a particular stance in the world, what beliefs are at play? The response to questions of this nature can lead to certain core beliefs and lessons at play, for this is part of the mirror effect in regard to race relations and human relations in the person's personal, societal, and global life spaces.

HOW UNIVERSAL ENERGY LAWS WORK IN RELATION TO THE PERSONAL ENERGY SYSTEM TO "MIRROR" AND EVOLVE THE HUMAN RACE GAME

Knowing what I have called Universal Energy Laws and how a person's Personal Energy System works in accord with them is also important for such an undertaking as evolving the human race game. I will adapt Michael and Heideman's description of seven Universal Energy Laws (see C. Heideman's *Searching for Light: Michael's Information for a Time of Change*, 1994). However, many guides, teachers, and authors have described these laws in various ways (e.g., Li, Woods & Lugo's *The Theory of Multi-Dimensional Unified Universal Energy*, 2008; Lee's *The Universal Life Energy*, 2010). The intent here is not to engage in a full discussion of these laws, but rather to reference them as tools of higher consciousness in actualizing the mirror effect in accord with many of a person's subconscious core beliefs and programming. Likewise, a person's higher consciousness uses these laws to create the possibility for mirroring higher ideas. I, therefore, refer readers to Heideman's *Searching for Light* for a much fuller discussion of these laws.

The seven Universal Energy Laws may thus be referenced as follows: (1) The *law of attraction*, (2) the *law of polarity*, (3) the *law of neutrality*, (4) the *law of consequences*, (5) the *law of intention*, (6) the *law of allowing*, and (7) the *law of universality* (See Table 1). It is important to study and to understand these laws in order to become a more constructive conscious creator or co-creator with one's higher consciousness. Understanding these laws sets the stage for developing more potent visions, strategies, and techniques for evolving the human race game.

Table 1.	Seven Universal Energy Laws
Law of Attraction	Energy of any form magnetically attracts similar Energy, the intensity of emotions causing a more intense attraction in both speed and quantity.
Law of Polarity	Energy always contains a duality or polarity, creating an unending array of choices within choices for you to select a preferred polarity at each crossroads.
Law of Neutrality	Perfectly matched polarities create a state of neurality, providing a third choice outside the two polarities of any Energy.
Law of Consequences	Enery moves through time and space, always touching other energies, creating reactions, and thus consequences.
Law of Intention	As Energy moves in all directions at once, it can be focused and aimed with Conscious intent, influencing Energy going out and magnetically attracted back.
Law of Allowing	As general Energy moves into open pathways only, stopping or moving around blockages, intentional Energy can open a closed pathway but only when allowed by a change in preference.
Law of Universality	All is available. All flows around you at every moment, but you experience only what you prefer. The Universe reflects you, and you reflect the Universe. All is.

In terms of universal energy, when a person formulates ideas at the level of their personality or ego, from an energy vibrational point of view, the person is saying to their higher self that this is what they want or prefer to attract into their life spaces at this time. The higher self then employs the law of attraction and the law of intention to bring the appropriate forms and contexts into the person's life spaces. But, the law of polarity may present various polar options, and the person must choose and decide on the path most appropriate for their growth.

However, when a person uses free will to choose a path and it does not work, or it results in mental, emotional, and physical harm or pain to the self or to another, the person's higher self, if the person allows themselves to listen, will attempt to assist them with spiritual dispatches in various intuitive forms for corrective action. These spiritual dispatches or intuitive forms might include, for example, illuminations, inner hearing, dreams, and symbolic synchronicity experiences with relevant people or events. If a pain/joy option for growth presents itself for evolving the human race game, I recommend a path of joy. Most people know too well the path of pain and suffering as a method of growth. It is time as human beings, individually and collectively, to develop and to affirm approaches for nurturing one's emotions, relationships, sexuality, bodies, money, work, and spirituality that will mirror paths of Joy.

Hating racism, wars, power struggles, poverty, etc., will not change those conditions. In fact, in terms of the Universal Energy Laws, doing so will only lead to more of the same kinds of conditions. However, a love of peace, abundance, and a positive regard for self and others will create the alternate conditions. In this regard, it is important to use the law of neutrality when one is not clear about what one wants. If a vision for positively evolving the human race game is fuzzy, use free will to create a conscious focus, or if there is only clarity about what one does not want, use the law of neutrality. It is important not to give energy to what one does not want. In the context of Universal Energy Laws, the mirror effect is the feedback that a person receives in accord with the law of attraction, the law of consequences, the law of allowing, and the law of universality.

The primary implication of these Universal Energy Laws and their connection to a person's higher consciousness is that they can allow the person to more efficiently evolve the human race game, when employed wisely. As a person learns how to consciously work with these Universal Energy Laws, they become a conscious creator or co-creator with their higher consciousness. I recommend that every person hasten their efforts in this regard. One need not feel alone in this process, however. There are many souls in Western society and in the world whose higher focus is to assist, to be companions, and to share their own ongoing process of uncovery of the Greater Self. Indeed, they may enter a person's race-related or other-related dramas in a variety of ways to mirror for the person particular kinds of lessons and vice versa.

The role of the mirror effect in evolving the human race game, therefore, is to be a user-friendly tool in providing feedback for learning how to grow with joy. There is no intent in the use of the mirror effect for self-blame or blame of others. Indeed, in terms of evolving the human race game, a person resonates with the archetypal energy Wisdom when they understand their self-limiting core beliefs and how they may be mirrored as the person interacts with others and their self-limiting core beliefs.

If a person understands the law of universality, they come to know that energy is vibrating everywhere and that everything they see or sense is a form of this vibrating universal energy. A much more difficult understanding is that the universe reflects the person and the person reflects the universe. Indeed, one of the roles of the mirror effect is to show each person this reflection and to assist that person in knowing how to work with the energy that is available to them.

At the level of the individual, therefore, it is important to understand that energy flows through the body, as well as within every physical object on the planet. It is also important to understand that as human beings, each person knowingly and unknowingly moves and manipulates energy through what is known as the chakras, the person's Personal Energy System. Although there are many methods for doing this, a principal method is the use of visualization, creating a visual image of what one wants to accomplish. There are seven primary chakras, as many already know, although there are a number of others that handle smaller and larger amounts of energy.

In all instances, it is the same energy. However, depending on the degree, kind, state, vibrational frequency, or level of consciousness (i.e., animal world, plants, minerals, structures, objects, locations, cetaceans, humans), and a person's soul age (as implied in the spiritual and soul-centered model, there are younger souls to more experienced older souls), energy may be processed in varying ways that are unique to the person as a CU or consciousness-energy entity. As fully sentient beings, human beings have the highest potential to consciously process energy on the planet, and this requires developing one's sensitivity to energy and developing one's skills to manage energy wisely. Developing this sensitivity and these skills, then, will help in evolving the human race game as conscious creators or co-creators.

There are numerous self-help books that are available to assist people in developing their sensitivity and skills to manage energy wisely. So, I suggest that each person allow themselves to be guided to those materials that feel right. I resonate with the methods presented by Seth, Lazaris, Michael, Orin, DaBen, Jaiwa, the Group, Abraham, and several other higher entities with which some readers are familiar.

THE PERSONAL ENERGY SYSTEM AND HOW IT RELATES TO THE HUMAN RACE GAME

The chakra system, a person's Personal Bio-etheric Energy System, has been described in many ways (e.g., Weuter's *Chakras and Their Archetypes: Uniting Energy Awareness and Spiritual Growth*, 1997; Johari's *Chakras: Energy Centers of Transformation*, 2000; Saradananda's *Chakra Meditation: Discover Energy, Creativity, Focus, Love, Wisdom, and Spirit*, 2008; White's *Using Your Chakras: A New Approach to Healing Your Life*, 2009). Again, it is through the chakra system that each person experiences the universe, the vibrating universe. I offer a brief overview here. In part, it is in regard to the processing of energy through this system that racially-linked energy blocks have occurred to fuel what I have called lower self race games, mirrored as the distortions I discussed earlier surrounding race relations specifically and human relations generally.

It is through a person's Personal Energy System that the person engages in sending and receiving energy in the vibrational world. Through the vortexes of the personal energy system, some chakras both send and receive energy, while others primarily send or receive energy during external energy exchanges. For example, the First (Root), Second (Navel or Sexual), Fourth (Heart), Fifth (Throat), and Seventh (Crown or Head) chakras are capable of both sending and receiving energy, although the fourth chakra is strongest in this regard during external energy exchanges. The Third Chakra (Solar Plexus or Power) is usually only capable of sending energy and so is not that much involved with receiving energy during external energy exchanges. The Sixth Chakra (Brow) is usually only capable of receiving energy, primarily collecting and processing it through what some know as the Third Eye, the intuition energy vortex.

In terms of internal energy, universal energy, which is vibrating within and as everything all around each person, typically enters the body at the base of the spine or through the top of the head, becoming a person's personal energy. Universal energy is thus processed in its various archetypal forms, as well as other forms, as it moves up, down, in, out, through, and around the body as a person engages in external energy exchanges.

In this context, a person's beliefs vibrationally attract particular kinds of energies and also frame and focus the nature of the processing. A person's imagination, on the other hand, vibrationally frames and focuses the person's intentions. Both the person's beliefs and their imagination thus act as triggers and conduits for the processing of energy through the person's Personal Energy System.

Energy, in a manner of speaking, vibrationally follows a person's imagination. If, for example, a person visualizes a world with abundant energy (the person's vision or imagination) and embraces and nurtures a belief in abundance (the person's focused thoughts), the conditions are created for processing higher soul qualities, such as abundance, compassion, peace, clarity, or joy (archetypal energies), through the personal energy system. That is, in accord with the Universal Energy Laws, these conditions or energy vibrations may be channeled through the person's personal energy system. And, they may be mirrored or experienced in the outer, vibrational world of experience in the person's life spaces, as they attract, perceive, and interact with people of all races, objects, events, and circumstances, if the person does not create energy blocks.

The authentic energy essence or soul qualities mentioned (abundance, compassion, peace, clarity, or joy) would enter through the head chakra and would be collected and processed through the sixth chakra to create a vision. Vision, then, may be intuitively felt, accepted, harmonized, and practically transmuted through the fourth chakra. If allowed by the person's personality or ego, a person's vision, then, could transform racially-linked energy blocks as well as other energy blocks associated with the second chakra in terms of the nature of the person's external energy exchanges in their life spaces. With enthusiasm and hope (archetypal energies), the person may then embrace beauty and humor (archetypal energies) related to the diversity in their world, for no longer would the person create others as a threat to the amount of energy in their world. The person's world would be creatively viewed and experienced as having and being filled with abundance energy, enough for everyone.

In practical terms and in terms of the human race game specifically and generally, what this means is that a person would no longer feel threatened materially or otherwise. That is, the person would no longer feel that they must use beliefs in scarcity and in the lack of energy to justify what they may perceive as protective acts against another person with a racial form or human experience different than their own. The person's strategic vision for evolving the human race game may even become focused on assisting others to gain the tools for accessing both a perception of and the experience of the archetypal energy abundance.

The abundance scenario that was just described represents a possibility, if a person would allow the Greater Self to create it or choose to be open to their higher energies. In spring 2008, the TV personality Oprah Winfrey modeled and created opportunities for others to model how such abundance possibilities can be mirrored in personal, societal, and global life spaces. This was done through a TV program called "The Big Give" and through a worldwide Internet event focused on the personality Eckhart Tolle's book *A New Earth*.

A person's higher qualities, however, can only find form and expression through that person, and their personal energy system, as that person chooses to access them. The challenge of the mirror effect is to assist the person in recognizing what they are currently choosing to create, along with others, and to learn how to consciously access one's higher qualities and direct this energy toward creating what they want with joy. Embracing enthusiasm and humor helps a person to move toward joy. The mirror effect, therefore, in a manner of speaking, allows a person to study the self, the Greater Self, or rather the soul, by looking at their world. In accord with the law of universality, a person's vibrational world is a reflection of that person. Everything around a person represents a part of that person.

Table 2 summarizes the types of archetypal energies (soul qualities) that flow through the various chakras, and the types of specific race games to which these higher energies are related. To some extent, this is very generic, as the various energies can and do eventually flow through all of the chakras at some point. As I have indicated earlier, I will discuss the nature of

Table 2.	The Chakras, Base Colors, Types of Archetypal Energies, and Types of Race Games (& Psychic Potentials) That May Be Mirrored by the Energies		
Chakras (Body Centers)	*Base Colors in Aura of Your Various Bodies*	*Types of Archetypal Energies (Soul Qualities) & Their Nature*	*Types of Race Games Mirrored (& Psychic Potential When Archetypal Energies Are Not Blocked)*
First or Root or Base Chakra or Center (Base of the spine)	Red	*Trust*: life-promoting Energy, vital, physical Energy, security, survival of the body, safety, self-protection, groundedness, presence, confidence	Security Race Game (Spatial Intuition)
Second or Sexual or Naval Chakra or Center (Lower abdomen to navel area)	Orange	*Enthusiasm, Humor, Beauty, Hope*: love as reserve Energy, sex and reproduction, sexuality, creativity, sensuality, intimacy	Sensory Race Game (Clairsentience)

Third or Power or Solar Plexus Chakra or Center (Above the navel, below the chest	Yellow	*Flexibility, Courage:* growth and healing, life-preserving Energy, power, control, taking independent action, self-image, accomplishments	Power Race Game (Sensitivity to "Vibes" from other people and places)
Fourth or Heart Chakra or Center (Center of the chest)	Green	*Love, Acceptance, Inclusion, Harmony:* love Consciousness as mental Energy, giving love, receiving love, self-love, forgiveness, surrender	Transformational Race Game (Authentic Empathy)
Fifth or Throat Chakra or Center (Throat area)	Blue	*Understanding, Truth, Wisdom, Patience, Inspiration:* volition, communication, expression, spontaneity speaking and hearing the truth, *discernment*	Inspirational Race Game (Clairaudience)
Sixth or Brow Chakra or Center or Third Eye (Center of the forehead, between the eyebrows)	Indigo	Abundance, Compassion, Peace, Joy, Clarity, Vision: transitional Energy, synthesizing Energy, seeing the Energy aspects of the world around you, Spiritual Vision, connectedness to all of Humanity	Altruistic Race Game (Clairvoyance)
Seventh or Head or Crown Chakra or Center (Top of the head, which opens to the the Soul or Monadic Body with three Higher Centers:	Violet (Ultra- violet)	Oneness, Unity, Serenity: integration, sending in- tentions, receiving in- sight, Soul awareness, Universal (Unconditional) Love, connectedness to All-That-Is	Soul-Source Race Game (Telepathy)
			(Cosmic Consciousness)
Causal Body, Compassionate Body, Atmic Body)	(Clear or White) (Silver) (Gold)		

the various types of race games later. The purpose here is simply to illustrate how the various types of specific race games are connected to the energy that flows through one's personal bio-etheric system.

Another purpose is to suggest that, at least in regard to the lower self race games, distortions have occurred due, in part, to racially-linked energy blocks in people's personal energy system, the chakra system, individually and collectively. These racially-linked energy blocks have manifested as self-limiting beliefs in regard to a person's current racial forms and who the person is. They also have manifested as distorted ideas in regard to the nature of the universe (one's vibrating universe), one's psychic potentials, and the energy that surrounds one's physical self (outer self) and others in a person's world.

In regard to the human race game, the mirror effect is showing each person, individually and collectively, many of the racially-linked, self-limiting beliefs and distorted ideas. On the other hand, the mirror effect also can and does show each person those areas where nurturing and human care beliefs are at play and can be applied to evolve the human race game.

The lower self race games are thus projective games, mirroring where there are racially-linked energy blocks in people's personal bio-etheric systems. The racially-linked energy blocks, then, are materialized in a person's life spaces, individually and collectively, pointing to various kinds of personal, societal, and global lessons that are important to learn if the person is to create paths of *joy*. I am suggesting that these lessons are related to how to creatively and physically manifest or give authentic expression to the archetypal energies that I have identified.

LOWER SELF RACE GAMES AND THE PERSONAL ENERGY SYSTEM

The way that many in Western society and in the world currently play the human race game is, to a large extent, in terms of what I have called lower self race games. The ego aspect of a person's personality structures lower self race games. In a manner of speaking, a person's lower self race games represent the struggle of their ego to make sense of their vibrational world, as the person identifies with what they consider the objective aspects of their self. In regard to the phenomenon of race in relation to a person's human experience, miscalculations often have led the person to focus their consciousness on particular physical aspects of their self. These physical aspects have included, for example, a focus on skin color, the size and shape of bodies, the size and shape of eyes, noses, and lips, the texture of hair, the use of the tongue in speech, the sounds of speech, and various other body postures and gestures.

In turn, lower self thoughts about one's human experience, the phenomenon of race, and the physical aspects of one's self often have served to trigger underlying fears, negative emotions, and over-identifications. Fear, then, generated by self-limiting, race-linked beliefs, is a common source for lower self race games.

Such fears, negative emotions, and over-identifications jam the free flow of energy or create spasms in the processing of energy, particularly archetypal energies, through one's chakras or personal energy systems. I have called these kinds of jams or spasms racially-linked energy blocks.

The fears, associated with race-linked ego-thoughts, produce racially-linked energy blocks and are mirrored as lower self race games as a person acts out individually and collectively in their personal, societal, and global life spaces. It is important to develop, therefore, an understanding of when one is acting out of one's lower self and what types of race games are created in one's human experience as one acts out in relation to the phenomenon of race.

How to Know When One is "Acting Out" of the Lower Self

The following ideas may assist a person and serve as guides in knowing when they are acting out of their lower selves. As I resonate with material presented by Robbyn and His Merrye Bande and many others, I have adopted their ideas here (see "Why Have An Ego?" in *Spirit Speaks*). A person is acting out of their lower self when they:

- Tell someone that they created their own reality when they're in great pain and need the person's compassion.
- Want to be right more than they want to be whole.
- Want their beliefs to be right.
- Want their favorite teacher to be right.
- Expect the people they admire to live up to their expectations.
- Expect the people they love to share their beliefs.
- Expect the people they love to accept them for what they think they are, to accept them how they want to be accepted.

- Seek validation outside of one's self.

- Want people to acknowledge them.

- Want to find something or someone to blame for who and what they are today—parents, schools, siblings, country, their own or another's race and so on.

In the above context, the ego-thoughts (self-limiting beliefs) of a person's lower self, along with their underlying fears, structure their outer, vibrational world of experience. Such self-limiting thoughts become centered on the themes of safety and security, sensory stimulation (what are known as the five senses and the person's feelings based on these senses; I will refer to them as the person's sensory feelings), and power or a sense of potency in the person's world. Given the various lenses (e.g., race, ethnicity, gender, culture) that are typically used to understand a person's outer, vibrational world of experience, the self-limiting thoughts serve to structure how the person's lower self may act out the three themes of security, sensory feelings, and power in relation to the various lenses.

Applied to the phenomenon of race in relation to the human experience, if a person's ego-thoughts remain self-limiting, the person may then act out three types of lower self race games in their personal, societal, and global life spaces—the Security Race Game, the Sensory Race Game, and the Power Race Game. Let's now take a closer look at these three types of lower self race games that a person may find their lower or outer self acting out, often unconsciously or rather subconsciously, to be more accurate.

Following is a general discussion of the three types of lower self race games, along with examples of how they may be acted out (or may manifest) in a person's personal life space and societal life space. For purposes here, I will delay for another time a focus on global life space, as a person is more likely to identify with their personal and societal life spaces.

THE SECURITY RACE GAME

As possibly recognized, the Security Race Game is highly linked to how the ego aspect of a person's personality focuses on beliefs and ideas in regard to the safety, security, and survival of the person's physical body or one's current racial form. Many of these beliefs and ideas are self-limiting. In this context, the person or rather a personality's ego holds the idea that the physical body is the self, which must be protected in order for their consciousness to survive. This is not to suggest that self-protection, or the safety, well-being, and trust of one's physical body, is unimportant. Indeed, the function of the ego is to help each person to survive in the physical form. Safety, well-being, trust of one's body, and the development of one's psychic capacity for spatial intuition are some of the very soul lessons, from a spiritual and soul-centered perspective, for which a person's innermost self (soul) created their ego and their current physical form.

The archetypal energy seeking unique form and authentic expression at this level of consciousness is Trust. In this context, one's physical body is to be affirmed as an expression of who the person is in this life, as that person understands it. It is important and necessary that one's physical body be nurtured, maintained, enjoyed, and appreciated as the person uses it to engage in various earth lessons. In a manner of speaking, then, a person is nurturing their soul as they do so. The problem arises from a person's over-identification with the body and a misunderstanding about the relationship of the person's physical body to their consciousness.

When a person over-identifies with the physical body or their current racial form as giving rise to their consciousness, rather than the other way around, ego fears may emerge to fuel and to reinforce a belief that the death of the body is the annihilation of consciousness. If a person thinks that those who are perceived to have a different racial form are a threat to their current racial form, racially-linked energy blocks, fueled by fear, may then occur. When a person perceives a racial difference as a threat to the survival of their body or perceived body type, fear emerges and the person constricts the flow of energy at this level of consciousness.

At this level of consciousness, energy is primarily processed through the root chakra where fear can easily be evoked. Fear has the effect of closing the chakras of a person's personal energy system. If racially-linked ideas such as those above are allowed to direct energy subconsciously at this level of consciousness, the personality (or person) may increasingly find their outer self isolated from anyone who is perceived to be physically different. They may then act out in their personal and societal life spaces a variety of fear-driven, race-related dramas, believing that they are protecting their selves from unsafe circumstances and the potential annihilation of their consciousness.

For example, racially-linked energy blocks may be subconsciously acted out in accord with a person's transparent core beliefs about safety and security. Such beliefs would be mirrored by who the person chooses for friends or intimate encounters, where the person chooses to live, who the person chooses to love, what the person chooses to do in and with their time and space. The person may live in de facto segregated neighborhoods. The person may be suspicious that those who are racially different will attack them on the street or steal something from them. The person may view them as violating the law more quickly than their self or someone from the group with which they identify. Or the person may view them as causing property values to decline.

In more dramatic race-related dramas, in the name of safety and security, the acting out may take the form of what is called institutional and cultural racism. Or it may take the form of groups believing and promoting the concept of racial purity and the racial superiority of their physical body or their current physical or racial form. Such has been the case with what are called hate groups in American society, groups such as the Aryan Nations, the Ku Klux Klan, the World Church of the Creator, and the Church of Jesus Christ-Christian. Notice that such groups may evoke religious dogma to cloak insecurities and fears and to provide justifications for preserving their consciousness through what group members believe is a superior physical body or racial form.

Indeed, it was only in the decade of the late 1960s that the United States Supreme Court declared it unconstitutional to create laws to ban interracial marriage, ironically in a decision known as Loving v Virginia. Loving v Virginia, 388 US 1, 1967, was a landmark civil rights case in which the United States Supreme Court declared unconstitutional Virginia's anti-miscegenation statue, the "Racial Integrity Act of 1924," thereby overturning Pace v Alabama, 1831. This ended all race-based legal restrictions on marriage in the United States.

In 2006 and 2008, it was observed that hate crimes continued to rise in various parts of the United States. In a November 19, 2007 Associated Press article, Michael Sniffen reported that, according to FBI reports, hate crime incidents in the United States rose in 2006 by nearly 8 percent, and that was with only 12,600 of the nation's more than 17,000 local, state, and federal police agencies participating in the hate crime reporting program. In 2008 FBI reports, law enforcement agencies reported that 4,704 offenses among single-bias hate crime incidents were racially motivated and that 72.6 percent of these incidents were motivated by anti-black bias. Hate crimes involving racial bias also are committed against both persons and property. In 2009 FBI reports, 61.1 percent of all hate crimes were against persons, while 38.1 percent were crimes against property. Of the 4,057 recipients of racial bias, 71.6 percent of the incidents happened because of an offender's prejudice against blacks.

Collectively, at this level of consciousness, in the name of safety and security, laws and practices may also be co-created to justify or rationalize race-linked, discriminatory behaviors. For example, the state of Arizona in April of 2010 passed what it called an anti-immigration law supposedly to protect its boundaries against what state residents considered illegal immigrants. Entitled the "Support Our Law Enforcement and Safe Neighborhoods Act," the law in Arizona essentially made every undocumented worker in Arizona guilty of a criminal offense and required state and local police to go after them. More specifically, it allowed police to arrest anyone who was in the United States illegally and to charge them with trespassing, required police to attempt to determine the immigration status of anyone they encountered, outlawed the hiring of day laborers off the street, and prohibited anyone from knowingly transporting an undocumented immigrant for any reason. Other states, like Indiana in February 2011, Utah in March 2011, Georgia in April 2011, Alabama in June 2011, and South Carolina in October 2011, enacted similar laws.

Since most immigrants within the boundaries of Arizona are of Hispanic descent, the inadvertent consequence of this law was to create opportunities to justify or rationalize discrimination against anyone who may look Hispanic, and to allow those in authority positions to knowingly or unknowingly engage in or exhibit what is called "racial profiling." The law was subsequently challenged in the federal court system of the United States, and was temporarily blocked in July of 2010. Interestingly, in October 2011, a federal judge refused to block Alabama's anti-immigration law. Despite this, as of this writing, the US Justice Department continued to challenge the constitutionality of these laws in all of the aforementioned states, the US Senate in June 2013 passed a comprehensive immigration reform bill that reportedly boosted border security while providing a special thirteen-year pathway to citizenship, and the US House of Representatives continued to be energetically blocked by a variety of perceived and entrenched security concerns and political posturing.

If a person is playing the human race game at this level of consciousness, there are some fundamental questions, then, that are important to explore within their selves as each person seeks to uncover their earth lessons. Do you experience the universe as a safe place or as a fearful place? Do you feel that the universe supports your well-being, or is the universe arbitrary in this regard? Do you have an intuitive sense of your special space in the universe or not? Do you trust your self (the universe), or do you have difficulty trusting? Do you use race as a screen through which you judge others in regard to your safety, well-being, trust of the world, and space in the world? Exploring these questions may reconnect a person with the authentic essence of their soul lessons.

Here is an exercise that may assist a person with self-explorations at this level of consciousness. First, start an Evolving the Human Race Game Journal. Use the mirror effect and in the journal make a list of what makes you feel safe and what makes you feel unsafe. Be honest. Ask your innermost self the kinds of questions presented above and use the mirror effect to develop your safe/unsafe list. As one develops a safe/unsafe list, one will be assessing their current stance in the world in regard to one's ideas about security as it relates to race as well as to other issues or other areas of one's life. The answers to these questions and the safe/unsafe list will indicate whether or not and how a person is acting out the Security Race Game using self-limiting ideas. I will discuss later ways to begin to transform such self-limiting ideas.

THE SENSORY RACE GAME

If a person is acting out of their lower self in regard to sensory stimulations and sensory feelings, they may be engaged in the Sensory Race Game. In this regard, a personality's ego now holds the idea that the physical body and the emotional body are the self. At this level of consciousness, the soul also may have chosen for the self other important soul lessons that a person may not have recognized yet. At the physical level, the soul or consciousness unit is in its most isolated form. And, while it is necessary in the physical form to have and to maintain good personal boundaries, the true intent of this state of affairs is to pull each person into a search for more connection and spiritual blending.

Having good personal boundaries simply means that a person has learned that they are responsible for their own sensory feelings and for living their share of life. The person would have learned, in other words, the lesson of personal responsibility. The person also would have learned that blaming and judging others for their own sensory feelings or the sensory feelings of others and for their own life circumstances or the life circumstances of others ultimately diminishes the self (self-pity) and their own sensory feeling or sense of personal boundaries. Further, the person would have learned how to give to others and one's self and to receive from others and one's self. These lessons are required before unconditional love is possible, as well as before a person's psychic potential for clairsentience can emerge.

At the sensory level, each person is in search of and engages their passions to explore their sensory feelings and ways of relating to others. Seeking unique forms and authentic expressions through a person's passions and sensory feelings at this level of consciousness are the archetypal energies Enthusiasm, Humor, Beauty, and Hope. Toward these archetypal energies, many people unfortunately may have created energy blocks that are experienced sensorially as their negativity. That is, the negative feelings that a person has in this context indicate energy blocks that separate the person from the authentic experience of these archetypal energies. I will elaborate.

At this level of consciousness, passionate energy is primarily processed through a person's second chakra, as the person attempts to create connections and spiritual blending. Through the screens of what is known as the five senses, each person may feel intensely negative or positive about another person, situation, object, issue, or race. In a manner of speaking, this represents how intensely the person feels, at a sensory level, a sense of separation from (negative) or connection to (positive) their innermost self, the archetypal energies associated with this level, and the experience of Love—the love inside of one's self and the love that is one's self.

If a person feels negativity, that person has allowed their sensory feelings to guide their consciousness away from the integrative experience of love and authentic expressions of the archetypal energies associated with this level. Love as an integrative experience is usually experienced as flowing through the fourth chakra, the heart or authentic feeling center. However, when a person's second chakra energy is lifted up to the heart center, loving energy is felt in the gut at this level of consciousness, allowing the person also to experience the other associated archetypal energies.

"I love you," for example, experienced as harmonious energy flowing through the heart center and felt in the gut, simply means when a person is in the presence of the other person, they feel in touch with the love inside of one's self. What the person experiences as negative emotions based on sensory stimulation simply mean that they feel out of touch with or separated from the love inside of one's self. This, in turn, limits the person's capacity to authentically experience and express enthusiasm, humor, beauty, and hope in relating to others.

A racially-linked energy block here would mean, therefore, that if a person feels negative when they are in the presence of someone that has identified the self as belonging to another race, the person is, in a manner of speaking, not in touch with the love inside of one's self. The person is thereby also limiting their human experience of the associated archetypal energies in regard to the phenomenon of race.

If the person has not developed trust and a sense of security in one's self and in one's world, it becomes difficult to accept that they have created their own negative feelings. The person would engage their five senses to point out "relevant external data" to justify what they are feeling. It would be difficult for the person to accept that they have created a negative connection with others, or with the race toward which they feel the negativity. The person would deny or be unaware of how they strongly identify with the other person or other race and how they project their negative feelings about aspects of one's self out onto the other person or the other race and rage against the projected qualities. It would be difficult for the person to accept that at a sensory level, that other person or other race represents an aspect, or aspects, of one's self that they fear and that await their love.

In turn, it also may become difficult, at a sensory level, for the person to feel positively connected with others in their world. When the ego aspect of a personality feels out of touch with the innermost self or authentic essence and the love inside of one's self, the person is allowing the ego to direct their consciousness and their senses toward feeling alone and frightened in their world. The person may not recognize that they have been subconsciously thinking, or holding the self-limiting belief, and experiencing sensory feelings, which suggest that to be alone and frightened is the nature of life. Reactively, a person's ego may then engage the physical senses in an alternate fashion, passionately looking for ways to feel positively connected in their world.

While the person may recognize that they have been acting out negatively, they also may still not recognize that subconsciously they hold the belief that to feel anything in order to connect has been the name of their game. Having exhausted their ego with the negativity, the person, then, may try to engage in what they think is the polar positive opposite. There is a potential pitfall here, however, if there are racially-linked energy blocks at the sensory level of consciousness.

In terms of the Sensory Race Game, a person's ego may focus passionately on the physical cues of people. The person may, then, erroneously reason that the only or primary way to feel connected positively to their own authentic essence is to relate only or primarily to those who appear to be physically similar, for surely they will understand. That is, surely they will share their beliefs and feelings and love who and what they are. The projective game becomes one of attempting to feel connected positively to one's authentic essence through relating only or primarily to others who appear, at a sensory level, to be similar to the person's physical self. Out of fear and a lack of understanding of the true intent of personal boundaries, the person rejects those who appear at a sensory level to be different. The person does so in order to avoid what they believe will be negative connections.

Implied in such ego reasoning, therefore, is that the ego aspect of a person's personality has been unable to comprehend being in a state of harmony with anyone who appears, at a sensory level, to be physically different. As I have previously implied, even God may then be viewed as looking like the person's physical self. And, the ego may play "I'm the good guy and you're not" as a way to feel passionately and positively connected to one's greater self or innermost self and the world.

Members of so-called hate groups such as the skinheads in America and Russia, for example, represent extreme cases of those who may be caught up in such good guy-bad guy ego reasoning at the sensory level. In such cases, the members may act out their fears in violent ways, extending and directing their fears toward those they consider racial and ethnic immigrants in their country who threaten their world. At a sensory level, the members of such hate groups may even experience pleasure from their violent acts.

At a sensory level, members of such hate groups view the world in "we-they" terms, and often reason that those who look like them share similar views and want to create and maintain rigid individual and group boundaries. In Russia, for example, "...thousands of far-right nationalists and neo-Nazis marched through Moscow (11/4/11)...calling on ethnic Russians to 'take back' their country as resentment (grew) over dark-complexioned Muslim migrants from Russia's Caucasus...They chanted 'Russia for Russians' and 'Migrants today, occupiers tomorrow,' along with anti-Muslim and anti-Semitic slurs and obscenities...Violent xenophobic groups have flourished in Russia over the past two decades. Their members kill and beat non-Slavs and antiracism activists, and crudely denounce the influx of immigrants from the Caucasus and from Central Asian countries that were once part of the Soviet Union" (Mansur Mirovalev, 2011, *The Boston Globe*, p. A4). At play here are numerous distortions, at the sensory level, flowing from ego fears and energy blocks related to individual and group boundaries.

Having good personal boundaries, however, means creating and having harmonious boundaries in one's vibrational world. It means honoring the love inside of one's self and honoring the love inside of others. It also means allowing one's outer self to experience, or be open to the possibility of experiencing, e*nthusiasm*, h*umor*, b*eauty*, and h*ope* (archetypal energies) as one relates to others who may appear, at a sensory level, to be different than one's outer self. Certain skills are necessary, however, to honor the l*ove* inside of one's self and others. The skills include the abilities to appropriately and harmoniously adjust one's personal boundaries. That is, a person develops at least four kinds of abilities: (1) the ability to expand, (2) the ability to reduce, (3) the ability to monitor the appropriateness of, and (4) the ability to hold firm boundaries in regard to the pushes and gaps between one's self and another person.

If a person is acting out of their lower self in the manner just described without harmonious boundaries, the person's consciousness may be stuck at a sensory level. And, through the Sensory Race Game, the person is also engaging others who appear to have different racial forms in a highly selective manner. It is all a distortion, however. The ego aspect of the person's personality has lost sight of the Truth (an archetypal energy) of who they are and is seeking *outside validation*. In its sometimes limited view, the ego aspect of a person's personality often is unable to see that learning to connect extends beyond racial forms, or current racial forms. Indeed, Perennialists would argue that each person has had many racial forms, as one's consciousness is pre-causal and does not require outside validation.

Out of touch with one's inner beauty, feeling hopeless, and fearing life, the ego aspects of a personality may also create distortions in regard to one's "sexual energy" and the phenomenon of race. Sexual energy is also processed through the second chakra, which assists the person in learning relationship lessons. Sexual energy pulls a person toward a connection with another person. Again, this is one of the ways that a person learns relational soul lessons concerning devotion and cooperation with others.

Sexual energy also helps a person to experience their passion, their hope and enthusiasm (archetypal energies) for life. If racially-linked energy blocks occur here, the Sensory Race Game may involve a variety of forms of interracial love-hate sexual dramas which may get acted out through how a person values, structures, and connects with other races (or ethnic groups) perceptually and sensorially in their personal, societal, and global life spaces.

Throughout history, for example, as currently understood, many acts of brutality have occurred under the guise of protecting the sexual virtue of a race. Such dramas are often acted out by men in relation to the perceived role of women. At a personal level, then, a person is playing and acting out the Sensory Race Game if their choices of friends or lovers are based on avoiding or hating another race (or ethnic group) or their own. A person is "acting out" the Sensory Race Game, if the person secretly or openly holds beliefs that create fears about the mixing of their genetic pool ("What about the children?" the person might ask). And a person is acting out the Sensory Race Game if their conversations overtly or subtly, within their circle of relationships, involve looking at another race in stereotypical or derogatory ways to affirm self-worth and self-value.

At a personal level, as a person plays and acts out the Sensory Race Game, the ego is creating jams and spasms in the second chakra of the personal energy systems. At a societal level, a person is acting out the Sensory Race Game if they create or support societal laws or social practices where the subconscious intent is to maintain segregation of the races in real or de facto terms. Likewise, at a societal level, the jams and spasms may be acted out to create or maintain institutional energy blockages through subtle or overt institutional practices, codes, or laws.

In other terms, as I have suggested, those, for example, who espouse hatred for someone of another race or for another person are very identified and attracted to the objects of their hatred. Indeed, a person cannot hate something or someone they do not identify with and care about. At a more subtle level, in American society, for example, many people who identify the outer self as white often engage in the ritual of "tanning" their skin as an indicator of beauty (an archetypal energy). On the other hand, many people who identify the outer self as black often play what I call the "light skin-dark skin" game, with either light skin or dark skin being used as an indicator of beauty. Each of these acts may be about one race mirroring the physical form of the other race and identifying with one another at some level.

There is nothing inherently good or bad or right or wrong about getting a tan or valuing one's skin color. What is important, however, is whether or not a person's intention, often subconscious, involves self-hatred or hatred of others and whether or not the person recognizes that the authentic essence of their beauty comes from within. Indeed, there are people in both groups, and in various societies, who may engage in both acts (tanning and valuing skin color) for reasons other than to look like another race. From a multicultural point of view, as many understand it, different meanings and values may be ascribed to the same or similar behavioral acts.

For their own reasons, for example, such people may want to enjoy and celebrate the life-giving and nurturing energy of the sun or joyfully and playfully affirm aspects of the self in this life or simply hold no particular value for such acts per se, except in a playful way. Those with such awareness recognize that there is nothing against which they must defend themselves and that validation is an inner process. It is important, therefore, for each person to honestly assess their race-related feelings and their stance in regard to these kinds of acts, to uncover whether or not they are seeking outside validation for who they are. Is this one of the ways that you as an individual unknowingly play the Sensory Race Game?

THE POWER RACE GAME

When a person creates value judgments in relation to skin color or in relation to what they have labeled as other race-related physical features (e.g., body size; hair), and they attempt to manipulate or control others in their personal, societal, or global life spaces on the basis on these judgments, believing that one color or physical feature is superior to another, they are now playing the Power Race Game. At this level of consciousness, the ego now holds the idea that a person's physical body, emotional body, and mental body are the self, to the exclusion of the person's authentic essence.

It is at this level of consciousness that the ego is most externally focused, as energy is primarily processed through the third chakra (the solar plexus). It is at this level that the ego primarily sends energy out externally, but typically does not engage in external energy exchanges in terms of externally receiving energy. In psychic terms, however, when the third chakra is open and unencumbered, a person can enhance their sensitivity to the vibes from others and places, which currently is often not the case at this level of consciousness. It is at this level of consciousness, then, that the ego identifies, or rather over-identifies, with a person's intellect and with the person's beliefs about who they are.

In terms of the Power Race Game, a person acts out their racial identity (and other identities) in terms of who and what the ego thinks they are at this level of consciousness. Viewing life as a series of competitive moves and countermoves, the ego-based beliefs about a person's racial identity (and other identities) structure the person's competitive racial dramas (and other dramas). That is, the person's competitive moves and countermoves are based on ego thoughts about their racial identity (and other identities) in their personal and societal life spaces. At this level of consciousness, therefore, a person's beliefs about their racial identity (and other identities) are very connected to how the ego aspect of one's personality thinks about a person's social status in their personal and societal life spaces and the person's desire to please others. As a great deal of racially-linked energy blocks are acted out in the world through the Power Race Game, I will extend the exploratory discussion somewhat here.

There are many soul lessons that a person can learn at this level of consciousness. One of the more important lessons is how to honor one's own free will and the free will of others. This is also connected to lessons about personal power (or whether a person uses their forceful will or wise will to do things) and personal responsibility, and to lessons about understanding the nature of harmonious boundaries. One aspect of these lessons is learning that harmonious boundaries involves being in touch with the archetypal energies *courage* and *flexibility* as a person engages in learning the nature of various spiritual blendings.

Courage and flexibility flow through the wise and appropriate use of a person's free will. They nurture the expression or actualization of mutual empowerment. However, when a person forcefully violates the free will of others by evoking a variety of false ego power games based on self-limiting beliefs and fear, the person is, in a manner of speaking, violating the soul and its path of growth. The person also stifles their psychic sensitivity to the vibes of others and places. Using one's free will as if there is an opposing force actually creates opposing forces where there are none. Honoring free will, therefore, is a key to evolving false ego-based power games. As a person does so, the person attracts higher ideas and expresses higher energies such as courage and flexibility. Honoring free will thus fosters self-love and self-mastery.

True power, therefore, has little to do with having power over another. Rather, it is a knowing-ness that one has the power to act. It is a knowing-ness that one has the power of choice and the power of action. And it is a knowing-ness that one can nurture and maintain harmonious boundaries as one chooses and acts. This kind of power leads to win-win conditions rather than win-lose conditions. Win-win conditions are created with a magnetic and wise will that does things with loving and creative thought, planning, and intention. In contrast, win-lose scenarios are created with the use of force and insensitive aggression. Unfortunately, win-lose conditions have guided the nature of many aspects of the human experience and the Power Race Game.

In personal and societal life spaces, the ego, to a large extent, has become immersed in and addicted to playing the Power Race Game. This is true when a person acts out in such a way that they use the phenomenon of race to subtly or overtly control others, employing the control dramas of which I spoke earlier (i.e., intimidation, interrogation, aloofness, and victimization) (see p. 77). This is true when a person blindly uses racial labels in ways to manipulate or control interracial relations. This is true when a person entertains self-limiting beliefs in regard to race to evoke divisive tactics or to engage in discriminatory acts. This is true when a person uses a divide-and-conquer approach to engage others in one's world.

Two beliefs, among others, underlie the Power Race Game—the belief in scarcity and the belief in the lack of energy. If the ego aspect of a person's personality holds such beliefs, the personality, based on the person's perceived racial identity (or other perceived identities), creates power games to get enough stuff for the self. The ego fears, in other words, that there is not enough stuff and energy for everyone in the world. In general terms, the ego is actually telling his or her outer self that he or she is not enough. The ego then forms many ideas for getting and protecting what it now considers the stuff of its personal boundaries, social position, and racial identity (or other identities).

Unfortunately, approaching life in terms of power games will be resisted by the power games of other people. Such games evoke defensiveness and do not invite other people to help the person get what they want. Applied to the phenomenon of race, as the personality addictively acts out moves and countermoves to try to control race relations in the environment, the third or power chakra closes and energy often becomes jammed in the person's personal energy system. The person will often experience the jam as a knotting in the area of their solar plexus. That is, the person will often experience a knotting in the solar plexus when they think about race relations or when the person has or anticipates having interracial encounters that involve adjusting their personal boundaries. The possibility of interracial intimacy and/or interracial sharing of resources may evoke such a reaction if there are racially-linked energy jams in the person's personal energy system related to power games.

Throughout history, as it is understood, the phenomenon of race has become a convenient tool for the frightened ego to try to manipulate or control the environment by playing the Power Race Game. That is, the frightened ego seeks to control the environment and to maintain its view of its racial identity in that environment. The person may then act out a variety of unexamined subconscious beliefs, in addition to the two beliefs identified above.

Again, unexamined subconscious beliefs may be acquired through exposure and acquiescence to the beliefs of significant others and/or to societal or cultural beliefs regarding the nature of the self and reality. Some of these unexamined subconscious beliefs are so culturally entrenched and internalized individually and collectively that their association to the racial dramas of the Power Race Game may not be self-evident. Some beliefs, for example, are connected to a person's ideas about life and death, day and night, the waking state and the dreaming state, the unknown, the nature of consciousness and the nature of the unconscious. They are also connected to a person's ideas about the God and Satan concepts. I have conducted empirical or scientific research into this matter and a full discussion can be found in my book, *A New Perspective on Race and Color* (1997).

For purposes at this point, I again refer briefly to American culture and to some of the unexamined beliefs uncovered in my research. My research uncovered a variety of what can be called associative thought patterns that may impact the meaning of race in American culture (See discussion of "associative thought patterns" in Ferguson's *A New Perspective on Race and Color*, 1997, p. 38-64). The thought patterns identified may emerge if the ego aspect of a personality is frightened or is being judgmental in acting out lower self race games, particularly the Power Race Game.

For example, for those who may be more outer-oriented in American culture, the research revealed that internalized beliefs about "The Nature of Death" are likely to trigger race-related associative thought patterns to structure the acting out of interracial power games. That is, the research revealed that associative thought patterns involving fears or fearful attributions in regard to race, religion, color, the dreaming state, and to some extent waking state fears or fearful attributions may become more salient as a person becomes frightened when thinking about the nature of death.

Further, the research revealed that when outer-oriented respondents applied evaluative judgments in thinking about the nature of death, they tended to directly link their evaluative thoughts (evaluative attributions) in regard to the color black and the black race to their evaluative thoughts (evaluative attributions) in regard to the waking state and the nature of a personalized unconscious.

As I have suggested, associative thinking of this nature, to a large extent, is connected to the old paradigm and to the current view that a person's current racial form gives rise to their consciousness, rather than the other way around. Again, in this kind of cultural context, the death of a person's current physical form may be perceived or represents the annihilation of the person's consciousness. Within this framework, giving validity to and having a sense of the self as a soul with pre-causal consciousness and a multidimensional nature would be a difficult proposition to accept.

Even those in American culture who think they are more inner-oriented were found to share some aspects of the above way of thinking. For example, the research revealed that when inner-oriented respondents applied evaluative judgments in thinking about the nature of death, they tended to directly link their evaluative thoughts (evaluative attributions) in regard to the black race and the unknown to their evaluative thoughts (evaluative attributions) in regard to the nature of God, life, the waking state, and to some extent the unconscious in general and personal terms. However, interestingly, if the inner-oriented respondents become frightened when thinking about aspects of the unknown, they may directly associate the race-linked color black to their fears or fearful attributions in regard to the black race and the nature of the unconscious, the dreaming state, and Satan.

For both groups in the research study, the race-linked colors white and black were respectively attached to the religious concepts of God and Satan, albeit in somewhat different ways. Interestingly, therefore, the religious overtone was revealed to be part of many aspects of the associative thought patterns uncovered in this scientific or empirical research concerning the phenomena of race, color, consciousness, and the unconscious.

The religion overtone can be said to stem, in part, from the connotative meanings or value judgments attributed to light and dark that surrounds religious dogmas (i.e., God being the God of Light and Satan the Prince of Darkness). These attributions have been misapplied in American culture, as well as in other cultures, in regard to source energy/spirit or All-That-Is and soul-centered and spiritual reality. Indeed, in physical terms beyond connotative meanings, the misapplication has become even more evident as some scientists have already discovered that light and dark are necessary for optimal health. Light, for example, helps with growth, while dark releases the melatonin necessary for the immune system.

What does all of the above mean? It means that if a person is to truly understand how lower self race games are acted out and if a person is to truly understand how they relate to their *current racial form* and one's self, it is important to examine the contents of one's mind to uncover the nature of one's beliefs.

As a reader, what do you believe about "The Nature of Life" and about "The Nature of Death"? Do you see "The Nature of the Unconscious" as the dark or black side of consciousness? Do you believe that your consciousness is a derivative of matter or the other way around? Do you validate the concept of a soul or do you require scientific proof for all aspects of your existence and your world? What meanings do you apply toward the phenomena of light and dark? That is, to you, are they opposites, positive or negative, or neutral, or are they complementary or blended to you as aspects of a spectrum, for example? How do you relate to the shadow aspect of your self? Are you able to embrace all of who you are?

Here is an exercise that may assist a person in their process of uncovery as related to the above questions. Take a piece of paper and draw a line down the center or start an *Evolving the Human Race Game Journal* and use pages from that journal. On one side of the paper, write the words "The Nature of Life"; on the other side write the words "The Nature of Death." Next, underneath each of these headings, write down as many word or image associations that come to your mind. Do not judge them. Simply relax and allow the associations to come and write them down as you focus on each heading.

Do the same process with the following headings: "The Nature of the Waking State During the Day" and "The Nature of the Dreaming State During the Night"; "The Nature of Consciousness" and "The Nature of the Unconscious"; "The Nature of God" and "The Nature of Satan"; "Light" and "Dark"; and "The Known" and "The Unknown."

Once you feel complete in your process, set the papers aside for a day or so. Then, go back and review the lists of associations as if they belonged to someone else. Call upon your observer self. See if you can discern patterns of thought and where fear is at play. Where you discern fear, decide that this is an aspect of your self that awaits your love.

Go into meditation or close your eyes and relax and send love to the frightened aspect of your self, recognizing that you have been exploring your inner psychic reality. Visualize energy in the form of a golden or greenish liquid light flowing from your fourth chakra toward the fear and where you may be experiencing fear in your body. If you have difficulty sending love to this aspect of your self, give this aspect a name and in your imagination and in writing, ask it what it is trying to teach you. Have a dialogue with this aspect of your self in your journal. Realize that this fearful aspect is meant to lead you beyond itself and that you do not need to use control dramas to manipulate others you perceive to be from a different race. This exercise, therefore, may assist a person in uncovering and transforming major areas of racially-linked energy blocks, operating at a core level of the person's personality.

COMMON INTERRACIAL ROLE RELATIONSHIPS "ACTED OUT" IN LOWER SELF RACE DRAMAS

Throughout history, as it is understood, there have been three common personal, societal, and global interracial role relationships that the frightened ego has attempted to establish in the world to control the environment individually and collectively. These common interracial role relationships are: (1) the Bully/ Victim roles, (2) the Pursuer/Distancer roles, and (3) the Parent/ Child roles. These roles represent complementary or matching energies that are sent out through a person's Personal Energy Systems and acted out by the frightened ego.

In terms of lower self race games, however, those who have sought to establish and perpetuate these roles have always been met with resistance at some point in history. While the respective sets of roles do match, energetically, to create auras that touch, they mirror the participants' inabilities to adjust their personal boundaries harmoniously. They also do not allow the parties to make true energy contact and to authentically experience the essence of another.

And so, these roles mirror for the frightened ego areas of life that await the actualization and manifestation of acceptance, love, inclusion, and harmony (the four basic transformational archetypal energies). These transformational archetypal energies await authentic expression as a person co-creates and acts out various roles in their three life spaces and creates, and as a person co-creates, and acts out institutional rules, policies, and practices, societal laws and cultural norms, and collaborative, global enterprises.

THE BULLY/VICTIM INTERRACIAL ROLE RELATIONSHIPS.

In accord with the circumstances just described in relation to the *Power Race Game*, as energy is processed and sent out through the third or power chakra, the Bully (an individual, group, or society), as aggressor and/or persecutor, overextends energy toward the Victim. In this context, the bully is seeking to touch the aura of the victim (an individual, group, or society), without, however, recognizing that there can be no authentic, external energy exchange in this manner. In lower self race games, then, particularly in relation to a person's personal life space, the bully gravitates toward the victim in asserting a racial identity (and other identities). The bully believes that there is not as much resistance with the victim as is found in the rest or other aspects of his or her life. The victim, on the other hand, who restricts the outward flow of aural energy, believes that the bully is the only kind of person who can touch her or him. As a result, the victim may inappropriately acquiesce for a time to this kind of "closeness."

In extreme cases, in a person's personal life space, the frightened ego of the bully may resort to acting out angrily or violently or to engage in rigid stereotypic thinking about the victim. Under such circumstances, all persons who are categorized as belonging to a particular race, or other group, may be viewed by the bully as having qualities that the bully finds objectionable. What the bully is objecting to, however, are qualities or aspects of their own personality that are objectionable or frightening. The bully further may have been "taught" and may have "internalized" certain ideas about another race, or an other group, which have not been questioned. Or, the bully may be generalizing a whole set of rigid ideas onto another race, or other group, based on a few unpleasant experiences with a few persons from another race, or other group.

Applied specifically to the phenomenon of race, the bully, in fearing to look at particular aspect of their selves, or in fearing to question certain rigidly held race-related ideas, may, at times, disguise the acting out by proclaiming that such acts are fueled by a love for their own race, and not a hatred of another race. The ego then gets to feel a sense of false pride, not recognizing that this false pride is based on needing to have another race in the victim role. The victim, in turn, may also proclaim a love for their own race reactively and retreat into a same-race preference attitude. The victim believes that all people who belong to the identified race of the bully will tend to act out just like the bully under particular circumstances. Rigid categorical thinking thus holds together the acting out of these two roles.

The underlying motives for both the bully and the victim are that both want to blame the other for particular life circumstances and both want to be acknowledged. Both then engage in a dance, until the bully violates the victim's relatively flat personal boundaries too much. At this point, transformation of roles is required and must occur. As both parties have difficulty harmoniously adjusting their personal boundaries, reactions can often be covertly or overtly very confrontational and has sometimes been violent.

At a societal level, there are many examples of acts that represent violations of personal boundaries. Such acts may include, for example, the use of authority and what is called racial profiling to discriminate or to withhold services by targeting and prejudging members of a particular race. Those in certain societal roles, such as police officers, may use unnecessary displays of force toward someone from another or targeted race. Cab drivers may refuse to pick up someone from another or targeted race, or department store security guards may use what has been called consumer racism explicitly or implicitly to target individuals of a particular race. However, it need not happen this way when certain relational lessons are understood and certain archetypal energies, particularly the transformational archetypal energies, are given authentic expression. I will discuss more specific aspects of relating constructively in energy terms later.

PURSUER/DISTANCER INTERRACIAL ROLE RELATIONSHIPS

Other lower self racial dramas have been enacted through the roles of Pursuer/Distancer. In energy terms, these roles are quite similar to the roles of bully/victim, except that the underlying motives are somewhat different and energy may be processed through the first, second, and/or third chakras at various points. The Pursuer (an individual, group, or society) overextends energy toward the Distancer (an individual, group, or society), subconsciously chasing qualities that the pursuer believes are external to the self, which the distancer represents. The distancer, wanting outside validation, may consciously or subconsciously view the pursuit as a form of validation of self-worth and self-importance, while at the same time using a variety of defense mechanisms to keep the pursuer at bay in order to create a safety buffer. In this way, the distancer remains a mystery to be pursued.

Both parties, however, fear authentic energy contact, creating illusive and addictive intimacy dramas while believing in a need for a safe buffer. Sometimes there may be explosive consequences. When the pursuer tires of the pursuit as the pursued qualities are experienced as too elusive to obtain, roles switch and the parties can go back and forth in an endless dance.

In terms of lower self race games, the acting out of the pursuer/distancer dance often occurs in concert with internalized stereotypic beliefs about racial groups (or other groups) from the participants' societal life spaces. For example, the pursuer at a core level may see another race in societal life space as representing the passive, lazy or relaxed, intuitive, spontaneous, uninhibited, rhythmic, sensual, lustful, or natural aspects of the self or the more active, energetic or anxious, intellectual, knowledgeable, visionary, organized, focused, civilized, or wise aspect of the self. The pursuer may fear and/or desire these qualities, often at the same time.

The pursuer pulls in the distancer through the universal energy law of attraction and the distancer acquiesces to the dance in accord with his or her own beliefs. The pursuer then engages in a pursuit of these aspects of the self externally by creating a variety of interracial love-hate dramas at the personal or societal levels.

In a person's personal life space, for example, the pursuer, rather than validating certain qualities as aspects of the self, may obsessively project out the qualities onto someone(s) from another race and either tries to emulate the person(s) or acts out in angry outbursts toward the person(s) for having the projected (desired and/or feared) qualities. To some extent, the distancer represents the other half of the self to the pursuer. That other half of the self also may be what some would call the Shadow of the Pursuer.

The distancer, therefore, at times may feel flattered, admired, or confused, but is nevertheless attracted to the pursuer. The distancer, however, will only allow the pursuer to get so close. In interracial terms, the distancer may create a safe buffer by indicating or implying, "You can never really understand who I am because you are from a different race (or other group) and you can not know what I am experiencing in my world or from my vantage point in society," or by letting the pursuer know, "You should stay with your own kind." This does not imply that genuine love and authentic energy contact do not or cannot occur interracially in a person's personal life space. Indeed, many people in a society have managed to transcend these kinds of roles in their personal life spaces and are mirroring Higher Ideas.

At a societal level, pursuing and distancing may be subtler. These roles may be acted out in real or de facto terms through institutional practices, institutional roles, and unspoken codes, or through de facto segregation of the races (or other groups) by what are called reservations, ghettos, the inner city, the suburbs or other forms of racial, ethnic or other group enclaves. Have you ever wondered why in American society, for example, the inner city seems to be filled predominantly with people of color while the outer realms of the city, the suburbs, are not?

At the societal level, therefore, the pursuer and distancer may get to pretend to have authentic contacts at various societal settings (such as work or school) with other races or other groups (who stereotypically represent the qualities projected out and attributed to the racial or other groups), while retreating back to their racial, ethnic, or other group enclaves at the end of the day. Again, this is not to imply that there is not or cannot be genuine or authentic energy contact in these settings, for indeed there are. I am simply describing how the pursuer and distancer dance may operate in these settings.

At work sites, for example, the pursuer and distancer may get to act out what is called politically correct codes with those from other races or other groups, or may get to pretend that all racial or other group matters in society have been resolved or at least substantially resolved. At school sites, the pursuer and distancer may even sit and learn together while in a classroom or while working on a common project. Yet, during breaks such as time spent at a cafeteria, they may sit apart or sit primarily with their own self-identified racial or other group, quite aware of one another's presence. They may consciously or subconsciously feel uncomfortable when alone with one another.

Both the pursuer and the distancer, nevertheless, may cite work-related and school-related relationships as proof of the reality of their current positive attitudes in regard to race or other-oriented relations. At the same time, both may deny or ignore underlying fears that often result in them having little or no contact with anyone from another race or other group outside of the work-related or school-related roles. In interracial terms, however, the pursuer/distancer roles, at the societal level, at least allow the participants to simulate having authentic energy contact and intimacy in accord with societal projects and products.

PARENT/CHILD INTERRACIAL ROLE RELATIONSHIPS

A third most common set of interracial role relationships enacted by the frightened ego to control the environment is the Parent/Child roles. Energy for these roles may also be processed through the first, second, and/or third chakras at various points. In terms of actual parents and children, these two roles ideally and developmentally can result in well-balanced, pleasant emotional and energetic contact, as each learns to negotiate and renegotiate boundaries during natural developmental phases. However, when these two roles are misapplied specifically in terms of the human race game, one race (or majority group) may attempt to control another race (or minority group) by assuming it has the truth and "knows best" as Parent the correct way to be in life. Those seeking to play the parent role in lower self race games often assume, therefore, that they must treat other races (or minority groups) indulgently as children (the Child position), while fearing that the child will somehow escape certain prescribed boundaries. Those enacting the parent role may thus act out paternalistic attitudes toward other races (or minority groups).

When the Parent role is taken to the extreme, as has happened in history, this role may be misapplied even further into acting out a variety of forms of interracial dramas. These dramatic forms include, for example:

- *"master/slave" interracial dramas* (Note: As was the case most recently and in the not too distant past of South African and American societies);

- *"jailer/prisoner" interracial dramas* (Note: When one race may be disproportionately imprisoned in a society, literally and figuratively, while another race is disproportionately represented as jailers, literally and figuratively, for whatever reasons);

- *"leader/follower" interracial dramas* (Note: Where one race predominantly occupies positions of authority and decision-making in a society, for example: (1) the United States only recently was able to truly conceive of having a person of color as president, that real possibility emerging in Spring/Summer of 2008—i.e., in Spring/Summer of 2008, Barack Obama became a legitimate and viable Democratic Presidential candidate and was indeed elected President in November 2008; (2) in numerous work settings in the United States, there exists what is called "a glass ceiling," an institutional practice whereby persons of color are consciously or subconsciously, yet systematically or consistently, overlooked for promotions and/or receive inequities in pay for the same work— e.g., 2001 case of Georgia Power & other subsidiaries of Southern Company; 2005 Retailer Abercrombie & Fitch $40 million settlement; 2006 Tyson Food Inc. $1 million settlement; 2007 discrimination suit against Chuck E. Cheese); and

- *"rescuer/saved" interracial dramas* (Note: Where one race in a society seeks to impose a way of life onto another race based on the belief that their way of life rescues or saves the other race from a life of ignorance or wrong thinking and acting).

Again, at the core of all of these interracial dramas is fear—fear concerning what is subconsciously believed to be the power of the untamed energies of the child that has to be harnessed, controlled, and molded or must be held in check. It is important, therefore, for each person to face their fears and to move through them.

Those caught up in the child position in these kinds of interracial dramas, in innocence, may acquiesce for a time, out of a perceived need for acknowledgment. They believe at some level that there will be a time for renegotiations. Ironically and unwittingly, the child position at times may also become that of teacher for those seeking to touch through the parent role—that is, the child position often mirrors the individual and collective inadequacies and "miss takes" of the parent position.

For example, some people in American society have begun to hold up stereotypically those who are called Native Americans—that is, Native Americans are stereotypically held up as teachers of wisdom regarding how to relate to nature. At the same time, many Native Americans may be living on what are called reservations in less than satisfactory living conditions. Mirrored, therefore, are lessons for society-at-large regarding quality-of-life conditions that remain to be manifested and lessons for a majority group regarding the themes of the importance of self-respect and respect for others, the environment, and nature. I am not suggesting, however, that there are untruths here regarding wisdom teachings. I am simply noting that such interracial role relationships do not allow for authentic energy contact, as perceivers would tend to view and relate to the individual in stereotypic terms.

Likewise, those in American society who are called African Americans mirror for society-at-large a myriad of inconsistent and ongoing individual and societal value conflicts that exist in relation to stereotypes at a core level in personal and societal life spaces. That is, individually and collectively, there are unfulfilled, yet espoused core societal values in American society that are mirrored through the discrepancies of the ongoing and daily experiences of African Americans. These include, for example, unfulfilled values such as the equality of all persons created and the inalienable rights of the individual.

When equality is espoused while also subconsciously believing that to be different is to be unequal, a society sets up a conflict in values that must be resolved. The society has set up the equations that only sameness equals equality (Equation 1: sameness=equality), while difference equals inequality (Equation 2: difference=inequality). And so it is, that the acting out toward African Americans in American society has reflected the conflicting, ongoing, and unresolved value struggle behind these internalized equations. One possible resolution is the equation that difference equals unique (Equation 3: difference=unique), as indeed no two people on the face of the planet are exactly the same, not even so-called identical twins or what we think will be clones.

There is thus a kind of role reversal in regard to the child position under certain circumstances, such that the child position in various interracial dramas may inadvertently be recast into a sort of parental-child position. Again, however, because these dramas and these roles derive their thrusts from fear, authentic energy contact does not actually occur.

The fears often masks old wounds or hurts related to shame, which, at a personal level, often stem from earlier periods of a person's life, as the person understands it, or at a societal level, earlier periods of a society's history. In terms of the soul-centered model (Figure 2), however, these fears or hurts may also stem from other lifetimes. In interracial terms, those in the parent position project their fears related to the pain of the child aspect of themselves onto another race. They may have been wounded by the deeds and ideas of their own parents or other significant figures. Another race, in a manner of speaking, represents this child aspect of the self to them.

On the other hand, those in the child position may also be caught up in their own hurts related to earlier feelings of help-lessness and rejection. Therefore, to mask the hurt or pain, or to avoid feeling the hurt or pain, both parties use protective mecha-nisms. One of the most profound protective mechanisms used is numbness. Again, this is part of what is called the shadow aspects of the self. When a person acts out the bully, pursuer, and parent roles toward another race in accord with what they con-sider the shadow aspect of the self, or allows the self to be acted upon through the victim, distancer, and child roles, they are in effect mirroring the numbness in one's soul, or more accurately a numbness toward one's authentic essence or self.

It is important for each person, therefore, to seek understand-ing (an archetypal energy), and to examine the source of their fears in order to release the blocked energies. Through under-standing, a person positions the self to release such energies and comes to know that their release is not the same thing as acting them out.

Numbness is often a useful and realistic protective device used by the ego to ward off feelings of hurt, rejection, and help-lessness. It is a device used to protect one's personality against contradictory responses, impulses, and reactions. However, when numbness becomes a habit, as is the case with many of the interracial dramas of lower self race games, it often results in insensitivity toward one's own pain and insensitivity toward the pain of others. Racially-linked energy blocks are then cre-ated as the numbness emerges, often at the level of the second chakra, restricting the flow of emotional energy. One's passion becomes distorted, stifling its transformation into or alignment with compassion.

A person thus denies the spontaneous, caring aspects of the self. The person becomes indifferent and may even act out cruelly towards others. The person may first experience numbness toward the self, then numbness toward others, and ultimately act out by inflicting pain. The person indifferently violates the free will of others. If a person is in such a state, transformation of the numbness is necessary.

MIRROR EFFECTS OF NUMBNESS AND ADDICTIVE ENERGY BLOCKS IN LOWER SELF RACE GAMES: "SYMBOLIC REFLECTIONS" FROM THE TRAYVON MARTIN AND MALALA YOUSAFZAI CASES

Sometimes, lower self acts of violence, flowing from common interracial role relationships, may be acted out without much conscious awareness. Common interethnic role relationships may be described in a similar fashion. At play are numbness and addictive energy blocks which cloud the intermingling of internal, underlying issues related to safety and security, sensory sensations and sensory feelings, and/or power and value judgments linked to external cues and/or dogma. In the Trayvon Martin case, the intermingling of various interracial roles and internal lower self issues were/are symbolically mirrored. In the Malala Yousafzai case, the intermingling of various interethnic roles, coupled with lower self religious and cultural dogma, were/are symbolically mirrored. Both cases also were/are symbolic mirrors for the ongoing, unresolved wound in the national psyches of two sovereign, yet interdependent nations as of 2013—the United States on the one hand and Pakistan on the other hand.

On the evening of February 26, 2012, seventeen-year-old Trayvon Martin, an African American youth, was shot and killed in Sanford, Florida, while walking home from a convenience store. The shooter, George Zimmerman, who has an ambiguous racial appearance (i.e., the son of a Peruvian mother and a white father), was a neighborhood watch captain, symbolically representing addictive energy blocks related to the illusion of power. Zimmerman, a 200-pound 28-year-old with a history of violence, claimed self-defense, even though Trayvon Martin, a tall and lanky 140-pound adolescent, had no criminal history and nothing more than candy and an iced tea in his hands.

The incident occurred in a "gated community," symbolically representing fear-based ideas and addictive energy blocks related to safety and security. Zimmerman, spotting Martin who wore a gray hoody as he was returning to a family's townhouse, told a police dispatcher, "This guy looks like he is up to no good—he is on drugs or something." Although told by the police dispatcher not to approach Martin, Zimmerman ignored the dispatcher's instructions. Symbolically and addictively, sensory stimulation and value judgments related to external cues were at play here, apparently overriding rational thought and influencing Zimmerman's immediate choices. Although different views emerged about what subsequently happened, the ultimate outcome of these immediate choices was the shooting incident.

When the Sanford police department was slow to release details of the shooting and did not immediately bring charges against Zimmerman, this sparked a national discourse about the case, revealing, according to some observers, a history of institutional and cultural racism (i.e., forms of addictive energy blocks) in Sanford, Florida. Petitions followed and Zimmerman was eventually arrested and charged with second-degree murder and manslaughter. Florida's controversial "Stand Your Ground" law emerged for review, and other collateral dramas involving deception and bail also unfolded.

On June 19, 2013, Zimmerman's trial began and on July 13, 2013 a jury of six women, five of whom were white, acquitted him of both the second-degree murder and manslaughter charges.

Zimmerman did not take the stand during his trial, and therefore was not cross-examined. As of this writing, the US Justice Department was looking into the possible violation of Treyvon Martin's civil rights, and the legal team for Martin's family was considering a wrongful death civil case against Zimmerman.

For many, particularly for African Americans, the verdict and the unfolding circumstances were/are viewed symbolically as mirroring yet another example of injustice in a long history of a struggle for social justice in the United States regarding race relations. Even the non-white juror noted in an interview that she thought Zimmerman "got away with murder," but given how the law and charges were constructed and given the instructions and evidence provided to the jury, she ultimately felt she had no choice but to go along with an acquittal.

In the case of 15-year-old activist Malala Yousafzai, on October 9, 2012, she was on her way home from school in Mingora, Pakistan, when unidentified men, reportedly with the Pakistan Taliban, stopped the school van. One of the men then reportedly asked which girl was Malala, and then proceeded to shoot Malala in the head and neck. Two other girls on the bus were also wounded and were treated at a nearby hospital. Strong in higher will, Malala lived. After being stabilized at a Pakistan hospital, she was transported eventually to a hospital in Birmingham, England, to see specialists.

Reportedly a spokesman for the Pakistan Taliban, Ehsanullah Ehsan, used dogma to justify the shooting, proudly taking responsibility. Ehsan reportedly said that Malala "has become a symbol of Western culture in the area" and had expressed admiration for President Obama. Ehsan is further quoted as saying, "She is a Western-minded girl. She always speaks against us... We will target anyone who speaks against the Taliban." He also reportedly said that although she was young, "she was promoting Western culture in Pashtun areas," referring to the ethnic group in northwest Pakistan and eastern Afghanistan whose conservative values the Taliban claims to defend (see The Lede—Blogging the News With Robert Mackey, October 9, 2012).

The Taliban reportedly said it was not only "allowed" to target young girls, but it was "obligatory" when such a person "leads a campaign against Islam and sharia." However, the Taliban's attempted assassination sparked outrage inside Pakistan and around the world, transforming Malala, who first came to prominence through her blogging, into an international symbol of defiance against the radical Islmaic group that continues to wield influence in parts of Pakistan. Some clerics in Pakistan also denounced the shooting and declared Malala's shooting as "un-Islamic." These clerics labeled as extremists those involved in this shooting drama. As of this writing, six suspects were arrested for the shooting, but were later released for lack of evidence. However, police named 23-year-old Atta Ulla Khan, a graduate student in chemistry, as the shooter. As of this writing, he remains at large.

Since the age of 11, Malala was an outspoken advocate of education for girls. Her message was simple—everyone should have access to an education, regardless of gender. Yet those addictively holding fear-based, self-liming cultural beliefs and dogma were/are threatened by this young voice. They thus acted out in violence against this courageous youth (see Ferguson's "Beyond Self-Limiting and Addictive Cultural Scripts," and "Beyond Dogma" in *AHP Perspective*).

Since the shooting, Malala has healed and her voice has become even stronger, symbolized by the United Nations inviting her to speak at the UN on her 16th birthday, July 12, 2013, dubbed "Malala Day." In her speech, she called for worldwide access to education. She also courageously stated:

"The terrorists thought they would change my aims and stop my ambitions, but nothing changed in my life except this: weakness, fear and hopelessness died. Strength, power and courage was born ... I am not against anyone, neither am I here to speak in terms of personal revenge against the Taliban or any other terrorist group. I'm here to speak up for the right of education for every child. I want education for the sons and daughters of the Taliban and all terrorists and extremists." (Michelle Nichols, July 12, 2013. "Pakistan's Malala, shot by Taliban, takes education plea to U.N.". Reuters. Retrieved 23 July 2013).

Regardless of the final outcomes of both of these cases, their significance is contained in the symbolism and addictive energy blocks connected to the dramas themselves. The mirrored effects were/are to illustrate how much healing still is required in regard to healing wounds in national psyches that are race-linked and linked to ethnic phenomena, as of 2013. In broader terms, the symbolism surrounding these events calls attention to the need for transformation related to the numbness, the addictive quality, and the energy blocks that are often at play in regard to lower self race games.

TRANSFORMING THE NUMBNESS, THE ADDICTIVE QUALITY, AND THE "KARMIC" ENERGY BEHIND LOWER SELF RACE GAMES

The first step in transforming and evolving the numbness toward the self, one's authentic essence, or one's soul is to acknowledge and honor one's emotions. A person's emotions will lead them to what they believe to be true about the self. These ego-held beliefs are causing the experience of numbness.

To get in touch with these ego-held beliefs, a person can again use their journal and have a dialogue with Mister or Miss Numbness. Ask what the numbness is masking or is trying to keep you from seeing or experiencing. What do you believe is too painful for you to look at? Realize that a belief is not necessarily the truth and that it is the belief that is generating the feeling-state of numbness.

Realize further that no feeling is static and that feelings are always in motion. *E-motions* are energy in motion. As such, any pain or hurt is not a static state. It only appears to be so at times because the person holds it in place with their beliefs and fears, giving it energy.

When a person examines their beliefs, faces the fears and goes through them, the hurt or pain dissolves. They discover that they have separated themselves from love and that when the hurt or pain dissolves, love is what is left.

As a person examines their hurt or pain, they also may discover that their second chakra energy has become stagnated and attached to their ideas about destructiveness. That is, the pleasure principle underlies and guides second chakra energy. Distortions, therefore, may have taken place such that the person may have misapplied the pleasure principle insensitively and/or destructively. In regard to lower self race games, then, a false sense of elation may temporarily occur as the person acts out insensitively and/or destructively toward those they identify as belonging to another race.

It may be difficult for a person to recognize that they have accepted the idea that harming another person somehow makes them feel good temporarily. Such reasoning, however, is behind all acts of what people call revenge and retribution on behalf of one's self, another, or a group with which a person identifies. A person may even delude their outer self into believing that somehow their acting out in such a manner is righteous and/or is an act of justice.

Doing harm to another, however, is never justified when there are no inner or outer agreements, for whatever reasons, from a spiritual and soul-centered perspective. If there are such agreements, a person must also understand that when they act out in such a manner, they are creating an energy imbalance. As a result, they also begin a process of energy movement toward reestablishing the balance. This is what is known as *karma*, in certain spiritual teachings, whereby a person is creating an energy loop with another entity such that they, at some point, will be experiencing the other side of the loop. From this perspective, karmic imbalances, therefore, are behind some lower self race games that are acted out face-to-face at an individual level.

From a spiritual and soul-centered perspective, then, it is important to choose inner and outer agreements carefully at all levels. From this perspective, it is also important to know that one can change any agreements that they may have established prior to and during an incarnation. In accord with the soul-centered model, people do this constantly already in what is known as the dream state. And, in resonance with the soul-centered model, there is some truth, therefore, to the notion that if one is uncertain about an action, they may want to sleep on it overnight.

More specifically, I encourage readers to try this experiment. Before you go to bed, give your self the suggestion and ask for possible solutions to racial or other problems that you may have identified. In a dream journal, record your dreams and examine them for themes. Calling upon your observer self, see your dreams as having certain storylines as if you are watching a story on television. Contained in these storylines of your dreams are possible solutions or information that can be helpful to you.

Remember that the language of one's dreams is in terms of what people think of as symbolic language or inner imagery or pictures. A person's symbolic language, however, is ultimately unique to that person—it is one of the ways that the soul communicates with the ego aspect of a person's personality, and one of the ways that the soul provides information to a person about their inter-dimensional travels. From a spiritual and soul-centered perspective, then, it is important to use one's dreams to understand one's agreements and to make newer, more constructive interracial or intra-racial agreements.

Beyond the level of agreements, lower self race games also have what might be called an "addictive quality" to them. That is, in lower self race games, often a person habitually operates unaware of certain beliefs or unaware of certain underlying ways of thinking and feeling. Or, a person repeatedly acts out behaviors that violate the spirit of original, nurturing, and cooperative agreements involving interracial dramas. For the most part, as a person acts out lower self race games, they operate unaware of how they are addictively misusing certain universal energy laws.

The addictive quality of lower self race games represents jams or spasms in a person's personal energy system, fueled by transparent core beliefs. These addictive energy jams or spasms tend to distort the person's heroic impulses for interracial and other forms of human collaboration, cooperation, and spiritual blending.

When energy is jammed or there are spasms in the flow of energy through a person's personal energy system, the energy gets distorted. If then the person directs that distorted, blocked energy toward the phenomenon of race, the person may keep the self and their consciousness stuck. The person acts out the now racially-linked energy blocks in a variety of self-limiting interracial dramas and unproductive or destructive interracial role relationships. It is important, therefore, to evolve the addictive patterns that have characterized much of lower self race games. It is this stuck energy that must be understood, released, and/or evolved.

Addictive patterns are interrupted with increased awareness and a conscious intent to shift preferences. By the law of universality, what a person experiences is a matter of preferences, what the person focuses on, knowingly or unknowingly. To shift one's preferences, the person may use their creative imagination, a tool of the mind for conscious intent.

Creative imagination is one of the most powerful tools that can be used for growth, change, and transformation. If a person cannot imagine their self or a circumstance being different than the way they currently are or the way the current circumstance is, then nothing will change. It is important, therefore, for a person to first use their imagination to create the possibility that they can be different, beyond their addictive patterns, than the way they currently are. In doing so, the person shifts their focus, and experiences are vibrationally created in alignment with this new preference.

This shift requires, however, becoming more open to one's higher self and to one's soul qualities or the archetypal energies that support the outer self. This shift also requires understanding the Universal Energy Laws and how to wisely use them. As a person does so, they will become more aware of how to bring into the physical plane various archetypal energies for evolving the human race game toward what I have called higher self race games.

In terms of personal, societal, and global life spaces, for example, the Barack Obama presidential and political drama in the United States may be viewed, individually and collectively, as one of a number of emerging or unfolding stimulus events that can be used for growth, change, and transformation. That is, these kinds of emerging or unfolding events tend to provide people with opportunities to choose to become open to their higher self and the archetypal energies, for shifting preferences and addictive patterns, and for entertaining the possibility for evolving the human race game toward higher self race games.

HIGHER SELF RACE GAMES AND ARCHETYPAL ENERGIES (OR SOUL QUALITIES)

To some extent, higher self race games mirror an ever-expanding, vibrational world of possibilities that resonate with archetypal energies, awaiting activation, form, and authentic expression. At the soul-centered and spiritual level, the phenomenon of race, as implied in the soul-centered model, does not exist, as the rules of manifestation are somewhat different. Theoretically, as a CU, or consciousness unit, in a Monadic body and its reality, the higher self can become any form that it can conceive. The higher self also can be content without form, as implied in the soul-centered model. At this level of consciousness, as the higher self thinks, so it is and so the higher self is. The higher self is not separate from its creations. Cause and effect are more immediate.

In addition, the higher self may, if it wishes, sense reality in a similar fashion as exists in physicality and in just as real terms. However, depending on the plane from which the higher self has consciousness, the sensing may be more of an emotional, mental, or unencumbered energy connection to wholeness and unity.

Part of the current process of evolving, therefore, is to bring more and more aspects of each person's higher self into the physical realm. Evolving the human race game, then, is part of this process. It is important, therefore, for each person to develop a sense of their own connection to their higher self, as well as to develop an understanding of when they are acting out of their higher self and what types of specific race games may evolve as they act out from this vantage point in accord with the phenomenon of race.

How to Know When One is "Acting Out" of the Higher Self

As I did with an examination of the lower self, I offer the following ideas as guides for how to know when a person is acting out of the higher self (see "Why Have an Ego?" in *Spirit Speaks*) and when the person is in alignment with their authentic spiritual essence in the physical realm. A person is acting out of the higher self when:

- They can empathize and offer comfort to someone in great pain without taking over their problem or trying or needing to fix them.

- They can let go of their need to be right about anything.

- They can accept that all beliefs serve someone at some time, even if they don't understand them or if they think theirs are better.

- They can accept that their favorite teacher(s) must present truths apparent to them that may not be apparent to the person at this time, or may never be apparent to them.

- They can accept the people they admire as human beings with just as many issues as any other human being.

- They can accept that the people they love have a right to do what they want and to be who they are, regardless of their personal tastes.

- They can accept that the people they love are not obliged to grow or to see them in any way but how they see them.

- They seek validation only from within, knowing that whatever response they get from the outside world reflect only something from within anyway.

- They acknowledge their self as the wonderful, unique being they are.

- They know that everyone in their life added to their growth, and they can see that addition as positive or negative to their overall growth and development, and they can have compassion for their role.

In the above context, who a person is, their Being-ness, frames the nature of their experience. In other terms, archetypal energies or the soul qualities of a person's higher self reflect the nature of the person's being-ness and serve as underlying urges or messages, or spiritual dispatches, to assist the person in their outer creations. In this light, a person's outer creations are intended to mirror the nature of the person's being-ness as the person gives form, context, development, and expression in accord with the properties of their thoughts, emotions, and actions and the Universal Energy Laws. Unencumbered by ego fears, then, a person's outer creations would mirror their higher ideas or soul qualities.

ARCHETYPAL ENERGIES (OR SOUL QUALITIES) THAT CAN HELP EVOLVE THE HUMAN RACE GAME

What, then, are some of these archetypal energies and how do they connect to the process of evolving the human race game? I am tempted, at this point, to offer specific definitions of some of the archetypal energies and hesitate here, as it is important for each person to give these energies unique and authentic expression. Definitions have a tendency to create boxes, rather than allow a person to expand in accord with their own purposes and experiences. So, what I offer are meant simply as guides and are not meant to be definitive descriptions of these archetypal energies. The descriptions are also based on a blending of thoughts from many sources.

I recommend, therefore, that when one reads the descriptions, they ask their outer self what their world would look like if these archetypal energies were at play in their personal, societal, and global life spaces. More specifically, ask the outer self in what ways it can allow more of these archetypal energies to enter its world or life spaces. What would it mean to be these qualities? If some or all of these archetypal energies are already at play in one's world or life spaces, affirm that this is so and simply ask the outer self in what ways it may more efficiently use them to evolve the human race game.

The following list of archetypal energies, therefore, is not meant to be exhaustive. I am presenting twenty-five of them, as these twenty-five will assist a person in evolving the human race game. I use common and familiar names, as these names will evoke a common sense of familiarity with the energy.

Again, archetypal energies are higher universal, transcendent, governing, vibrational energy-imprinting principles within the cosmos at work within individual lives and psyches. A person tends to experience them as "creative urges" that move one toward their optimal selves and optimal realities. The nature of these archetypal energies, however, is much more significant than the labeling process itself.

These archetypal energies easily blend and flow together. I have already mentioned a number of these archetypal energies elsewhere in this discussion. In reading the descriptions, one may sense the higher energy behind the printed words. I have lengthened the descriptions for this reason.

I will first list the twenty-five archetypal energies (see Table 3) and then provide the guiding descriptions. The list is in terms of those archetypal energies that often function to open up the lower self to growth and integration with the higher self through engaging in and experiencing various earth lessons. Three general types of soul-linked earth lessons are: (1) Foundational Lessons for the lower self; (2) Transformational Lessons for the observer self; and (3) Spiritually Integrative Lessons that involve both the lower self and the higher self. Again, I am identifying particular archetypal energies that are helpful in regard to these lessons.

Table 3.	List of Archetypal Energies or Soul Qualities	
Higher Energies For Lower Self Foundational Lessons	Higher Energies For Observer Self Transformational Lessons	Higher Energies For Spiritually Integrated Self Lessons
•Trust	•Love	•Understanding
•Enthusiasm	•Acceptance	•Truth
•Humor	•Inclusion	•Wisdom
•Beauty	•Harmony	•Patience
•Hope		•Inspiration
•Flexibility		•Abundance
•Courage		•Compassion
		•Peace
		•Joy
		•Clarity
		•Vision
		•Oneness
		•Unity
		•Serenity

Foundational Lessons are those lessons that help each person form or establish a personality structure, a foundation, which has qualities that allow the person to entertain the possibility of choosing to grow, to expand, to move higher, and to do so by choosing a path of growth with joy. I am identifying, therefore, particular archetypal energies that support this kind of process of becoming.

Transformational Lessons are those lessons that focus on the heart center of each person's personal energy system. The lessons at this level pertain to the changes in the foci and preferences of a person's consciousness and the nature of various blending, transformations, transcendences, and transmutations of energies as the person makes authentic contact with their higher self and as souls make authentic contact.

Spiritually Integrative Lessons are those lessons that help each person to mirror the integration of the person's lower and higher selves and to be their truer self. To be one's truer self is to be and to act out one's soul qualities in one's world.

The archetypal energies that are identified here will be each person's unique expression of those qualities of their higher self. Ultimately, when a person consciously recognizes and engages the outer self in any of these lessons and applies those lessons to the human race game, the person may view their outer self as involved in the process of evolving the human race game.

Some of the archetypal energies, therefore, can be identified and described as follows:

FOUNDATIONAL ARCHETYPAL ENERGIES

- *Trust*—is an energy aspect of authentic essence or a soul quality that brings a sense of security to a person's unique consciousness and their unique being-ness in the universe. Trust brings a sense that the person's consciousness and being-ness cannot be destroyed, only transformed. Trust is a knowing-ness about one's unbreakable energetic connection to source energy/spirit or All-That-Is as each person is an aspect of source energy/spirit or All-That-Is, a knowing-ness that one's consciousness and being-ness are protected and nurtured. Trust also guides the creation of contexts so that a person experiences the Universe and their self in the universe as safe, mentally, emotionally, physically, and spiritually. Trust thus acts as one of the major energy components for relating to others, that is, for creating and establishing authentic soul contacts and soul relationships as well as more surface, ego or personality contacts and relationships.

- *Enthusiasm*—is an energy aspect of authentic essence or a soul quality that stimulates and excites a person's inner and outer senses as the person engages in acts of relating and spiritual blending. Enthusiasm seeks to sustain a person's interest and focus, internally and externally, so that the person can successfully direct energy toward their goals and toward creative acts and creative expressions that nurture their whole self. Enthusiasm directs the pull of energy on a person to seek out and to experience various forms of relating and spiritual blending, while fostering a sense of well-being. Enthusiasm is also an aspect of a person's authentic essence or soul, connected to source energy/spirit or All-That-Is, that creates a context for stimulation, aliveness, and excitement as the person experiences and focuses on her or his reality, whether alone or with others.

- *Humor*—is an energy aspect of authentic essence or a soul quality that urges a person to smile and to laugh with their whole self and others. Humor assists a person in seeing the lighter side of an apparent polarity with perspective, facilitating the movement of the person's emotional body toward that lighter side. In this regard, humor brings to the person a quality of healing to lift and alter their perspective in regard to those matters they may have taken too seriously. That is, humor urges a person to question if they have judged their outer self too harshly. Humor lightens the person's energy, allowing the person to laugh at their outer self and not weigh one's whole self down with bleak thoughts and emotions. Humor, therefore, is one of the practical sides of learning to live with joy in the moment and to engaging others in play in the moment.

- *Beauty*—is an energy aspect of authentic essence or a soul quality that holds all in awe for the magnificent blending of spirit with its infinite forms. In recognizing this quality in all, there is a direct recognition and a direct experience of the wonder of the universe and the eloquence and elegance of spirit in the world in its various forms. Beauty seeks to frame the nature of a person's inner and outer senses as the person creates and shapes their world. Beauty is one of the qualities, along with harmony, that sets the stage for the emergence of joy.

- *Hope*—is an energy aspect of authentic essence or a soul quality that assists a person in continuously moving toward their optimal future. It helps the person to maintain a sense of optimism when what appears to be so does not quite match the person's desires in the present moment. It is a precursor for and establishes the foundation for allowing the larger energy of vision to manifest. It supports the person's desires as the energy of the person's unique aspect of vision is being actualized.

- *Flexibility*—is an energy aspect of authentic essence or a soul quality that guides the free flow of energy in relation to permeable and personal boundaries, creating an atmosphere for honoring and nurturing free will as connected to spirit. Flexibility is also an energy aspect of authentic essence or soul quality that urges a person to find, to recognize, and to acknowledge the meaning of and behind all possibilities or probable creative acts or events. Flexibility urges a person to expect the best and to seek out the good in relating to others. Flexibility nurtures a person's process of becoming, letting the person know through its urges that their energy may have become stagnant or stale. In this light, the person comes to know when to let go and when to allow the outer self to grow, to change. Flexibility assists a person in becoming open to viewing and valuing their world and others in their world from many perspectives.

- *Courage*—is an energy aspect of authentic essence or a soul quality that assists a person in asking for what they want and in making the person's dreams come true. Courage allows or gives a person the ability to say yes and no to energy exchanges that nurture and do not nurture the person, to begin again, or to let go of something that is not in alignment with the person's higher purpose(s). Courage encourages a person to act in behalf of their higher good and highest expression. Courage supports the person in being open to their higher self, to their connection to source energy/spirit or All-That-Is, and to all other higher qualities. Courage supports the person in actualizing their higher ideas and beliefs, supports the person during times of self-initiated change, and allows the person to see their whole self as a radiant spirit and being of light with power. Courage also guides the development of greater confidence and helps the person to reach farther out, strengthening their ability to live by the authority of their own soul. Courage allows the person to bring in new sources of life energy.

TRANSFORMATIONAL
ARCHETYPAL ENERGIES

- *Love*—is a state of being and feeling and a state of doing. Energetically and vibrationally, it is the source feeling-tone and authentic essence or soul quality behind all creative acts. Love has no limits, nor does it perceive anything against which it must defend itself, for indeed it is a part of all creations. Love is the authentic essence of who a person/consciousness/soul is in their infinite expressions and multidimensional forms, as the universe has given a person/consciousness/soul birth with it. Love is ever-emerging, unconditionally, and ever-expansive. Love is the only feeling that transmutes, transforms, and transcends all levels of consciousness. As the prime moving force, love is the strongest and gentlest force in one's universe. Love is and is to be freely given and received. Love grounds a person and is one's birthright. However, love can only be given by the giver. Love is the primary line of communication to All-That-Is.

- *Acceptance*—is an energy aspect of authentic essence or a soul quality that repositions a person internally and externally and urges the person to examine, to embrace, and to love all aspects of who they are and what is so. In this regard, acceptance has a function of opening the door for love so that love can transform and transmute other energies, a function that ultimately also allows a person to transcend what may appear as opposites or polarities at some levels of consciousness. Acceptance acts as a bridge between lower and higher centers of consciousness and serves as a doorway to and for a person's creative imagination. As such, acceptance is a doorway for envisioning alternative possibilities. Acceptance is also a doorway for experiencing the wholeness of one's self and for seeing more of the whole or source energy/spirit or All-That-Is.

- *Inclusion*—is an energy aspect of authentic essence or a soul quality that urges a person to expand their consciousness as they become more and more of who they are. In expanding one's consciousness, this archetypal energy assists the person in embracing more and more of one's self as an aspect of source energy/spirit or All-That-Is from the standpoint of one's unique perspective. Inclusion functions to nurture a person's movement through the doorway that acceptance opened so that love can expand and move forward (outward), allowing the person to experience more and more of one's self. Energetically, then, inclusion works along with or is a companion for the archetypal energies love and acceptance. In this light, inclusion also urges a person to seek and to find communality with others.

- *Harmony*—is an energy aspect of authentic essence or a soul quality that facilitates the creation of constructive outcomes for all spiritual blending. Harmony also encourages, nurtures, and supports the give-and-take of all energetic exchanges—physical, mental, emotional, and spiritual—using the principle of balance. Harmony is one of the qualities, along with beauty, that sets the stage for the emergence of joy. Harmony facilitates the vibrational and energetic work between a person's higher and lower consciousness and soul contacts by acting as an ideal maintenance form to move toward, once acceptance has created a bridge and opened the door for love. Harmony is therefore the archetypal energy that emerges when aspects of the person's self and/or others are touched by love (i.e., the person gets in touch with the love inside of them and others) and is the archetypal energy that remains as a vibrational and energetic reflection (the reflected outcome) of the nature of love.

SPIRITUALLY INTEGRATIVE ARCHETYPAL ENERGIES

- *Understanding*—is an energy aspect of authentic essence or a soul quality that guides the nature of inner and outer comprehension of the whole or source energy/spirit or All-That-Is. Understanding urges a person toward a comprehension that apparent polarities have a single source. Understanding is a companion of truth and creates the context or establishes the contextual outcome for acceptance. Understanding works with truth to unveil and comprehend the nature of the many forms and manifestations of spirit without judgment. In this light, understanding brings order to the contents of the higher and lower aspects of one's mind. Its nature guides a person as the person gets to know all aspects of their self. Understanding also guides the nature of inner repositioning such that a person's acts of choosing or developing preferences can be comprehended as acts of alignment with the person's spirit and acts of movement toward the person's growth and wholeness.

- *Truth*—is an energy aspect of authentic essence or a soul quality that urges a person to look at and see what is so. In this sense, truth is neutral and thus sets a person free as the person lets go of judgments in seeing beyond illusions, beyond the images a person lives by and the roles a person plays. The doorway to deeper truth is awareness, paying attention to energy and to one's thoughts and emotions, and holding every situation up to the light of what is really so. When a person acts and speaks from their truth and integrity, the person lightens their energy. Truth thus offers a person an opportunity to clean up one's energy, evolve one's self, and move higher. Truth is meant to be expressed, with the guidance of love. Truth also gives birth to compassion as a person sees the truth behind one's passions and allows higher guidance for one's passions.

- *Wisdom*—is an energy aspect of authentic essence or a soul quality that harnesses, focuses, and nurtures a person's ability to be conscious of what is happening around them, to see the higher truth, and express one's self with compassion. Wisdom is a quality that fosters a person's ability to discern, without judgment, which messages to pay attention to and which to release, that supports a person's ability to learn what is one's own thoughts, one's own expectations, and what is another person's, and that sustains a person's ability to know when to act and when not to. Wisdom is also knowing when to help and when not to. Wisdom, therefore, is the ability to know what is important in one's life and what is not, what are distractions in one's life and what are soul urges. Wisdom is the ability to sort through all the input into one's life and to select only those things that contribute to one's sense of well-being. Wisdom brings together what a person knows intuitively with what the person knows intellectually. With wisdom, a person comes to believe that everything is happening for their higher good and it does.

- *Patience*—is an energy aspect of authentic essence or a soul quality that gives a person the ability to play with the phenomenon of time and the natural flow and rhythms of universal energies. Patience provides a person with the ability to slow down time so that one can sense the larger vibrational and energetic connections of events and people, as well as to sense the unfoldment of soul contacts and connections. Patience helps a person to develop the ability to create a pause when the intellect wants to control everything, losing sight of its soul connection and the natural ebbs and flow of energy. Patience can and often does use the universal energy law of neutrality whereby a person chooses both sides of a polarity until the person is clear about what they want. In this way, patience keeps a person from sending energy to that which they do not want, thereby creating it. Patience often paves the way for the archetypal energies *truth* and *clarity*. Patience urges a person to develop one's problem-solving and relationship-building skills.

- *Inspiration*—is an energy aspect of authentic essence or a soul quality that urges a person toward the fulfillment of their higher abilities, higher goals, and higher good as aligned with the person's soul purpose(s) or path for growth. Inspiration also aids a person in making soul contacts in ways that assist others to move toward the fulfillment of their higher abilities, higher goals, and higher good as aligned with their soul purpose(s) or path for growth. Inspiration thus functions to lift up or to raise to a higher level the vibrations of other energies that may have become stagnant or that may require expression or release. Inspiration is an expressive energy and is thus instrumental in all forms of communication. Inspiration provides a person with motivation to act. Inspiration is, in other words, the underlying archetypal energy that promotes and sustains a person's motivation. Inspiration promotes and sustains a person's motivation to act by transmitting and translating spiritual meaning to the person. As an expressive energy for spiritual meaning, inspiration can, therefore, refine or reframe other energies such as understanding, truth, wisdom, and patience in terms of experiencing more enhanced motivational urges.

- *Abundance*—is an energy aspect of authentic essence or a soul quality that urges a person to recognize that energy in its many forms is always available to the person and is ever-emerging. In this light, abundance links a person to the unlimited abundance of their soul or their higher self. Abundance encourages a person to affirm their connection to unlimited and ever-emerging energy and it supports the person's existence in terms of their value, worth, and uniqueness in the universe. A person, therefore, comes to know that they are the source of their abundance and that whatever one focuses on is what they get, for energy follows thought. That is, when a person focuses on what they love, what they want, the person vibrationally and energetically draws it to them. Thus, what a person knows as positive emotions and thoughts draw what the person wants to them, while what a person knows as negative emotions and thoughts bring only what the person doesn't want. The former, therefore, attracts abundance and the latter repels abundance. By thinking, expressing, and radiating one's higher qualities, a person becomes the source of their abundance. Additionally, by allowing their outer self to have more, feel good, or love something, the person contributes to the planetary path of abundance.

- *Compassion*—is an energy aspect of authentic essence or a soul quality that urges a person to develop and to have the ability to put one's outer self in the other person's shoes. Its parent energy is truth and so in a manner of speaking, to have compassion means coming from one's deeper truth as a person gives compassion expression and acts in accord with one's truth with others. Compassion urges a person to uplift others by having the ability to see and to reframe an unfortunate experience in terms of issues of growth. In terms of service to others, compassion facilitates one's communication to others in terms of knowing when and how to say things to nurture another's growth. Compassion is not the same thing as having sympathy, which means feeling sorry for others and seeing what is happening in negative or bad terms. Rather, compassion urges a person to authentically share what may be useful to others without judgment.

- *Peace*—is an inner state of being and an energy aspect of authentic essence or soul quality that functions to move a person toward itself in regard to self-growth and urges a person to handle and release those emotions and emotional attitudes that separate the person from the experience of it and love. To do this, peace urges a person to use the gift of forgiveness. Those separating emotions and emotional states include anger, hurt, self-pity, fear, anxiety, worry, confusion, and doubt. In addition to itself, peace urges a person to replace those separating emotions with other higher qualities such as love, trust, enthusiasm, and serenity. Peace, in other words, creates high expectancy for a way to be.

- *Joy*—is an energy aspect of authentic essence or a soul quality that creates lightheartedness and guides the nature of spiritual blending in terms of relating and connecting such that it is experienced as fun. Joy guides the nature of play in the universe. Joy naturally emerges in response to any soul contact and comes from creating order with harmony and beauty. Joy resides beneath the surface of apparent polarities in the core of one's being and springs forth in response to soul contacts. Joy is the primary note of the planet Earth, guiding the evolutionary plan.

- *Clarity*—is an energy aspect of authentic essence or a soul quality that emerges to support truth and to assist a person in their decision-making and their movements toward one's vision and one's higher good. Clarity helps a person to set specific and clear short-term and long-term goals as well as immediate and eventual goals. Clarity helps a person to create and to have what might be called optimal futures.

- *Vision*—is an energy aspect of authentic essence or a soul quality that nurtures the birth of and supports all seed thoughts for manifestation, seeing and synthesizing all relevant energies that may be desired and/or required for a creative enterprise. In this light, vision functions to give birth to and to support one's creative imagination and is thus seen as one of the principle underlying energies that is important to tap and to use in accord with the art of manifestation. Vision also gives a person a sense of destiny and meaning.

- *Oneness*—is an energy aspect of authentic essence or a soul quality that urges a person toward one's wholeness. Oneness functions to facilitate the perception and the experience of the integration of the inner and outer self and the perception and experience of one's connection to source energy/spirit or All-That-Is. Oneness can be experienced physically, mentally, emotionally, or spiritually. As a soul quality, oneness also functions to expand one's consciousness as a person utilizes the universal energy laws of allowing and of universality.

- *Unity*—is an energy aspect of authentic essence or soul quality that urges a person toward soul contacts as well as a contact and connection to source energy/spirit or All-That-Is. Unity is the quality that functions in accord with the universal energy law of universality and helps a person to comprehend how everything that surrounds a person is a reflection of the person as an aspect of source energy/ spirit or All-That-Is. In other terms, unity urges a person to create opportunities to connect with other Souls through Spiritual blending or what is called "soul linking."

- *Serenity*—is an energy aspect of authentic essence or a soul quality that urges a person to balance one's emotions and acts as a motivator for developing, nurturing, and sustaining inner peace. In this light, serenity is a companion to inner peace, often carrying a person deeper and deeper into the pool of one's emotions to clear the way for the establishment of a deeper sense of inner peace.

THE RELATIONSHIP OF ARCHETYPAL ENERGIES TO HIGHER SELF RACE GAMES

Now, if one looks closely at the above descriptions, one may discern that Love, Acceptance, Inclusion, and Harmony have unique functions in regard to the other archetypal energies and to the process of evolving. I refer to them as "Transformational Archetypal Energies." Together they function to create soul-centered pathways for the spiritual blending of other archetypal energies that are processed in relation to one's personal energy system (chakras). Together they function to transform blocked lower self energies so that they may blend or align with higher self spiritual energies. Together, they also enhance one's psychic potential for Authentic Empathy. I will be discussing the function of these Transformational Archetypal Energies in more detail later when I explore what I am calling the Transformational Race Game and the Path of the Bridger.

At this point, I will note that all archetypal energies flow from the higher vibrational dimensions, in relation to one's physical body and one's personal energy system. They initially enter through the top of one's head or the head or crown chakra (I have

called these energies "spiritually integrative archetypal energies")
or through the root chakra or the base of one's spine (I have
called these energies "foundational archetypal energies").

The archetypal energies are processed through the various
Chakras, and, in accord with the soul-centered model, they are
to be given unique form and authentic expression through one's
heart chakra or heart center. As implied in the soul-centered
model, unencumbered, as they are allowed to flow, a person
becomes aware of and also awakens a sense of one's Monadic
body and its reality. A person further begins to raise their vibrations to align with these energies as one gives them unique form
and authentic expression. In relation to one's higher self and the
human race game, one's current racial form is one's unique form
on the physical plane that provides a person with opportunities
for authentic expressions of one's authentic spiritual essence.

Now that I have provided general descriptions of some archetypal energies, I suggest it is these archetypal energies that can
assist a person in evolving the human race game. They do so as a
person opens to allow their outer self to connect to their deeper
or higher self and become more and more of their truer self. In
this light, a person can evolve and can act out what I am calling
three types of higher self race games in their personal, societal,
and global life spaces.

HIGHER SELF RACE GAMES AND DEVELOPMENTAL STAGES OF THE SOUL IN THE PHYSICAL WORLD

The three types of higher self race games can be called the Inspirational Race Game, the Altruistic Race Game, and the Soul-Source Race Game. Let's take a closer look at these three types of higher self race games that a person can evolve and act out by consciously creating or co-creating them. In this discussion, I will provide a brief overview of the three types of higher self race games, along with descriptions of ways they can manifest in a person's personal life space and societal life space. I will then suggest a model or perspective for how these higher self race games mirror soul lessons and stages of a person's soul development in the physical world as each person's soul contributes to evolving the human race game in specific and general terms.

THE INSPIRATIONAL RACE GAME

First, a person begins to act out the Inspirational Race Game when they actively and consciously engage the outer self in processes of uncovering, understanding, and expressing who they are authentically in their world, including an understanding that they have constructed their racial identity. In this context, the person opens up possibilities for rich forms and forums for sharing and communication.

Because the person's intent is one of embracing the soul quality or archetypal energy *understanding* and their consciousness is focused in this regard, the person is not threatened by what they uncover in their self and others. Differences and diversity are viewed celebratorially as opportunities for new learning and expansion of consciousness.

Indeed, at this level of expanded consciousness, such contacts with the self and with the self of others are experienced as soul contacts and therefore are often experienced as inspirational. Therefore, it is when a person engages their self and others they identify as belonging to a different race in this manner that the person will be acting out the Inspirational Race Game.

In accord with the soul-centered model, at this level of expanded consciousness, a person begins to open to their higher mind and to be inspired by new ways of mentally understanding and perceiving their world. The person indeed is able to view their self as a conscious creator or co-creator of the kind and quality of human, racial, and multicultural relationships that they foster in their personal life space. The person begins to understand their mental constructs and how thoughts, their core beliefs, structure their reality in regard to the phenomenon of race. The person is also able to view the phenomenon of race as an opportunity for learning in their societal life space.

Further, in terms of the soul-centered model, the person's experience in their world will not be one of reacting to external cues, but will be one of mentally resonating to their inner urges and inner guidance, to the vibrational urges of archetypal energies from the causal reality and their superconscious mind. Such mental resonance also stimulates and enhances the person's psychic potential for experiencing clairaudience. The archetypal energies from the causal reality include the soul qualities that I call understanding, truth, wisdom, patience, and inspiration.

One of the underlying soul lessons that are at play at this level of cognition is the lesson of *discernment*. Discernment involves making life choices without the use of good-bad value judgments; this involves aligning one's heart center with particular archetypal energies and allowing them to serve as guides.

Calling upon the archetypal energies *wisdom*, *truth*, and *patience*, a person may come to understand the function of the people in her or his personal life space, including those who the person has identified as belonging to a different race. The person may come to understand the function of the interracial societal issues, dramas, personalities, and events that they pay attention to overtly or covertly in their societal life space. It is not accidental that they are there. The person has invited them or caused or allowed them to be there for their own reasons.

Most often they are there to help a person recognize and understand the nature of harmonious personal boundaries. That is, a person learns to discern what works and what does not work in regard to creating, nurturing, and maintaining harmonious boundaries in relating to others.

They may also be there to provide the person with opportunities to actualize their authentic spiritual essence more harmoniously by opening up to and expressing their understanding, wisdom, truth, and patience with others. They may be there, in other words, to provide the person with opportunities to understand and to celebrate their unique soul qualities and the unique soul qualities of others.

To a large extent, at this level of expanded consciousness, a person may be inspired to transform all of the interracial power or control games that may have been at play in the person's personal, societal, and global life spaces. The person may use their courage and flexibility, the foundational archetypal energies nurturing the growth of their personality, to patiently find and discern, and not to manipulate, the truth about their self as a soul in their current physical or racial form.

At this level of consciousness, a person is inspired to transcend the tendency to think in terms of "you or me" or "us or them." A person is inspired to fully comprehend and embrace a way of thinking that is "you and me" and "us." Indeed, by the Universal Energy Law of Universality, what a person does to others, mentally, emotionally, and physically, in their personal, societal, and global life spaces, they are at some level, in energy terms and spiritually, doing to one's self. At this level of cognition, a person may mentally sense this kind of higher reality and be inspired to act accordingly.

It is at this level of expanded consciousness that a person realizes that their racial identity is a construct that they have created and that they are the meaning-maker in regard to this construct. This construct may be composed of what has been called subpersonalities or partial selves as aspects of one's personality.

Subpersonalities or partial selves related to the phenomenon of race may include, for example, a self-righteous racial self, a frightened racial self, a child-like racial self, a spontaneous racial self, a parent-like racial self, a caring racial self, a rejecting racial self, a vain racial self, a greedy racial self, an angry/hating racial self, an attached or addicted racial self, an obedient racial self, a rebellious racial self, a confident racial self, or a lustful racial self. These subpersonalities may get acted out through the Bully/Victim, Pursuer/Distancer, or Parent/Child interracial role relationships and interracial dramas that I discussed in another section (i.e., master/slave, jailer/prisoner, leader/follower, and rescuer/saved interracial dramas) (see pp. 134-135).

At this level of expanded consciousness, a person embraces the truth of the development and acting out of their personality and subpersonalities or partial selves. The person looks to understand, acknowledge, and step outside of all of the images they live by and the role(s) that they and others have played and do play at the level of their personality. The person begins to lift the veils of illusion, as they comprehend that their soul, their core self, hold their deepest truth.

As a person is inspired by their higher motivations (their archetypal energies) from their superconscious mind, the person also begins to comprehend at a mental level that all of the dramas in their outer life, including their interracial dramas, have been gifts, in a manner of speaking. The person begins to realize that even those interracial dramas that they may have interpreted as negative have been gifts. They are gifts in that they have provided the person or do provide the person with opportunities to grow, to raise their energy vibrations higher, to clean up one's energy.

A person realizes further, however, that they have been using the human race game in both specific and general terms to grow with pain and that they need not continue to choose to grow in this manner. A person realizes that every drama, including their inter-racial dramas, is a reflection of a drama in their inner life, a drama involving their subpersonalities. Everyone that the person interacts with in their outer life who they identify as belonging to another race symbolizes an interaction of energy that is going on within them. Each person's challenge then is to learn to grow with joy.

At this level of expanded consciousness, a person forms what I will call an Archetypal Energy Loop (see p. 197) that inspires the person to raise the vibrations of their energy in their world. This is done by using the transformational archetypal energies related to the heart center to create inspirational pathways to and from the person's higher self in their mind, their mental body.

In terms of the Inspirational Race Game, the inspirational pathways serve as conduits for the foundational archetypal energies *courage* and *flexibility* to transform racially-linked energy blocks. Through the inspirational pathways, these two foundational archetypal energies are lifted up to blend with the spiritually integrative archetypal energies *wisdom*, *patience*, and *truth* that are initially processed through one's fifth chakra or throat center.

The focus of one's consciousness thus shifts in such a way that a person now seeks understanding. A person then expresses their truth with wisdom and patience. It is in this context that a person invites their subpersonalities or partial selves to participate with them to evolve the human race game. To do this, however, it is important for a person to have dialogue with their subpersonalities, or with these aspects of one's self.

I will discuss archetypal energy loops and the process of dialoguing with one's subpersonalities in more detail later. The purpose at this point is to suggest that at this level of consciousness, a person is inspired through seeking understanding to mentally expand one's consciousness even more. A person becomes more inclusive in their thinking and ways of being. As one does so, a person cognitively begins to work in harmony with one's higher self and the soul level or one's soul-source in evolving the human race game. Intuitively, a person begins to develop a mental sense of one's vibrational connection to source energy/spirit or All-That-Is and a person begins to use their creative imagination with understanding to consciously create or co-create one's reality.

THE ALTRUISTIC RACE GAME

As a person develops a mental sense of their whole self and its multidimensional nature, the person experiences more and more of an inner shift away from primarily an egoistic approach to life toward an even more expansive, emotional approach to life. Using their intuition, from an energy vibrational point of view, the person emotionally begins to recognize that their service to others is also a service to their self.

In service to their self through their vibrational and emotional connectedness to others, a person's interracial dramas now become opportunities to enhance their service to and play with those they have identified as belonging to a different race. In other words, a person's acting out toward those they have identified as belonging to a different race becomes altruistic in nature as the person now engages in what I am calling the Altruistic Race Game.

It is at this level of expanded consciousness that a person's emotional body and its reality expands or opens to become aligned with their compassionate body and its reality and the archetypal energies of the messianic plane. The archetypal energies at this level of consciousness include abundance, compassion, peace, joy, clarity, and vision.

These archetypal energies are processed initially through the sixth chakra or brow center or what is called the Third Eye. They are then aligned with the foundational archetypal energies *enthusiasm*, *humor*, *hope*, and/or *beauty* through the heart chakra or the heart center of the person's personal energy system. It is in this kind of context that a person's psychic potential for clairvoyance develops and is enhanced.

As may have been discerned by now, all alignments or spiritual blending of higher energies that are given authentic expression through a person's lower self on the physical plane, take place through the person's heart center.

At this level of expanded consciousness, reality is viewed in terms of abundance energy to nurture the self and to altruistically and compassionately share with others. A person also becomes aware of and learns methods and techniques for tapping into this abundance. As a person allows their outer self to be guided to those resources that may be useful to them (e.g., books, people, techniques, strategies, inner qualities, etc.), they open to the possibility of greater abundance. One resource book that I am particularly fond of is Orin & Roman's *Creating Money-Attracting Abundance*.

At this level of expanded consciousness and recognition of the archetypal energy Abundance, empathic racial and cultural encounters become commonplace in that the person's actions are guided by a personal compassionate vision. The person is no longer ego-driven, desiring instead to be of service to humanity. Here, the altruistic nature of the person's actions toward those they may have identified as belonging to a different race may now be characterized as actions that promote human care.

If, then, one were a parent, the way that the person may act out the altruistic race game in their personal life space would be expressed through the ideas and values they teach their children about the phenomenon of race, as they are related to human care. The person's altruism may also be acted out through the choices they make for actions they engage in to emotionally bridge perceived barriers to their higher self and perceived racial and cultural barriers. Are these ideas and values expansive, accepting, inclusive, and loving? Do they foster a sense of harmony, collaboration, and cooperation?

By raising the vibrations of one's energy to envision or simply to imagine the possibility of a messianic plane, a person begins to recognize that reality works cooperatively through vibrational matches. The person recognizes that their altruistic actions are in actuality a mirror to manifest on the physical plane more of what is so for their higher self. The person discovers the power of giving through service, for in giving and wisely using the universal energy laws the person also receives all the gifts of abundance in return. Through their altruistic actions, therefore, the person further recognizes that, in larger terms, who they identify as the other is providing them with an opportunity to grow into a greater awareness of how to give and receive from their higher self.

It is important, however, for a person to be clear about their higher foci or purpose(s) here and not simply to follow someone else's script. This is not to suggest that assistance from others is not useful or warranted. Indeed, a person's experience on the physical plane of existence requires an understanding of the nature of collaborative enterprises and the wise use of co-creative energies. The point here, therefore, is to seek to develop and to nurture altruistic scripts that work for one's self and for others, flowing in accord with one's higher foci.

To do so, a person needs to look within, establish contact with their higher self and ask what their higher foci are for this life.

Ask what archetypal energies might be helpful in realizing their higher foci. Ask also how one may use their higher foci and the archetypal energies to create bridges of subtle-energy across perceived racial and cultural barriers.

It is at this level of expanded consciousness that a person may uncover particular life themes (see Micheal & Heideman's *Searching for Light* and Sylvia Browne's *The Other Side and Back*), some of which are associated with the person's current racial form in relation to lessons for allowing their abundance energy to manifest itself. It is, therefore, not accidental, that a person's soul chose their current racial form. This is not to suggest that one racial group is more prone to particular qualities or lessons than another. Rather, the point is that a person's soul is aware of probable and perceptual realities that can enhance the person's growth.

There are many methods for establishing contact with one's higher self and there are many resources that can serve as guides for a person. It is important to use methods with which one is familiar and comfortable already, or to allow one's outer self to be guided to resources that resonate with one's inner self.

I offer at this point one method that readers might want to try. From an energy vibrational point of view, it involves using one's creative imagination and one's intuition to emotionally tap into what others and I call the akashic record. To maximize the effectiveness of the method, I recommend that a person use their own voice or that of a trusted friend to tape record the steps of the method first (presented below) and then to play them back to their outer self as they guide their outer self through the method.

First, use 3 x 5 cards and a magic marker to create a set of twenty-five cards with the names of the twenty-five archetypal energies I have identified. Now, sit quietly for a moment or two in a comfortable chair with a pencil and a pad of paper nearby along with the twenty-five cards. Close your eyes and progressively relax your body, beginning with your feet and moving upward to your shoulders and head. Breathe deeply and feel your entire body relaxing. Pause.

In this relaxed state, imagine a radiant light moving toward you from a distance. Make it as beautiful a color as you can imagine. It might be light blue or rose or another color. Invite it to come closer and feel your self merging with this light. Feel the radiance of its love and peace and fill your body with this radiance. Pause.

Now, imagine that you are surrounded by light, as if you were in a bubble. In your imagination, see your self floating in this bubble higher and higher, as high as you can imagine until you reach what might be called the Akashic Library, where there are records of all your lifetimes. In your mind's eye or imagination, what does this library look like to you? What does the door of the library look like?

Now, picture yourself entering this Akashic Library and being greeted by a high being. Request to see a book on your current lifetime and immediately find yourself in front of the appropriate shelf. See yourself picking out the book for this lifetime and opening it.

Each page has words or pictures that have meaning only to you. The first page shows you what authentic essence qualities you chose to develop during this lifetime. See what is written or shown here. Pause. The second page shows you what mental features you chose to emphasize during this lifetime. Again, see what is written or shown. Pause.

The third page shows you what emotional features you chose to emphasize during this lifetime. What do you see? Pause. The fourth page shows you what physical features you chose to emphasize this lifetime. See what is written or shown here. Pause. Assure yourself that you can remember what is written or shown on each page.

After seeing what is written or shown on the first four pages, flip to the next page as you now ask yourself what you want to explore or to learn in relation to each of the features. The fifth page shows you possibilities. What are some of the possibilities that are written or shown here? Pause.

Now, ask any other questions that you may see as relevant at this point, flip the page and see what is written or shown. Pause. When you feel complete, you will see your guide again. Give thanks for the service, surround yourself again in your bubble of light, and picture yourself floating back down and into the present moment.

Slowly open your eyes and record your impressions on the pad of paper that you had nearby. Pause. Continuing in a relaxed state and continuing to feel the presence of light around you, create a dialogue with your higher self in which you may ask any clarifying questions. Pose the question to your higher self by writing out the question. Then wait and write down any answer that comes into your mind, without forcing it or judging it. If it feels like you are forcing an answer, it's probably your ego posing as your higher self. Get the feel of the soft and gentle voice of your higher self that whispers, "I am with you." Pause.

Next, ask your higher self which archetypal energies might be useful to you now in evolving the human race game. As you focus on this question, shuffle the deck of twenty-five cards, place the cards next to you with the written portion faced down, and select three cards from anywhere in the deck. You will be selecting the three archetypal energies that can be useful to you now in evolving the human race game. After selecting the three cards, allow yourself now to become fully awake and alert and give thanks for all the gifts you have received.

It is important to know that a person can repeat this process whenever one desires, although it is advisable to give one's self time to integrate the gifts. For the next week or two, I suggest that the person find ways to express the three archetypal energies in their personal and societal life spaces. As the person does so, they will be evolving the human race game in specific and general terms.

THE SOUL-SOURCE RACE GAME

At this level of expanded consciousness, the focus of a person's consciousness is on spiritual unity, fueled by two urges: (1) the urge to accept and love all of who they are, and (2) the urge to express their love unconditionally. This state of being is often called agape and is aligned with what I have called one's atmic body and its reality. A person may also get a glimpse of the nature of what some have called one's cosmic consciousness. At this level of cognition, the underlying archetypal energies that dispatch, nurture, and support these two urges flow from the buddhaic plane.

The archetypal energies fueling these two urges are the energies *oneness*, *unity*, and *serenity*. It is at this level of cognition, therefore, that a person may sense their unencumbered energy connection to their soul and to source energy/spirit or All-That-Is, the source of a person's unique being. A person also may sense the spiritual or higher will of their soul and how it relates to the universal energy law of universality.

Illusions are further lifted at this level of expanded consciousness as the person awakens and identifies their self as a soul on the physical plane with a mind and a physical body, their current racial form. A person may also awaken to their psychic potential for telepathy. In this context, the person further awakens to the divine or universal energy behind the thought-form that views their self as a unique aspect of source energy/spirit or All-That-Is in their soul's current racial form on the physical plane, with the ability to manifest in alignment with their spiritual or higher will.

Prior to this expansion of consciousness, a person may have awakened to a mental and emotional connection to the divine or universal energy behind a thought-form. Now, a person awakens to an uncluttered or what some have called a purer energy connection to the universal energy behind a thought-form. As a person does so, they begin to learn how to transform and to manifest their experiences in alignment with seven qualities of their spiritual or higher will and the divine or universal energy.

As Orin and Da Ben suggest, seven qualities of a person's spiritual or higher will and the divine or universal energy include:

1. The Will to *initiate* expansions of consciousness, to *receive* insights and revelations, and to *initiate* activities that are in alignment with the divine probable plan of a person's life;

2. The Will to *unify*, to bring unity to a person's personality, soul, and spirit, and to *increase* the person's ability to know their soul, the soul of others, and to know other higher beings;

3. The Will to *evolve* both a person's consciousness and all the forms and circumstances in the person's life by further developing their vision, and to *increase* a person's ability to express the creative intelligence of their soul to create their highest or optimal future;

4. The Will to *harmonize* and to *deepen* a person's intuition by releasing limitations, to bring harmony to areas of conflict, and to *expand* the person's ability to create art, music, and beauty in all forms;

5. The Will to *act* in such a way as to achieve liberation by aligning a person's higher mind with their everyday concrete mind; the person's mind can then fulfill its purpose of being a channel for the inflow of higher mind energy (archetypal energies) and the person's personality can become a purer channel for their spiritual will;

6. The Will to *cause* through embodying high ideals and thoughts; thus a person comes to know the universal mind or the mind of source energy/spirit or All-That-Is which appear in one's mind as high ideals and thoughts; and

7. The Will to *express* and to *create* divinity-in-form in a rhythmic and orderly way through the use of a person's

strength, perseverance, enhanced courage, self-reliance, steadfastness, care in details, and precision in creating form (See Orin & DaBen Newsletter, Spring & Summer, 2000).

At this level of cognition, therefore, the human race game is recognized as a highly creative act, given the spirit of meaning only in so far as it evokes the pull toward spiritual unity. It simply becomes an opportunity, then, for a person to expand their consciousness through engaging in and making authentic energy contact with their soul and authentic energy contact with the soul of others.

In other terms, the human race game at this level of cognition becomes an opportunity to celebrate the miraculous oneness of spirit in its diversified forms. It further becomes an opportunity for a person to celebrate and to share their unique and authentic essence with the unique and authentic essence of others. Through making authentic soul contact, a person now resonates on a purer energy level with the inner qualities, the soul qualities, of another person.

At this level of cognition, a person may find a deeper sense of inner peace, known as serenity, as an aspect of their authentic essence in being their higher self. A person may also experience a sense of serenity in being with and playing with the authentic essence or authentic energies of others.

Rather than focusing or fixating one's ego primarily on the external, a person lets go of all racially-linked energy blocks and fears. What is left as a person does so is the person's unconditional spiritual love. In this context, a person may experience an energy resonance between their unique soul qualities and the soul qualities of others.

In physical terms, what this means is that the auras of a person's personal energy system vibrationally, energetically, and authentically touch those of others. In other terms, the auras of a person's higher self touch the auras of another's higher self. In one's current racial form, a person thus engages their self and others in what some authors have called "soul linking" (e.g., Roman-Orin, 1997).

In accord with the soul-centered model, the soul perceives no barriers. And so, in this context, the meaning of the phenomenon of race may only be relevant to a person's own personal psyche, their soul age, and the soul aspects that they wish to explore. Race as a physical phenomenon may then be viewed as one method the soul chooses to learn more about itself and to evolve as a CU to expand its consciousness.

At this level of cognition, therefore, a person comes to view people as evolving souls. As such, everyone is a potential teacher, guide, learner, and companion on the planet. People that may be identified as belonging to a different race now become soul actors in a person's interracial drama to mirror for the person their own inner dramas. They are there to assist the person in their soul growth. Likewise, a person may be a soul actor in other people's interracial dramas, mirroring for them opportunities for learning, growth, and love.

In terms of the soul-centered model and interracial dramas, and as evolving souls on the physical plane, the soul has chosen to experience the world in its current racial form in accord with its own divine developmental life plans. From the perspective of one's soul (see Figure 4 for Developmental Stages of the Soul), developmental life plans are primarily cyclical or broad, expansive, spiral blueprints for growth, given birth through free will and through which a person uses their free will to choose and to alter various paths, attitudes, and roles in accord with one's experiences. In these terms, no one race is more evolved than another as there are souls at all soul ages and at various cyclical or spiral developmental levels, so to speak, in and among all races. In these terms, there is also no better or worse soul age at which to be or better or worse level at which a soul may choose a broad blueprint for experience. Free will is the cornerstone for all growth, expansion of consciousness, and co-creative adventures.

Figure 4.   Developmental Stages of the Soul On
The Physical Plane

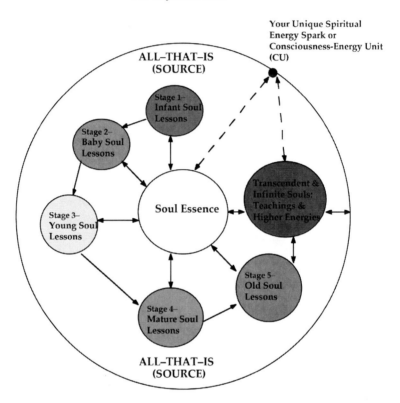

Among all so-called races, therefore, there is what some spiritual teachers have called *infant souls*, exploring what it means for an ego or personality to survive on the physical plane. In this state, the ego or personality may believe that this is the only life that it will have and may thus live life without regard for others, beginning what is known as *karmic entanglements* of energy.

There are *baby souls*, exploring what it means for an ego or personality to establish and to maintain order on the physical plane. In this state, the ego or personality begins to reach out to other people, animals, and nature. What I have called foundational lessons are often the foci of infant souls and baby souls.

There are *young souls*, exploring what it means for an ego or personality to have potency and to succeed on the physical plane. In this state, the ego or personality begins to focus on similarities with others rather than on why there is separateness from others; the process of understanding and remembering a sense of *oneness* with humanity and source energy/spirit or All-That-Is begins.

As consciousness expands, there are *mature souls*, exploring what it means for an ego or personality to have a group consciousness on the physical plane. In this state, the ego or personality learns to feel emotionally connected to others on both a small and broad scale, to be fulfilled with others, to have compassion for others, and to give and receive love without conditions. Spiritually, the ego or personality asks more questions and seeks to further understand its connection and oneness with all living beings, animal and human, and with source energy/spirit or All-That-Is. What I have called transformational lessons are often the foci of young souls and mature souls.

Then, there are *old souls*, exploring what it means to move beyond dogma on the physical plane and to teach and assist others in their chosen paths of spiritual development. In this state, the ego or personality is open to a sense of inner-directedness, is open to change and new concepts, takes responsibility for its life, feels a responsibility to assist in cleaning things up, and feels a desire to continually evolve. What I have called spiritually integrative lessons are often the foci of mature souls and old souls. In the soul-centered developmental model, therefore, with each new incarnation, a person may sense aspects of each of the various soul ages and the lessons and learning involved.

I have applied the above developmental model in relation to soul growth only because it is a model of development on the physical plane with which many people are familiar. As implied in larger terms, all development is simultaneous. As may have been surmised, therefore, beyond the physical plane, souls continue to evolve. Indeed, in accord with the soul-centered model, there are evolving souls that have chosen not to incarnate on the physical plane or who interface with the physical plane as *transcendent souls* through an agreement to temporarily use the body of an already incarnated soul or as aspects of *infinite soul.*

I realize that for the uninitiated, this kind of discussion may not resonate or may sound strange. I also realize that for others, some kind of scientific proof would be required for these kinds of claims. I simply suggest that each person trust their own intuition here and listen to the deeper aspects of their self. I further suggest that each person allow their outer self to be guided to other relevant resources, scientific (e.g., Stephen H. Martin's *The Science of Life After Death: New Research Shows Human Consciousness Lives On,* 2009; Gloria Chadwick's *Reincarnation and Your Past Lives: You've Been Here Before,* 2009; Jim Tucker's *Life Before Life: A Scientific Investigation of Children's Memories of Previous Lives,* 2008; Gary E. Schwartz's *The Afterlife Experiments: Breakthrough Scientific Evidence of Life After Death,* 2003; Tom Shroder's *Old Souls-Compelling Evidence from Children Who Remember Past Lives,* 2001; Dr. Ian Stevenson's *Children Who Remember Previous Lives: A Question of Reincarnation,* 2000) or metaphysical, to explore this kind of framework, but only if it is of interest to one's outer self.

For our purposes at this point, I have introduced these ideas here simply to note that among all races there have been and are evolving souls at all soul ages on various paths of spiritual growth and development, including *transcendent souls.* For the most part, however, at present on the physical plane, as it can be understood, there are more *young souls* in all races, seeking to mature in consciousness. Some spiritual teachers have suggested that this is an aspect of the next evolutionary step for humanity—to become more mature as souls on the physical plane. In this context, *transcendent souls* usually show up for short periods of time, as can be understood, to prepare the planet for large transitions. In accord with the soul-centered model, people can recognize them by their seemingly miraculous and inspiring works in service to humanity.

In terms of the soul-source race game, the physical plane may be viewed as an arena for engaging in soul lessons, using a racial form chosen by one's soul. One's soul knows that all so-called races flow from the same source and so does not have fear in regard to any soul lesson. All fears are ego-related and are at the personality level. In accord with the soul-centered model, soul lessons, therefore, are intended to be joyful lessons, as one creates unique opportunities for the spiritual blending of Energies. Such lessons could include, for example, the choice to grow and the lesson of interdependence.

Because humanity has free will, however, and as I have noted elsewhere, humanity often has chosen to use race as a phenomenon to grow with pain, using its forceful will rather than its wise will to manage its fears. I will have more to say about humanity's forceful will and wise will later. At this point, I simply want to indicate that when a person identifies their self as a unique aspect of All-That-Is, all fears dissolve. The person learns to play as they engage in their soul lessons. And, the person learns to grow with joy, nurtured by an unencumbered energy connection to the spirits of oneness, unity, and/or serenity.

It is important to ask one's self now how would one's world look if one genuinely expressed unconditional and universal love for one's whole self, for others, and for all races? What would one be thinking, feeling, and doing in their personal life space? How would one perceive, connect with, and experience others in their societal life space? How would one perceive, connect with, and experience others in their global life space? What kinds of resources would one direct toward enhancing the quality of one's life and the quality of the life of others? How would one, in other words, act out their *soul-source race game*? What would it mean to be one's truer self in one's world?

THE TRANSFORMATIONAL RACE GAME, THE PATH OF THE BRIDGER, AND THE TRUER SELF

It is in acting out what I am calling the Transformational Race Game that the process of evolving the human race game occurs. It is in the process of calling upon and/or being open to the four basic transformational archetypal energies—love, acceptance, inclusion, and harmony—that a person transforms or "lifts up, clears, and releases" racially-linked energy blocks and allows their truer self to emerge. It is in this context that the transformational archetypal energies assist a person in creating a bridge between their higher self and lower self.

In acting out the transformational race game, a person expands their consciousness to embrace their truth about who they are, without denying or negating the aspects of any level of consciousness. The person opens to the myriad of possibilities for how they may now give unique form and authentic expression of their higher qualities, their soul qualities, in this life.

The person is in effect opening their heart center to become more of who they are, to become and express their truer self with its deeper, higher qualities. In terms of the human race game specifically and generally, the person now begins to create and to view a multidimensional, multiracial world that is in alignment with all of their soul qualities.

When racially-linked energy blocks are lifted up, cleared, and released, a person will experience a shift in their consciousness. The person will also experience an expansion of their consciousness. The person's physical senses may get sharper, and their outer, vibrational world may appear more radiant and clearer to the person. Rather than placing so much value on outward forms, the person may now value the development of their inner qualities and how they can authentically manifest them with wisdom.

The person resonates to other human beings as people with their own unique consciousness and personal energy systems (as consciousness-energy systems). Like the person, they too are engaged in lifting up, clearing, and releasing their own energy blocks in the best way they know how. Psychically, as I previously mentioned, the person opens to and comes to know the nature of authentic empathy in energy terms.

Racial prejudices and negative attributions about one's own and/or other races are now viewed as various forms of racially-linked energy blocks. Individually, they are areas or challenges for personal transformation. Collectively, culturally, and institutionally, they are challenges for social transformation. In this context, cultural and institutional racial barriers and negative societal practices are viewed as mass energy blocks or pockets of energy blocks, held in place by self-limiting beliefs that are projected out and acted out individually and collectively through self-limiting shared codes, cultural scripts, and man-made laws.

Through the transformational race game, however, each person literally transforms the world through transforming and evolving their consciousness, individually and collectively. The transformation and evolution of each person's consciousness is in relation to each person's personal life space, each person's societal life space, and each person's global life space.

Each person impacts a personal world, society, culture, and institutions, therefore, through how that person acts out her or his transforming and evolving consciousness in those arenas, allowing their truer self to emerge. Each person's emerging and new preferences are new energy messages that are transmitted and translated vibrationally through the universal energy laws. They travel both through time and space and at soul-centered levels, when each person chooses to transform and to evolve her or his consciousness.

Through the mirror effect, then, the outer, vibrational world in various arenas of each person will begin to reflect that person's transforming and evolving consciousness. Being and acting out as one's truer self in various contexts, individually and/or as part of a group consciousness, the person thus becomes a bridge for evolving the human race game.

THE PATH OF THE BRIDGER: THE TRUER SELF AS A "BRIDGE" TO EVOLVE THE HUMAN RACE GAME

To transform and to evolve one's consciousness in regard to the phenomenon of race and in general, it is important to examine the content of one's mind for any strongly held self-limiting preferences. As I have noted, some of these preferences may relate to a person's transparent or core beliefs about the nature of their consciousness, the nature of their unconscious or inner life, the race-linked roles they may play, and their beliefs about the material and non-material worlds (see the journaling exercises I suggested in other sections for exploring beliefs about one's safe/unsafe world, and the numbness in one's soul that can assist a person in uncovering relevant core or transparent beliefs).

As a person does this examination, they can begin a process of shifting those self-limiting preferences toward more expansive preferences that truly serve the person's higher good. In turn, the person can allow their truer self to emerge. That is, the person can open to a path of living their deeper truth, beyond fear, and of playing growthful games in accord with their deeper truth.

As an archetypal energy, a person's truth, the truth of one's soul, recognizes that what the person believes at a personality level may or may not be true per se and may or may not be true for someone else. It is in this light that a person's deeper truth sets the person free from their ego fears—the fear, for example, of being wrong and the need to be right. It is in this regard that the person is set free from viewing the phenomenon of race in fear-driven, self-limiting ways. The focus of the person's consciousness shifts to integration, balance, and bridging, fueled by love. Indeed, mirrored for the person may be a multiracial, multidimensional universe that is safe, abundant, and friendly.

The Transformational Race Game is thus one of the games played by the self as a soul in relation to what I am calling the path of the bridger. This path allows a person to explore and to expand their unique consciousness through direct (face-to-face) and indirect (those experiences that are not face-to-face) trans-formational relationships. That is, the path unfolds through individual, group, and, sometimes, multidimensional relationships that invite transformation. One aspect of this path, therefore, is this race-linked game and how it engages each person in a process of transcending fear-driven, ego-based racial barriers as one's truer self emerges.

On this path, a person also explores the self by learning about harmonious boundaries and group consciousness, while affirming the value of and maintaining the uniqueness of one's truer self in the process. It is a path that looks at the relationship of energies and invites the bridging or spiritual blending of these energies through the use of what I have called archetypal energy loops (see Figures 5 and 6). In the process, a person's truer self and one's natural soul qualities emerge.

Applied to the *human race game*, a person's truer self emerges as a bridge to evolve the *human race game* specifically and generally as the person acts out the four basic transformational archetypal energies in their life spaces and in various life arenas in regard to the phenomenon of race. In other terms, the person, as their emerging truer self, opens the door for bringing together foundational and spiritually integrative archetypal energies. The spiritual blending of these energies allows the person to more appropriately view and to more constructively play the *human race game*.

On this path, a person's consciousness creates soul-centered bridges or pathways: (1) for transforming and transmuting energy, (2) for making soul contact, and (3) for relating authentically with others. It does so by using the universal energy laws and by focusing and directing energy with higher thoughts. Energy otherwise tends to move in all directions at once.

By evoking positive thoughts about race relations and other-oriented relations that are in alignment with the four basic transformational archetypal energies, a person becomes open to the *path of the bridger*. This means that the person, as their emerging truer self, will be choosing or preferring to transform relational energy blocks. A person can do this by allowing the transformational archetypal energies to serve as guiding and motivational urges for their inner self in creating relationships that work for the outer self and others.

Through aligning one's consciousness with the four basic transformational archetypal energies, a person will transform and evolve the essence of their interracial relationships and other-oriented relationships. And, the person will align their self with their higher good. In other terms, as a bridger, the person will be giving unique form and authentic expression to the four transformational archetypal energies in their personal, societal, and global life spaces.

Further, the person will be bringing together other archetypal energies and giving them unique form and authentic expression in evolving the human race game. In alignment with these archetypal energies, the person can vibrationally attract and/or create interracial relationships and other-oriented relationships for working together collaboratively to support their higher good and the higher good of others. In alignment with these archetypal energies, how the person in turn thinks about race, their self, their world, and the people or souls in their world are transformed. As a bridger, this kind of inner work leads to what I call aggressive collaboration.

The path of the bridger thus invites a person to shift their consciousness and to align their personality and soul preferences. It further invites the person to become involved in humanity's next evolutionary step. That next step involves raising the vibrational energy of the material universe so that humanity's consciousness can mature and learn how to grow with joy.

In terms of the human race game, the path of the bridger invites a person to allow their truer self, the external expression of one's soul, to emerge as a mature consciousness in their interracial encounters, and other human encounters, in one's personal, societal, and global life spaces.

Through the transformational race game, a person's soul, emerging as the truer self, will establish its focus in their world. And, the person may give way to evolving the human race game by acting out race relations more in alignment with what I have called higher self race games.

Through the transformational race game, for example, as archetypal energies align and blend together, the Security Race Game will evolve toward the Soul-Source Race Game. As a person trusts their self and their vibrational world, the urge to move toward spiritual unity and the expression of unconditional love emerges. The person will have learned the lessons of personal responsibility and harmonious boundaries.

In like fashion, the Sensory Race Game will evolve toward the Altruistic Race Game. As a person experiences their aliveness and the beauty of their world with enthusiasm, humor, and hope, the urge to create optimal futures with clarity and vision and to seed their world with ideas of abundance, compassion, peace, and joy emerges.

And, the Power Race Game will evolve toward the Inspirational Race Game. As a person learns the art of having and expressing flexibility and courage, the person will be inspired to move toward a higher truth about who they are. The person will give validity to their truer self as a soul, who can take many forms in the outer, vibrational world of experience, including their current racial form, and who can act with wisdom, understanding, and patience, among other soul qualities. The person will, therefore, inspire others to uncover their truer selves through being their truer self.

When a person's truer self emerges as a bridger and as an aggressive collaborator with others, the person may begin to resonate with and to act out a variety of roles. The person does not have to *do* anything to *be* in these roles as their truer self emerges. The person simply *is* these roles naturally through the expression of their truer self. Four generic kinds of bridger roles are:

1. The role of Relationship Builder/Harmonizer,
2. The role of Transformer/Catalyst,
3. The role of Illuminator/Teacher, and
4. The role of Spiritual Integrator/Healer.

In resonating with the role of Relationship Builder, a person's truer self seeks to stimulate energies for life and success, without judgment. That is, as the person authentically relates to others as their truer self, the person's personality will radiate various kinds of energy that support and move their outer self and others toward a focus on life and success, without judgment. The person's truer self also seeks to awaken a sense of creativity and beauty. In turn, this awakening stimulates the person's higher mental faculties for their practical work in the world as the person acts out harmoniously with others in their personal, societal, and global life spaces.

In resonating with the role of Transformer, a person's truer self guards against psychic imbalances or dangers and invites patience and balance for their catalytic work in the world and harmonious state of being with others. In this context, the person gets rid of or minimizes the effect of, and assists others in getting rid of or minimizing the effect of self-limiting beliefs and growth-limiting patterns of behavior. The person also embraces and assists others in embracing newer, more growth-filled beliefs and patterns of behavior. The person, therefore, often serves without effort as a mirror or catalyst for others who may be engaged also in a similar process of growth.

In resonating with the role of Illuminator, a person's truer self mirrors hope, illumination, and love. In this role, the person taps into, expresses, and mirrors for others intuitive teachings, spiritual duties, and the sacred aspects of the world as the person's personality and the personality of others awaken to a greater understanding of dreams and the role of one's creative imagination.

In resonating with the role of Spiritual Integrator, a person's truer self works with nature, spirit and energy. In this role, the person may use alchemy and vision to awaken their personality and those of others. In this context, the person consciously collaborates with others to co-create physical and emotional healings and to co-create opportunities, arenas, circumstances, and events in building bridges of harmony. The person may also naturally and effortlessly blend two or more of the other generic roles.

In a manner of speaking, those who choose the path of the bridger can be called Harmony Workers in their vibrational world (see Table 4). Harmony workers can be found in all walks of life and in all forms of group life. They may be in leadership roles or may fulfill their higher purpose(s) behind the scenes, so to speak. They may be more or less consciously aware of their chosen path, but will nevertheless feel the pull toward balance and harmony within themselves and toward others.

As a person's truer self emerges, therefore, they may find that they have chosen the *path of the bridger* and that one of their higher purposes is becoming and being a harmony worker in their world. And, since one of the foci of harmony workers is to enhance awareness and mastery of the harmonious flow of energy, the person may find that the nature of their work deals with transforming their own energy blocks and/or assisting others in the transformation of their energy blocks.

Table 4. PATH OF THE BRIDGER: THE TRUER SELF AND THE BRIDGING ROLES OF HARMONY WORKERS	
Bridging Roles of Harmony Workers	**How The Truer Self "Acts Out" These Roles**
Relationship Builder/Harmonizer	•Seeks to stimulate Energies for life and success •Seeks to awaken a sense of creativity and *Beauty* •Awakens the person's Higher Mental Faculties for her/his practical work in the world as s/he "acts out" harmoniously with Others in her/his personal, societal, and global life space
Transformer/Catalyst	•Guards against psychic imbalances or dangers and invites *Patience* and balance for the person's work in the world •Seeks to rid the person's personality and to assist Others in ridding their personalities of unproductive beliefs and patterns of growth •Serves without effort as a mirror or catalyst for Others on similar paths of growth

Illuminator/Teacher	•Mirrors *Understanding, Hope,* illumination, *Peace,* and, *Love* •Taps into, expresses, and mirrors for Others intuitive teachings, spiritual duties, and the sacred aspects of the world •Stimulates the person's personality and the personality of Others to awaken to a greater understanding of dreams and the role of the person's creative imagination
Spiritual Integrator/Healer	•Works with Nature, Spirit, and Energy •Uses alchemy and *Visions* to awaken the person's personality and those of Others •Consciously collaborates with Others to co-create physical and emotional healings and to co-create opportunities, arenas, circumstances, and events in building Soul-centered bridges of *Harmony*

Transforming Racially-Linked Energy Blocks with "Archetypal Energy Loops"

In relation to the Transformational Race Game, archetypal energy loops may be viewed as soul-centered energy links for transformational purposes. From an energy vibrational point of view, archetypal energy loops serve or function as soul-centered pathways to lift up, to clear, and to release racially-linked energy blocks in regard to one's self and to those a person has considered racially different. These archetypal energy loops can also function in a similar fashion for any energy-block that needs transforming.

In evolving the human race game, archetypal energy loops involve bringing together foundational and spiritually integrative archetypal energies to transform self-limiting, racially-linked beliefs. With the four transformational archetypal energies (acceptance, love, inclusion, harmony) serving as transformative bridges, the energy blocks that are attached to such beliefs are lifted up, cleared, and released from one's personal energy system.

As a result, the Self-limiting beliefs loose the emotional or energy charge behind them and no longer function to structure the person's reality. The person's consciousness expands to accept, love, include, and harmonize more of who the person truly is as they recognize how others mirror aspects of their self. The door is opened for the person's deeper truth and the authentic expression of their soul qualities.

Lifting up, clearing, and releasing racially-linked energy blocks, therefore, involves several kinds of activities or steps:

1. Identifying the core or transparent self-limiting belief;

2. Accepting what is so, and also accepting the identified belief as simply a belief and not necessarily the truth;

3. Forgiving one's self and others for one's own sake;

4. Sending love to the frightened aspect of one's outer self that has been limiting the whole self;

5. Including the possibility of change by letting go of a need for the old form or a specific form; and

6. Allowing one's outer self to be open to having harmonious boundaries at both the individual and/or group levels.

To identify a transparent core belief, one simple method is to use the mirror effect in accord with one's observer self and what may be called a *third party stance*. Experiment with the self. Using one's observer self, affirm that no one is at the mercy of any belief and that one always has three choices available in the *now* in relation to any belief one may have internalized or encountered.

Those three choices are: (1) to consciously *accept* the belief in order to consciously structure one's reality, if one so desires; (2) to *reject* the belief so that it does not impact one's outer self in a self-limiting manner; or (3) to *modify* the belief to fit one's unique life circumstances.

The next step in the method is to select a circumstance pertaining to race in one's life spaces—personal, societal, or global—that is unsettling to one's outer self. Then, using one's observer self, ask: what would someone have to believe in order for this circumstance to exist?

Then, using one's observer self, ask: how might this circumstance limit someone? If the circumstance is from one's own societal or global life spaces, as the observer self, ask: what do you feel when you think about someone having this circumstance in their personal life space? If it is already an aspect of one's own personal life space, re-identify with the circumstance and ask the same emotion question. How do you feel about having this circumstance in your personal life space?

The emotion(s) or knotting a person experiences in their solar plexus is the blocked energy charge behind the belief that is structuring the person's reality. This means that the natural expression of an archetypal energy was blocked and distorted due to the formulation of a frightening belief by the ego aspect of the person's personality, for whatever reason. When the person transforms that belief, that emotion and blocked energy charge will dissipate, and the circumstance or how the person relates to it will change.

To release the fear behind a self-limiting belief, such as a belief in scarcity, I invite readers to experiment in using focused thought, their creative imagination, meditation, and what I will call a Primary Archetypal Energy Loop (see Figure 5; if helpful, use the Figure as an inner visual focus for meditation). It might be helpful to tape record the process that I will present, using one's own words, or have a friend to read the process to one's self when there is a desire to release racially-linked energy blocks or other kinds of energy blocks.

Figure 5.   Primary Archetypal Energy

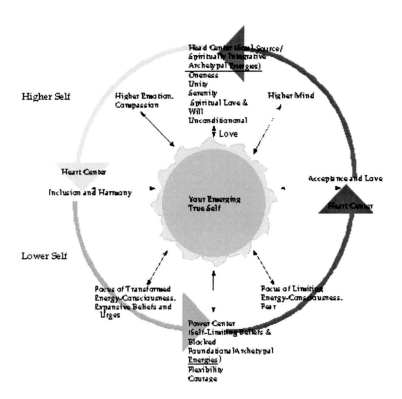

The description, therefore, is intended to have a meditative tone to it. As I resonate with the ideas of Abraham, readers may also want to use the idea of an Emotional Guidance Scale to assist the outer self in monitoring the shift in their emotions during and after the process (see Ester and Jerry Hicks' *Ask and It Is Given*). From an energy vibrational point of view, the scale involves twenty-two emotions, which essentially provide guidance for how a person's thoughts feel to their outer self.

From lower to higher emotions, the Emotion Guidance Scale vibrationally flows accordingly: (1) Fear/Grief/Depression/Despair/Powerlessness; (2) Insecurity/Guilt/Unworthiness; (3) Jealousy; (4) Hatred/Rage; (5) Revenge; (6) Anger; (7) Discouragement; (8) Blame; (9) Worry; (10) Doubt; (11) Disappointment; (12) "Overwhelment"; (13) Frustration/Irritation/Impatience; (14) Pessimism; (15) Boredom; (16) Contentment; (17) Hopefulness; (18) Optimism; (19) Positive Expectation/Belief; (20) Enthusiasm/Eagerness/Happiness; (21) Passion; and (22) Joy/Knowledge/Empowerment/Freedom/Love/Appreciation.

First, close your eyes, progressively relax your body, and go within. With every breath in, call upon the archetypal energies *acceptance* and *love* to enter your heart center. Your intent to do this is all-that-is required. Allow yourself to open to these energies, to get a sense of these energies in your heart center.

Then, with every breath out, ask acceptance and love to move to the frightened aspect of yourself as you try to sense the self-limiting belief and how it is generating fear or the frightened aspect of your self. Again, you may experience the fear in your solar plexus. If you do, ask love and acceptance to blend their energies with the energies courage and flexibility.

Continue to take deep breaths in and out and as you do, imagine that a "pathway" is being created by acceptance and love for this frightened aspect of yourself to be lifted up to your heart center. It is in your heart center that the self-limiting belief can be acknowledged for what it is trying to teach you. It is in your heart center that you may provide yourself with forgiveness.

If you get insights at this point, remember to record them later in your journal. Or, if you prefer, you may also pause here briefly and record your insights while still in a relaxed state. This is the First Soul-centered Bridge of the Primary Archetypal Energy Loop.

As you lift up the frightened aspect of yourself to your heart center, in your mind's eye, imagine that at a slightly higher level there is a clear, crystal, liquid-like space, like a spacious blue lake, which exists on this pathway. It is smooth and calm and represents your clear and calm higher mind as it is connected to your heart. Continuing to use your creative imagination, in your mind's eye, allow the frightened aspect of your self to enter this liquid-like space, washing away and cleansing all remnants of the blocked energy as you release your attachment to the self-limiting belief.

As you release your attachment, you may come to understand how you allowed this belief to misuse or misapply the universal energy laws in creating or allowing a particular circumstance. Realize that you are not at the mercy of this belief.

Allow whatever related thoughts or images that may come up for you at this point to be cleansed and released into the clear, calm, liquid-like blue space. Again, you may, if you desire, record them later in your journal. Let yourself and these thoughts or images blend with the transformative energies of the liquid-like blue space, allowing the belief to loosen its grip on you. As it does, allow yourself to get calmer and calmer with each breath of acceptance and love.

Now ask yourself, how would you and this circumstance look if acceptance and love were operating in your personal life space? Use your creative imagination and form a clear alternative picture with your calm mind and balanced emotions or simply allow a picture to emerge.

With this new picture in your mind and feeling emotionally balanced, imagine now that acceptance and love are continuing to form a pathway to your head center or crown chakra, where you may experience other higher energies. This is the Second Soul-centered Bridge of the Primary Archetypal Energy Loop.

Having released all attachment to fear, open now to other higher energies through your head center. They can assist you in refining your energies and your new picture.

Imagine that you are surrounded by spiritual love and your higher will, your unconditional love, and the light of your soul.

Allow yourself to experience a sense of oneness with your soul. As you make soul contact, you will know that fear does not exist at this level of consciousness and that the circumstance that exist is based on a belief formed at the level of your personality.

Imagine yourself now expanding your consciousness to blend with oneness and serenity. Now, release your new picture to your soul and affirm that your soul will materialize it in accord with your higher good.

In this expanded state, open yourself to your unconditional love and your higher will, and invite the archetypal energies compassion, inclusion, and harmony to support you in giving unique form and authentic expression at the level of your personality to your new picture. Recognize that you will relate to the circumstance with a new, transformed perspective at the level of your personality.

Imagine now that the archetypal energies inclusion and harmony are creating a return pathway to your heart center and will serve as guiding urges, along with unconditional love and compassion, for your outer actions. This is the Third Soul-centered Bridge of the Primary Archetypal Energy Loop.

In your relaxed state now, allow yourself time to integrate all the new energies and insights you gained. Again, record all insights you acquired from this process in your journal as a method of concretizing the information and grounding yourself for future guidance and action.

One can now function in the outer, vibrational world of experience with a Transformed Consciousness-Energy in relation to the circumstance. One may now accept, have, and act in accord with more expansive beliefs and urges.

Once a person gets the feel for working with the Primary Archetypal Energy Loop, they only need to relax, go within, and ask the following kinds of questions for future guidance. Ask, for example, what would *acceptance* do in this situation? What would *love* do in this situation? What would *inclusion* do in this situation? What would *harmony* do in this situation? And, what would *compassion* do in this situation?

In asking and receiving the gifts of the archetypal energies of one's soul, a person no longer resonates, at the level of their solar plexus, to self-limiting aspect of their self. The person's consciousness resonates now with the archetypal energies of their heart center and the archetypal insights of *compassion*. This approach thus allows a person to blend and to bring together the logical and intuitive aspects of the person's self.

As a person does this kind of inner work, it is important to recognize that they will also be working with the Universal Energy Laws in sending out new energy messages vibrationally and transpersonally to structure a new reality for their outer self and others. The new reality will be in alignment with the archetypal energies that the person calls upon through the Primary Archetypal Energy Loop.

It is important to recognize further that the Primary Archetypal Energy Loop connects and circulates archetypal energies from the power center (solar plexus chakra) through the four higher centers (heart, throat, brow, and head centers), transforming and transmuting energy blocks related to power and control games. As a great many energy blocks related to the human race game are specifically and generally connected to the power center, the Primary Archetypal Energy Loop can be an important tool that a person may use to dislodge and to transform energy distortions and to evolve the human race game.

There are other Generic Archetypal Energy Loops that may also be useful in evolving the human race game (see Figure 6). In creating soul-centered pathways for these generic archetypal energy loops, acceptance and love flow through the heart center to assist in lifting up, clearing, and releasing blocked energy as they move the energy to higher levels. Inclusion and harmony, on the other hand, flow through the heart center to assist in finding unique form with harmonious boundaries for the authentic expression of the transformed energy in the outer, vibrational world of experience.

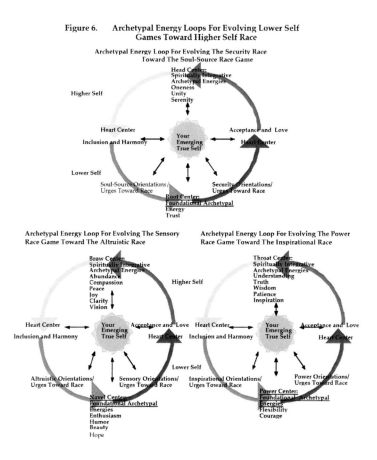

Figure 6.   Archetypal Energy Loops For Evolving Lower Self
Games Toward Higher Self Race

Thus, to assist in evolving the Security Race Game toward the Soul-Source Race Game, for example, one Generic Archetypal Energy Loop would bring together the foundational archetypal energy trust (root chakra) with the spiritually integrative archetypal energies oneness, unity, and serenity (the head center) through soul-centered bridges created by acceptance, love, inclusion, and harmony (the heart center) (see first Loop in Figure 6).

Likewise, to assist in evolving the Sensory Race Game toward the Altruistic Race Game, a second Generic Archetypal Energy Loop would bring together the foundational archetypal energies enthusiasm, humor, hope, and beauty with the spiritually integrative archetypal energies abundance, compassion, peace, joy, clarity, and vision (see second Loop in Figure 6).

And, to assist in evolving the Power Race Game toward the Inspirational Race Game, a third Generic Archetypal Energy Loop would bring together the foundational archetypal energies flexibility and courage with the spiritually integrative archetypal energies understanding, truth, wisdom, patience, and inspiration (see third Loop in Figure 6).

Let's look at a specific racially-linked circumstance attached to self-limiting beliefs and how the sensory and power race games that the participants were/are playing may be transformed using archetypal energy loops.

There was a trend in American society, very visible in the late 1990s for example, whereby some individuals in the majority group were raging against what they called reverse discrimination. In turn, some parents or others who identified with what is called the white race proclaimed that it was unfair that they or their children were denied entrance to particular schools because of their race. They used the same arguments that those who identified with the minority group(s) previously used to gain entrance to these same schools when they were being denied because of their race.

A deeper truth here, as may be discerned, is that the participants in this kind of interracial drama were/are holding onto a self-limiting belief in scarcity. The accompanying fear is that they won't get their share of what seems to exist in terms of the kind and quality of education or school they desire. They also believe that they are right. So, they seek to prove their righteous position by having it to be acknowledged at a societal level. If the ego frames this kind of societal issue along these lines, then sensory games and power struggles based on skin color are created that can go back and forth over time as participants try to get their fair share.

To transform this kind of circumstance if someone was/is one of those participants, the person could, individually and collectively, stop before taking action, go within, and receive guidance from their higher self about what appropriate action to take. The person would do the inner work first before doing the outer work. The person could go within and call upon the foundational archetypal energies flexibility and courage, for example, first to question the validity of the belief in scarcity and secondly to entertain the possibility of a win-win solution.

If someone was/is one of those participants and if the person questions the validity of the belief in scarcity, they may uncover what aspects of their self they have been denying and how they were/are acting this out through this interracial drama. The person may uncover, for example, that they have been denying their connection to one or more of the spiritually integrative archetypal energies understanding, wisdom, truth, inspiration, or patience. These archetypal energies would allow the person to see the essence of this kind of interracial drama or the bigger picture mirrored by this kind of interracial drama. The person may uncover, for example, that they have denied viewing their self as the source of abundance.

The person may come to understand that the beliefs behind this kind of interracial drama attract what appear to be opposing energies through the law of polarity (the haves versus the have-nots). The circumstance, therefore, serves as a mirror to provide the person and others with an opportunity to transcend that apparent polarity toward a belief in abundance, compassion, and peace.

The person may come to understand, then, that the kind and quality of a school may have more to do with how energy and resources are used (managed/mismanaged and directed/misdirected) than with the lack of energy and resources. The person may further come to understand that their experiences related to circumstances like the school situation may also relate to other life choices that they have made in regard to the phenomenon of race.

It is not accidental, for example, that people live in their current neighborhoods. The person may come to understand that they are the source of this kind of circumstance in their life spaces. The person caused or allowed it to be present in their personal or societal or global life spaces, for their own reasons, through what can be called vibrational harmony with it.

To further lift up, clear, and release the belief in scarcity, a person may use their creative imagination, go within, and call upon the archetypal energies *clarity* and *vision*. In the identified circumstance, the person may discover that they were/are sending energy to what they say they do not want, thereby creating win-lose scenarios. In calling upon clarity and vision, win-win solutions may present themselves.

For example, with a belief in abundance, the focus of a person's consciousness shifts from a focus on skin color to how to support what might be called a diversified quality-oriented consciousness process. Such a shift of consciousness would allow the person to support various methods for more efficiently and equitably managing, balancing, and directing an abundance of energy, money, and resources as they relate to the quality of education and schools.

If the person has a preference for social action, they may join with those of other races and direct their personal energies toward having those in key societal decision-making positions to create local, state, and federal budgets that truly reflect, beyond lip-service, a priority for having all schools be quality schools in all neighborhoods. The person would assist those decision-makers in understanding how they and others can win with such a priority. The money and resources that are being managed is public money, and there is indeed enough energy, money, and resources there to have this kind of educational possibility materialize.

The person may even involve their outer self in consciously creating diversified quality-oriented neighborhoods, unencumbered by racially-linked ego fears. Racial diversity and multicultural perspectives within schools, then, will be a natural outgrowth of the spirit or authentic essence behind a diversified quality-oriented consciousness, for indeed authentic essence seeks to manifest itself in as many diversified forms as possible. A person's multidimensional self is an outgrowth of their diversified quality-oriented consciousness. Quality-oriented schools will, therefore, naturally and effortlessly mirror this kind of consciousness or the nature of the truer self.

Further, what if it were very profitable through tax incentives for businesses to donate 10 percent of their profits toward public education or to donate other school-related resources? What if 10 percent of all lottery funds were earmarked for public education? What if it were very profitable for textbook publishers, computer companies, paper companies, etc., through tax incentives to donate these school-related resources for public education? What if there were a variety of educational tax incentives for individual contributors and philanthropists for public schools? The energy for initiatives along these lines is already available and seeks even greater manifestation.

There are also a number of philanthropists whose inner work has already guided them toward a diversified quality-oriented consciousness. One philanthropist, for example, through his inner work was inspired in January of 2000 to donate 100 million dollars to assist in creating quality schools by directing his dollars toward improving the quality of reading in the schools of Mississippi.

There are also more well-known philanthropists, like Bill and Melinda Gates and Warren Buffett, who, through their foundations, are focusing their resources toward enhancing the quality of education and health worldwide. Indeed, in June of 2006, Warren Buffett gave over 30 billion dollars or 85 percent of his wealth for worldwide quality education and health, joining his resources with those of the Gates, to model for the world a gracious and wonderful philanthropic expression of abundance.

The point is that money and resources, that is, abundance in many energy forms, surround everyone. It is a question of altering the preference of one's consciousness, individually and collectively, and allowing one's archetypal energies to provide one's outer self with guidance for expressing one's personal energy and attracting mutually empowering personal, societal, and global circumstances.

I realize that this approach may sound unrealistic and impractical to some. And yet, if people do not believe in *abundance* and that such win-win interracial scenarios are possible, then people will not take constructive action to materialize them, choosing instead to be reactive.

In using this kind of approach, a person would be tapping into the two Generic Archetypal Energy Loops I identified and described for evolving the Sensory Race Game and the Power Race Game. As a result, a person's power orientation for circumstances like the school situation would shift toward inspirational urges and the person's sensory orientation to skin color for this kind of situation would shift toward an altruistic orientation. The person's outer actions, therefore, in regard to this kind of situation would shift and the person may evolve the nature of this kind of interracial drama such that it can be played more in alignment with what I have called the altruistic and inspirational race games.

Transforming Racially-Linked Subpersonalities

Previously, I noted that every drama, including a person's interracial dramas, is a reflection of a drama in the person's inner life. A person's inner life dramas involve their subpersonalities or partial aspects of the person's personality and the interaction of energy within the person's self. I also previously identified some possible racially-linked subpersonalities that may get acted out through interracial role relationships and interracial dramas. For the present focus, I will re-identify these subpersonalities, but frame them now in terms of how a person might experience them and how a person might transform them. As people's lower self consciousness in its current state is largely focused on security, sensory, and power issues, some racially-linked subpersonalities may be described in these terms (see Table 5).

Through the Transformational Race Game, however, a person may invite their racially-linked subpersonalities to participate with their outer self in evolving the human race game. It is important to realize that these aspects of the outer self have been serving a purpose for the whole self and that it is important for the person to understand their purpose before they can invite them into a process of transformation.

To a large extent, they have functioned in regard to the person's assessment of potential pain or pleasure as applied or misapplied to the phenomenon of race. In this regard, many of them have also been fueled by the person's race-related fears that flow from their race-related ideas about security, sensory interpretations, and power.

More often than not, the strategies employed by many of the person's race-linked subpersonalities have been to avoid, to keep at a distance, or to try to manipulate those who are perceived to be racially different. Similar dynamics, likewise, apply to the person's ethnic-related fears, and fears related to other lenses for the person's human experience.

Table 5. Examples of Racially-linked Subpersonalities That Are Self-Limiting and Require Transformation		
Insecure Subpersonalities	Sensory-focused Subpersonalities	Power-Driven Subpersonalities
•Frightened Racial Self	•Child-like Racial Self	•Self-Righteous Racial Self
•Rejecting Racial Self	•Spontaneously Reactive Racial Self	•Parent-like Racial Self
•"Addicted" or Attached Racial Self	•Outer-oriented Racial Self	•Greedy Racial Self
•Blaming Racial Self	•Numb Or Non-caring Racial Self	•Controlling -Manipulative Racial Self
•Conflicted Racial Self	•Passionate-Driven Racial Self	•Powerless Racial Self
•Obedient Racial Self	•Angry or Hateful Racial Self	•Vain Racial Self
•Overcompensating Racial Self	•Lustful Racial Self	•Rebellious Racial Self
•Obsessive-Compulsive Racial Self	•Avoidant Racial Self	•Compliant Racial Self
•Overcautious or Reticent Racial Self	•Oversensitive Racial Self	•Overaggressive-Overconfident Racial Self

While there are many methods for working with one's racially-linked subpersonalities or partial aspects of one's personality, readers may want to experiment with an approach that I will describe. It involves calling upon the archetypal energies and working with one's journal, the mirror effect, and one's observer self. It also brings together a person's intuition and their logic.

First, relax, go within, and call upon the archetypal energies understanding, truth, or wisdom and any of the four transformational archetypal energies (acceptance, love, inclusion, harmony) to act as guides through this process.

Now, in your journal, without monitoring yourself, write down as many names as you can of people in your personal life space that you consider are from a race different than your own. Make sure that these are people with whom you have or have had some kind of face-to-face contact. They could be friends, relatives, acquaintances, co-workers, store clerks, past or present contacts, etc.

Next, look at the first three names. These are the primary people who, at this point in time, may be symbolizing for you a drama of your racially-linked subpersonalities and the interaction of the energy going on within you. Others on your list may also be symbolizing other interracial dramas, which you may want to explore later using this process.

If you have difficulty in making a list due to lack of other-race exposure in your *personal life space*, recognize that this is feedback to you from the *mirror effect* about the interaction of energy going on within you. Search your *societal* or *global life space* memories, therefore, for any other-race societal or global figures who resonate in your mind positively or negatively and use them as transitional or symbolic objects for your exploration of racially-linked subpersonalities.

Or, search your personal life space memories for encounters that only involved your observation of someone from another race, but was not a specific face-to-face interaction (e.g., witnessed an interracial incident or observed someone from another race on the street who stuck in your mind). If you do not remember or know a specific name of the person(s) and only remember the circumstances or incidents, give the person(s) a name. Realize that they are learners on the planet, just like you, and have unique life spaces and unique life histories.

Next, use the mirror effect and your observer self to assess the themes of these interracial relationships and/or interracial dramas in your personal life space. To do this, without monitoring yourself, list each name at the top of separate pages in your journal. On each page, write a response to the following questions, again without monitoring yourself: How would someone else describe the nature of your relationship to this person? If someone else was watching a real or imagined interaction between you and this person, how would they describe it or what would they see going on? Describe the scene. Write down your descriptions with as much detail as you can, recalling as best you can an actual interaction or creating an imagined interaction. After you have written these descriptions, set your journal aside for a brief period of time.

Now, go back and read what you have written as if these writings belonged to someone else. Look for themes. Do these relationships involve fear, rejection, addiction or attachment, blame, conflict, obedience, overcompensation, obsessions or compulsions, over-caution or reticence, childish urges, spontaneous reactions, outer-orientations, numbness or non-caring, passion-driven urges, anger or hate, lust, avoidance, oversensitivity, self-righteousness, maternal or paternal urges, greed, powerlessness, controlling or manipulating, vanity, rebelliousness, compliance, over-aggression or over-confidence? If they do, then you have uncovered the racially-linked subpersonality or subpersonalities that have been at play in these relationships, mirroring the energy going on within you.

If none of the examples of racially-linked subpersonalities I have identified fit you and the nature of these relationships, then create an appropriate description or label that does. Although racially-linked subpersonalities have a tendency to be limiting to you, they may not necessarily be so. To a large extent, they are meant to lead you beyond themselves.

Once you have identified a subpersonality, use your *journal* again to have dialogue with this aspect of yourself. Get relaxed in a comfortable place, go within, and ask this aspect of yourself questions about what it might be trying to teach you.

Write down any answers that come to you without monitoring yourself or judging the answers. Pose the questions in your *journal* in writing. Then, use a label or name for this aspect and dialogue back and forth with it in writing until the intensity of the energy dissipates or you feel complete or satisfied. Think about possible lessons that may be at play, but do not force an answer. Simply allow a response to come.

For example, you might ask the *angry* or *hateful racial self:* "Can you tell me why you are so angry/hateful when you think about those from another race?" Angry or hateful racial self might answer: "I give you the experience of anger or hate because you believe that they get preferences and rights that you do not get or have the attention that you believe you do not have or that you believe that you deserve. However, I am teaching you a lesson in caring."

Then, you might ask: "It feels right to be angry/hateful about these things, but how can this be a lesson about caring? And why am I walking around feeling bad and upset?" Angry or hateful racial self might then answer: "You cannot feel angry/hateful about something or someone without caring about that something or someone. You also cannot hate without identifying with the object of your hate. Otherwise, you would simply feel neutral. You have not yet recognized this. And so, I am showing you that you will feel bad and upset until you do come to such a realization and examine the limitations of your beliefs. When you do recognize how you have been limiting yourself, you will have learned your lesson."

You might continue: "Do you mean I must care about those people? Or do you mean I should not care about those people?" Angry or hateful racial self might then respond: "To care simply means that you are in touch with the *love* inside of you. The anger or hate is simply telling you that you have separated yourself from the *love* inside of you, that you have objectified people, that you have projected out your anger or hate (your feelings of separation from *Love*) onto those you have objectified, and that you do this when you think of someone from another race.

You see, you are really angry with your Self about this separation from love. And, hate is an extreme form of your anger about this separation from love. I exist therefore to remind you of this. You feel angry because you do not believe that they are open to your love since you are not open to your love. When you do become open to your love in this area, you will no longer need me to remind you about the qualities of caring and how you are now limiting yourself with the nature of your focus."

When the dialogue feels complete or you feel satisfied, without having a knot in your solar plexus, you would have released much of the blocked energy behind the angry or hateful racial self.

Now, to continue to transform such a subpersonality, if it is at play in one or all of the interracial relationships you identified, you may again call upon the four transformational archetypal energies and simply invite them to assist you in thinking differently about these relationships. You may also evoke these four archetypal energies by surrounding yourself in the greenish light of the aura of the heart center or by allowing a golden light to flow through your heart center.

Take a deep breath, relax, and use your creative imagination to form a bubble of greenish or golden light around you, flowing from your heart and surrounding your whole body. Bask in the warmth of this light. Send acceptance and love to this subpersonality and thank it for trying to take care of you.

Then, for each of the three persons you identified, as I have previously suggested, ask the following four questions:

- What would *Acceptance* do in this relationship?
- What would *Love* do in this relationship?

- What would *Inclusion* do in this relationship?

- What would *Harmony* do in this relationship?

Write down in your journal any answers that may come to you. If these relationships are part of your personal life space, past or present, what is your highest vision for each of them? Likewise, if they are in your societal or global life space, what is your highest vision for these persons or the highest ideas or ideals they can represent?

Next, imagine where these persons might be physically and in your mind's eye send the warmth of your greenish or golden light out to them from your heart center. You will be sending out the energies of acceptance, love, inclusion, and harmony from your heart center to them as you do.

Finally, if these persons are in your current personal life space, it is important for you to then act toward them in accord with your new insights and transformed consciousness energy.

I intentionally outlined this process with a focus on transforming subpersonalities related to interracial dramas. However, it is important to note that a person can also use the same process for transforming similar subpersonalities related to intra-racial dramas, or other human relationship dramas. As a person's subpersonalities transform, therefore, the person's race relationships and/or human relationships will also transform, mirroring a new, evolving race reality and human reality for the person in her/his life spaces.

THE TRANSFORMATIONAL RACE GAME, THE TRUER SELF, AND HARMONIOUS RELATIONSHIP PRINCIPLES

To create race relationships that work energetically and to create relationships that work in general, from the vibrational point of view of harmony, a person may also want to use what I will call harmonious relationship principles. Harmonious relationship principles resonate in general with how a person's emerging truer self can and will wisely use the Universal Energy Laws to construct life-nurturing relationships. They are also consistent with what Orin calls the universal laws of relationships (Roman, 1997), although I have adapted and expanded on Orin's insights.

As guides for a person's consciousness and their emerging truer self, harmonious relationship principles may serve vibrationally as magnet thoughts to attract and to nurture particular kinds of relationships for purposes of growth, facilitating authentic soul contacts, and creating bridges for the person's truer self to emerge through authentically expressing their soul qualities in and through relationships.

In terms of race relations and the Transformational Race Game, harmonious relationship principles will allow a person to invite and to have constructive, catalytic interracial encounters in their life spaces, particularly in the person's personal life space. That is, the person's interracial relationships will serve as a catalyst for their personal transformation and growth, as well as the transformation and growth of those who are identified as belonging to another race. The person may be a mirror and teacher for others in their interracial dramas and others may be a mirror and teacher for the person in her/his interracial dramas. In this context, the path of the bridger will immerse the person in and will provide the person with opportunities to implement harmonious relationship principles in her/his three life spaces (i.e., personal, societal, global).

I am focusing here on the nature of people's relationships because it is through evolving how a person thinks about and carries new images about their interracial and other personal and group relationships in their mind that the human race game will evolve in specific and general terms. Societal structures are held in place and institutional practices and polices are, to a large extent, carried out in accord with the "thought energy" that people give to the race-related "relationship images" (and human relationship images) that they carry in their individual and collective minds.

Knowing and working with harmonious relationship principles can, therefore, assist each person in evolving the human race game. In accord with the mirror effect, generally these principles may be helpful to a person in wisely applying the Universal Energy Laws to co-create the kind and quality of relationships that they say they want in their personal, societal, and global life spaces. As the person does this, the quality of her/his race relations (and other human relations) will also evolve.

HOW THE TRUER SELF CAN CREATE "HARMONIOUS BRIDGES" IN HUMAN RELATIONSHIPS, INTERRACIAL RELATIONSHIPS AND INTERRACIAL DRAMAS

The harmonious relationship principles may be described as follows (see Table 6 for summary):

Table 6. Harmonious Relationship Principles for Evolving the *Human Race Game* As Related To The Universal Energy Laws	
Truer Self Relationship Principles	**The Related Universal Energy Laws**
•**The "Reality" Principle.** You create your own Reality according to the nature of your beliefs. Adopt, therefore, "win-win" beliefs and attitudes.	**Law of Attraction**
•**The Focus Principle.** Do not send Energy to what you do not want. Send Energy only to that which you do want.	**Law of Polarity**
•**The Preference Principle.** When in doubt, adopt a neutral stance until you can get clear about what you prefer. Go within and ask for **Clarity**. Be patient with your Self. Do not choose the lesser of what you do not want.	**Law of Neutrality**
•**The Source Principle.** a. Beliefs are not truths per se. You are at the mercy of circumstances only if you "believe" that you are. Believe, therefore, that you are the Source of your life. b. To change the nature of "unhealthy" circumstances, you must first change the limiting belief(s).	**Law of Consequences**

•The Essence Principle. Focus on the "Essence" of what you want and do not become a persondded to "form" per se. When you know the "Essence," any form will work.	**Law of Intention**
•The Change Principle. You can only change your Self, not others. Allow your Self to change your preferences, and allow others to change theirs. Allow your Self, therefore, to change, to "be" your highest Qualities, and to "have" what you ask for. Likewise, allows others to change and to "be" Themselves	**Law of Allowing**
•The Healing Principle. The key to all "healing" and change, including healing racial relationships, is the use of your *creative imagination* and your preference.	**Law of Universality**

- *The Reality Principle.* You create your own reality according to the nature of your beliefs. Adopt, therefore, win-win beliefs and attitudes in regard to your relationships. This relationship principle is related to the universal energy law of attraction. By adopting win-win beliefs and attitudes in regard to one's relationships, the person's emerging truer self, in terms of vibrational harmony, is allowed to be open and to remain open to the nurturance of various archetypal energies in attracting people, objects, events, circumstances, and interracial dramas which mirror win-win conditions for their outer self and others in their personal, societal, and global life spaces. One such general transformative win-win belief, for example, is the belief that the world is safe, friendly, and abundant. I do not want to be overly simplistic here, but if enough people adopted such a belief, the world would look dramatically different in terms of how people would view (think and feel) and behave toward others in their life spaces. When a person acts toward others, knowing that the person has value and worth as s/he has value and worth, the stage is set for win-win beliefs and attitudes. Even so-called competitive events at individual and group levels can be experienced playfully and result in what I call aggressive collaboration to uplift spirit. That is, people collaborate with one another aggressively, energetically, and consciously for a creative and constructive enterprise. This requires, however, recognition of one's own free will and the free will of others and recognition that one has a right, as do others, to say yes and no to experiences that do not nurture one's own value and worth and that of Others.

- *The Focus Principle.* Do not send energy to what you do not want. Send energy only to that which you do want, to the qualities and highest ideals you want reflected in and through your relationships. This relationship principle is related to the universal energy law of polarity. Here, a person may invite in the archetypal energies *clarity* and *vision* to assist with their decision-making and co-creations of relationships and interracial dramas. With clarity and vision resonating and assisting one or more of the four transformational archetypal energies, the quality of a person's relationships, including their interracial relationships, will move with a clear intent toward the Highest Ideals contained in a polarity.

- *The Preference Principle.* When in doubt, adopt a neutral stance until you can get clear about what you prefer. Go within and ask for clarity. Be patient with yourself. Do not choose the lesser of what you do not want. This relationship principle is related to the universal energy law of neutrality. Here a person is choosing both sides of a polarity until they can get clear about what higher qualities they would prefer to emerge in a particular interracial relationship or interracial drama, or general relationship drama. This is somewhat different from tolerance. Tolerance implies that the person has already created an emotional response and has decided to ignore their feelings for the greater good, without fully understanding the original belief(s) behind the emotional response and how these beliefs may be self-limiting. In terms of interracial relationships, if the beliefs are left unexamined, this could result in the creation of racially-linked energy blocks in the form of resentment for choosing the lesser of what the person does not want. With neutrality, the person simply allows their outer self and the outer self of the other to just *be*, without creating an energy block since the choice of both sides of a polarity neutralizes the energy. In this context, the person's interracial relationships can at least remain civil and respectful, without causing harm to their outer self or to the outer self of the other. The person, therefore, acts with respect and civility toward others they consider racially different, until they can get clear about what higher qualities may be available to their outer self for emergence or what higher qualities their outer self would like to use to structure the nature of the relationship. Similar dynamics operate for human relationships in general where perceived differences are at play.

- *The Source Principle.*

    a. Beliefs are not truths per se. You are at the mercy of circumstances only if you *believe* that you are. Believe, therefore, that you are the soul-source of your life.

    b. To change the nature of *unhealthy circumstances*, you must first change the limiting belief(s).

These two aspects of the source relationship principle are related to the universal energy law of consequences. By realizing that beliefs are not truths per se, a person releases their self from giving their beliefs power over their self, and reclaims their own power by recognizing that they can accept, modify, or reject any belief in structuring their reality. The person realizes that they are the soul-source who lovingly gives energy to their beliefs, even when they may for a time appear to be self-limiting. Self-limiting beliefs may then be viewed as temporary survival-oriented tools the person may have adopted. But, if allowed, they will eventually lead the person beyond themselves when examined. When the consequences of a person's beliefs have resulted in unhealthy circumstances and relationships such as those related to lower self race games, the self-limiting belief(s) at play must then be examined and changed or released.

- *The Essence Principle.* Focus on the essence of what you want and do not become wedded to form per se. When you know the essence, any form, including the form for a relationship, will work. This relationship principle is related to the universal energy law of intention. The conscious intentions behind a person's thoughts vibrationally influence energy going out from the person and energy magnetically attracted to the person. As visually-oriented human beings in one's current racial forms, it is important to understand what one's intentions are behind their thoughts and how they get directed toward those they perceive to be racially different or different in general. Is the intent to honestly understand and to get to know other people? Is the intent to seek to control or manipulate other people? Is the intent to seek to avoid or to hold people in prescribed places in one's mind by using one's stereotypes or prejudices about the societal group to which those persons are thought to belong? Is the intent to work through karma with other people? Is the intent wedded to a particular way one wants to hold people in one's mind? This principle helps a person to transcend their race-related or other-oriented fixations and fears. The person embraces an intention to make authentic soul contact and focuses on knowing the authentic essence of one's self and others.

- *The Change Principle.* You can only change yourself, not others. Allow yourself to change your preferences, and allow others to change theirs. Allow yourself, therefore, to change, to be your highest qualities, and to have what you ask for. Likewise, allow others to change and to be themselves. This relationship principle is related to the universal energy law of allowing. If a person is caught up in an interracial or other-oriented drama that they find frustrating, often this is a sign that the person's outer self is not allowing a higher soul quality as an aspect of their truer self to emerge for their outer self to frame the nature of their experience. It is important to go within and meditate on what it is that one's outer self (one's ego or personality) may not be allowing one to see. It is important for the person to seek to understand how their outer self may be using fear to not allow their self to have particular kinds of interracial or other-oriented experiences. In practical terms, after meditating, it is important for the person to use their journal to record insights, and then follow their own inner guidance in finding ways to allow their outer self to change their preferences, to be their highest qualities, and to have what they ask for.

- *The Healing Principle.* The key to all healing and change, including healing racial relationships, is the use of your creative imagination and your preference. This relationship principle is related to the universal energy law of universality. It is through the use of a person's creative imagination that they shift their focus in their world, creating a visual seed or picture for calling forward the necessary energy from the universe for healing and change. A person's creative imagination is one of the most potent methods that they can use whereby they are saying to the universe, "This is what I now prefer." The person's creative imagination activates the mirror effect, whereby the person begins to send and receive the quality of energies they desire in their relationships, including their interracial relationships.

If these relationship principles were applied individually and collectively, people would be able to consciously use the mirror effect with wisdom for transformational purposes. In turn, people would be able to co-create relationships, including interracial relationships that work for their own outer self and others in their personal, societal, and global life spaces. People would co-create a kind of group consciousness that would mirror and nurture ongoing possibilities for harmonious, interdependent interracial relationships.

For example, in applying the reality and focus principles in their role as a bridger, a person's emerging truer self consciousness in their *current racial form* will focus on these following dynamics:

1. An ever-emerging Authentic Essence Reality, not personality;

2. The feelings or the qualities of love they want in their relationships;

3. The recognition of all the ways people are giving their outer self the essence of love, perhaps in ways they might not have noticed or acknowledged before; and

4. A reliance on the feeling of love, rather than on gestures or outer appearances.

In practical terms, what this means is that in one-on-one interracial or other-oriented encounters in a person's personal life space and as a soul actor in another person's interracial or other-oriented dramas, as a bridger one becomes a mirror for the other person. And, the person recognizes how the other person is a mirror for their outer self. The person will also view her/his encounters with others as opportunities to resonate with them soul-to-soul. The person genuinely relates to people in a soulful way, without needing a rigid we-they attitude to validate her/his own and their worth.

In applying the source and change principles in one's role as a bridger, a person's emerging truer self consciousness in their *current racial form* will focus on these following processes:

1. Releasing any feelings that they are (or have to be) a victim, and any feelings of self-pity, blame, or thoughts that they cannot have what they want because someone is holding them back;

2. Lifting up energy blocks to their heart center and allowing the soul's Will to Love to dissolve these blocks;

3. Enhancing their ability to express love and to radiate unconditional acceptance and love; and

4. Using the mirror effect to remind their outer self that they are the creator of their life.

In other words and in practical terms, applying these two principles will allow a person to understand that they have choices and that this is what they are presently choosing. The person recognizes further that they can make a different choice to create what they want, if they are not satisfied. The person needs only to change their beliefs and/or to release those beliefs that are limiting. In this sense, the person does not *need* others to give them what they want. Their outer self and their soul can create any life the person can imagine for their self. Each person is the soul-source of their own life, not others.

In applying the preference, essence, and healing principles in one's role as a bridger, a person's truer self consciousness in their *current racial form* will focus primarily on three issues.

1. First, the person's consciousness will tend to focus on what is working in their relationships, including their interra-

cial relationships, and on a certainty that the universe is working for their whole self.

2. Second, the person's consciousness will tend to focus on the thoughts they have about their relationships, including their interracial relationships. That is, the person acknowledges other people when they act in ways they like and the person shifts their focus away from any thoughts about what is wrong between their outer self and the outer self of others or about what the other person is doing that their outer self does not want.

3. And third, the person's consciousness will tend to focus on all that is high and loving between their self and the self of others and on how to radiate to the other person qualities they would like to receive.

I have suggested that each person vibrationally activates the harmonious relationship principles to create more authentic interracial relations or other-oriented relations through the use of their creative imagination. As they do so, it is important to recognize that one is making a decision to change their preference for how to view their world.

It is also important to recognize that one is additionally making a decision to activate and to be open to the archetypal energies, as they flow, blend, and are uniquely expressed through the person's personal energy system, their energy centers, in accord with the universal energy laws. The archetypal energies can then assist the person in their change of preference for how to view their world.

ACTIVATING CORE ENERGY ELEMENTS FOR CREATING HARMONIOUS RELATIONSHIP

To start the change of preference process, a person only needs to decide to focus on one of three higher energy elements. I call these three higher energy elements *core energy elements*, or the *TLC* for creating harmonious relationships (see Figure 7).

Figure 7. Illustrations Of How You "Open" and "Close" Your Consciousness To The Soul Qualities Of Your Emerging True Self As You Relate To Others

A. How An Emerging Spiritually Integrated Self (Your Emerging True Self) "Opens" To Archetypal Energies and Uses "Authentic Communication" (A-Com.) To Form "Harmonious Energy Relationships"

B. What Happens When The Flow Of Archetypal Energies Is Blocked: Fear, Mistrust, And "Mis-communication" (M-Com.) Are Allowed To Structure "Disharmonious Energy Relationships"

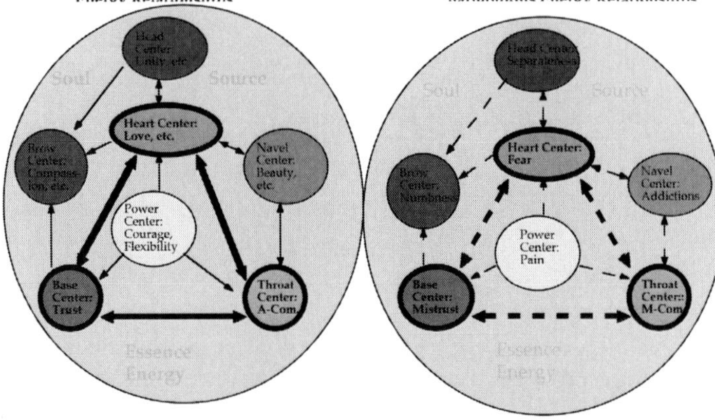

To "open" your Consciousness to establishing harmonious relationships, three core Energy elements (pictured in Figure A with bold lines) must be present: Love, Trust, and A-Communication (Authentic Communication resonates with the Archetypal Energies of Understanding, Truth, Wisdom, Patience, and Inspiration). Take one of the three core Energy elements away and you get a shaky relationship. When you "decides" to allow yourself to "experience" one of the core Energy elements in a relationship, that first core Energy element fuels one of the other two core Energy elements, flowing in either direction. That second core Energy element then fuels the third core Energy element, which in turn serves to increase the energy of the first core Energy element in advancing the quality of the relationship. You become "open" to your own Courage and Flexibility (Power Center Energies) as you authentically express who you are in the relationship. The quality of the relationship is then additionally reinforced and supported by the other surrounding Energies, establishing a "mature, caring, harmonious energy relationship." The arrows show how the Energies flow and blend together (solid lines=smooth flow of energy) or are blocked (dotted lines = interrupted flow of energy) in your personal energy system as you relate to someone energetically. Fear, mistrust, and miscommunication (M-Com= uninspired communication based on misunderstading, untruths, ignorance, and impatience) represent the flip-side of the three, triangulated core Energy elements; these three flip-side primary elements block the flow of Archetypal Energies (pictured in Figure B in bold lines). With these three primary elements, you become "closed" to your own authenticity in the relationship, which in turn gets expressed in the relationship primarily as perceived pain (The blocked Power Center). That is, the relationship is experienced as painful. The relationship is then additionally framed, reinforced, experienced through, or is characterized by the additonal energies of addictions, numbness, and a sense of separateness. Energetically, then, the elements of the flip-side work in a similar fashion to escalate "dysfunction" (immature, uncaring, disharmonious energies) in a relationship. In practical terms, the key to turning a dysfunctional relationship around (i.e., establishing or flipping a disharmonious relationship around to its natural, energetically flowing, harmonious state) is to embrace, practice, and give form and expression to aspects of A-Communication. Natural and flip-side elements are not really opposites energies per se. Rather, it is moreso the phenomenon that the two aspects of energy elements can not occupy the same "time" and "space."

Together, the core energy elements emit a golden glow when they are spiritually blended to support and nurture a relationship. There is kind of a triangulated, interdependent flow among the three elements as energy moves back and forth, in either direction, to establish stability.

The three core energy elements are:

1. The archetypal energy Trust (T), a foundational quality;

2. The archetypal energy Love (Caring) (L), a transformational and integrative quality; and

3. One or more of the archetypal energies underlying authentic communication (C) (A-Com.), the expressive qualities associated with the throat center (i.e., understanding, truth, wisdom, patience, and/or inspiration).

In a person's relationships, including their interracial relationships, the person therefore decides to evoke, invoke, or invite within their self one of the three core energy elements. When a person decides to evoke, invoke, or invite any one of the three core energy elements, the decision then serves as a vibrational stimulus to activate the two other core energy elements within the person's self and to invite the activation of those same elements in the self of others. The activation may go in either direction and the person gets back more of the original activating energy.

For example, if a person decides to evoke, invoke, or invite trust as their original activating energy, the person will find that they become open to engaging in and experiencing more authentic communication in the relationship. As the person communicates more authentically, they will find that they become more open to caring (love) in the relationship. As the person cares more, they will find that their capacity to trust in the relationship has increased.

Or, in an alternative direction, if a person decides to evoke, invoke, or invite trust as their original activating energy, the person will find that they become more open to caring (love) in the relationship. As the person cares more, they will find that they become more open to sharing and engaging in authentic communication. As the person talks more authentically in the relationship, they will find that they trust more in the relationship.

From a thought-emotional perspective, therefore, the original stimulus energy may flow vibrationally in either direction, blend with other energies, and flow back to the activating quality, enhanced and enriched to frame the quality of the relationship. In terms of a person's emerging truer self, then, their consciousness becomes more spiritually integrated through the blending of energies, and their outer self experiences the self as more open in relating to others.

Further, as a person activates the flow of these three core energies, the person also activates the flow of other energies and qualities associated with their personal energy system. That is, the person's other energy centers are stimulated to open, supporting the person to give more authentic expression to their courage and flexibility in their relationships as they experience more of their inner beauty and increase their capacity for compassion and unity (See Figure 7).

In due course, a person's interracial relationships and interracial dramas, as well as their other-oriented relationships and dramas, will be more constructively nurtured, reinforced, and supported as these other energies get expressed through the person's personal energy system. The archetypal energies will be authentically acted out in relation to other people in the person's personal life space, or in relation to the race-related societal or global issue or event in the person's societal or global life spaces.

The natural flow of the three core energies is blocked when the ego aspect of a person's personality fails to recognize the unique essence of another person, for whatever reason. The person will then experience the flip-side of the core energy elements—fear, mistrust, and miscommunication—reinforced by a sense of separation, a creeping sense of numbness, and a tendency to view the world in addictive ways. A person's energy centers, therefore, tend to close in such a state and the person will have difficulty and dysfunction in her/his relationships.

It is when a person *consciously* decides to engage in authentic communication, to be authentic, that the person can eventually turn this state of affairs around. A person's truer self then emerges as a *catalyst* to create harmonious bridges for their human relationships and human dramas, including their interracial relationships and interracial dramas. As a catalyst, the person's truer self will allow their archetypal energies to flow more naturally through their personality as they relate to the unique and authentic essence of the other. Authentic essence, in other words, implies worth, value, capability, and lovability.

EMERGING VISIONS AND PATTERNS OF INTERDEPENDENCE FOR EVOLVING THE HUMAN RACE GAME

As a person changes their preference for how to view their world, the person, in energy terms, will alter how they relate vibrationally to their own and another's ever-emerging, ever-creative, and ever-loving authentic essence. The person will also begin to encounter, through their mirror effect, emerging visions, patterns, tools, and opportunities for humanity's next evolutionary step. These emerging visions, patterns, tools and opportunities have implications for evolving the human race game.

For many people, this perspective is already a reality in their experience, and this book's material is simply an extension of their current self-explorations. For others, the reader will find their outer self attracted more and more to alternative frameworks, as they open their outer self to alternative ideas that expand their sense of self and their worldview.

What is now called the new physics, for example, is providing people with a scientific perspective or scientific mirror effect about an alternative way to view the world. The new physics now theoretically acknowledges an underlying consciousness-energy framework for understanding physicality and uses terms such as implicate order, explicate order, superimplicate order, supersuperimplicate order, holomovement and string/M-theory to explain the vibrating world and the substance and boundaries of matter (e.g., David Bohm; Fred Alan Wolf; Brian Greene).

I, therefore, will metaphorically integrate a few of the new physics ideas and their implications for evolving the human race game as I discuss a few emerging visions, patterns, tools, and opportunities associated with humanity's next evolutionary step.

EMERGING VISIONS ABOUT HUMANITY'S NEXT EVOLUTIONARY STEP: IMPLICATIONS FOR EVOLVING THE HUMAN RACE GAME

There are many emerging visions about humanity's next evolutionary step, all flowing from the paradigm shift that I have discussed. For purposes here, however, I will focus on three of these emerging visions, which have implications for evolving the human race game.

The first evolutionary vision is a vision of humanity as a telepathic species. Another way of saying this is that humanity is evolving in such a way as to be more open telepathically to one another, to better understand, vibrationally tune into, and trust its intuitive and psychic communication abilities. That is, the vision is that as people open telepathically to one another, from an energy vibrational point of view, people also open and learn to trust more their potential for other psychic abilities (i.e., spatial intuition, clairsentience, sensitivity to vibes from other people and places, authentic empathy, clairaudience, clairvoyance) in accord with their own interests and paths of growth.

This means that a person will be able to better sense or vibrationally connect with the subtle energies that interpenetrate their environment, and to more consciously use the nature of thought and intention as an energetic and electromagnetic force to consciously create or co-create the world with other people and source energy/spirit or All-That-Is. Some people have come to know this phenomenon as "the sixth sense," "psi," or the opening of the third eye (e.g., Naparstek's *The Sixth Sense*). For purposes here, I will refer to this evolving telepathic sense as a person's soul-centered sense in relation to evolving the human race game.

The second evolutionary vision is a vision of humanity having and developing the gift of visible auras. That is, as humanity begins to view itself as consciousness-energy self-aware beings, with physical bodies supported by interpenetrating subtle energies, people's ability to physically sense (to see, feel, and technologically view) these subtle energies and to vibrationally and energetically relate to one another in accord with these auras will be greatly enhanced (e.g., Roman's *Personal Power Through Awareness*; Heideman's *Searching for Light*).

I will refer to this aspect of a person's soul-centered sense as relating through extended or etheric perception. It occurs when the person begins to open and integrate their heart and head centers, although some people also simply call this phenomenon their intuition or an aspect of their ESP or extrasensory perception. This second evolutionary vision is very closely aligned, therefore, with the first evolutionary vision.

The third evolutionary vision is a vision that humanity's consciousness is maturing. As it does so, the vision is that the material world will become more spiritualized, as the vibrational frequency of the material world rises or becomes higher. Additionally, with a maturing consciousness, people, in addition to current forms of communication, will engage in relating more to one another through a process that has been and will be called soul linking (e.g., Roman's *Soul Love*).

It is in the third evolutionary context that people begin to enhance their perceptions and abilities in bringing together the energies that flow through their higher and lower centers. In a manner of speaking, therefore, the third evolutionary vision is simply an outcome of the other two evolutionary visions, mirroring what it means to be a mature human being who consciously co-creates the world through the extension and use of both inner and outer senses.

I will, therefore, offer some preliminary thoughts about each of the three evolutionary visions, or the three aspects of humanity's evolving soul-centered sense, and their implications for evolving the human race game.

HUMANITY AS A TELEPATHIC SPECIES

The evolutionary *vision* of humanity as a telepathic species is actually a more *conscious* recognition and acknowledgment of what already is so. That is, at inner levels, a *soul-centered sense* of telepathic connections already exists. Currently, people are aware that as human beings they communicate with one another through both verbal and nonverbal forms of communication. In a manner of speaking, then, telepathy is another, more expanded form of nonverbal communication.

In accord with the soul-centered model, each person has what might be called telepathic or soul-centered energy cords coming in and out of their self, whereby the person nonverbally communicates with people they now know, people they will know, and people they have known. These soul-centered energy cords can be thought of as electromagnetic waves or thought-forms vibrationally linking the person to others.

Consider now what this means in terms of the people in the person's *personal, societal,* and *global life spaces,* that is, people who are part of the person's awareness, and people that the person considers members of different races or members of their own race. It is not accidental, therefore, that they are there in the person's awareness. From an energy vibrational point of view, the person has attracted them there or allowed them to be there, through their telepathic or soul-centered energy cords, for whatever reasons. And, if they are in the person's *personal life space*, both the person and they have attracted or allowed one another into each other's *personal life space* through both people's telepathic or soul-centered energy cords, for whatever reasons.

In larger terms, then, a person's new dramas with those they consider to be members of a different race may be viewed as extended versions, alternate versions, or newer versions of older dramas with them. These dramas are attracted or allowed, and enacted in one another's personal, societal, and global life spaces to provide everyone involved with an opportunity to choose to grow. Or, alternatively, in larger terms, a person's new dramas with those they consider to be members of a different race may be other-oriented versions of older dramas with newer actors, again providing everyone involved with an opportunity to choose to grow.

So, how will a person know if other people, particularly those they consider to be members of different races, are inviting or allowing them to join them telepathically in a personal, societal, or global interracial drama, or if they are the primary initiator? With respect to the soul-centered model, in larger terms, of course, the question would not be relevant, for all operate by cooperation and by agreement through *vibrational harmony*. In the person's current physical reality, however, it is relevant only to the extent that such a question may guide the person toward a more comprehensive understanding of their personal energy system as it relates to telepathy.

First, with respect to the soul-centered model, it is important to realize that telepathic messages would come to a person through the vibrations set off by the thoughts of people. As energy that is experienced at a subtle level, telepathic messages would flow in accord with the universal energy laws. The closer a person is physically to another person, the stronger the telepathic reception (see Roman's *Personal Power Through Awareness*, 1986).

Second, with respect to the soul-centered model, it is important to realize that a person can receive telepathic messages both through the person's lower centers at an emotional level and through the person's higher centers at a mental level. However, the reception through the person's higher centers may be much more beneficial to their outer self in terms of maintaining a clearer sense of who they are. Telepathic reception through the person's higher centers, therefore, will enable the person to more efficiently discern the difference between their own feelings and thoughts and those of others. That is, the person can more efficiently discern what they feel like in their current racial form versus what others feel like in their current racial forms.

One of the primary ways, then, for a person to know whether they are invited or allowed to join others telepathically, or they are inviting or allowing them telepathically to join her or him, is to pay attention to one's own feelings first. This action enables the person to know their own energy and to discern what vibrational thought-forms, that is, what electromagnetic thought waves, the person is sending out or is picking up from others. Indeed, like other authors who have expressed this notion (e.g., Roman, 1986; Hicks, 2006), I am also saying that a person must know their own energy first before they can know what they are picking up telepathically.

A person can begin to know their own energy better by simply checking out how they feel each morning when they awake. Do what might be called a morning feeling check-in. Then, when the person encounters others during the day and their feelings alter during particular encounters, they can then be clearer about their own thought and emotional energy and the thought and emotional energy that they may be picking up from others.

I agree with Orin (Roman, 1986), therefore, that it is also important to understand that currently almost everyone on the planet experience emotional telepathy in their unique world, but few experience mental telepathy. Indeed, learning to experience mental telepathy is part of the next evolutionary step. As each person does so, they will be evolving the human race game, particularly when they begin to understand that telepathy is both a gift and a responsibility, but can be a problem when not understood (Roman, 1986).

People have not understood, for example, that many of their personal, societal, and global problems, racial and otherwise, are manifested in the world because they do not understand how they can and do affect others with the gift of telepathy. People also have not understood how others can and do affect them with this gift. Underlying these effects is what can be called the Principle of Vibrational Harmony—that is, for anything to enter and affect a person in their personal fields of experience, there must be vibrational harmony, for whatever conscious, subconscious, and/or unconscious reason(s).

For those who require scientific evidence of these effects, I recommend that they explore some of the research findings of organizations such as the Institute of HeartMath (see www.heartmath.org) and Bioresonance (see www.bioresonance.co.uk). The researchers at the Institute of HeartMath, for example, have focused on what they call the science of the heart and have validated that there are real (not metaphorical) electromagnetic connections and vibrational effects going on between people—heart to heart, heart to head, and head to head.

As humanity evolves toward becoming more of a telepathic species, people are also evolving toward a more comprehensive understanding of what it really means to be part of a group consciousness, part of a whole, part of source energy/spirit, part of All-That-Is. That is, while affirming the validity of who they are, each person will also be able to affirm that they are a unique portion of source energy/spirit or All-That-Is, as are those they consider to be the others.

Some people at this point will be tempted to make sense out of what I have described in other terms or to argue for or against this *vision* by evoking the framework of what is called science. Indeed, there are scientists in the world who are studying telepathic communication. Numerous experiments, using what is called modern Kirlian effect equipment, now seem to confirm the existence of direct mind-to-mind telepathic communication.

For example, a scientist known as Professor Bunzen in Russia, using what is called bio-electrography, in relation to what is known as the Kirlian aura effect, has provided scientific evidence that a thought appears in the aura before any electrical activity can be detected in the brain. That is, the evidence indicated that a response in the Kirlian aura seemed to precede (appears as soon or earlier than) electric processes in the brain during a decision-making process. It also was demonstrated that there was no detrimental effect on such communication at a distance of several hundred kilometers. In addition to the scientific findings of researchers like Professor Bunzen and groups like those of the Institute of HeartMath and Bioresonance, I also want to refer to the evolving notions of quantum reality.

In terms of the quantum reality that scientists are now exploring, what this vision means metaphorically and, to some extent, literally is that the quantum light particles that have been observed and that can exist in more than one place (the concept of nonlocality as some scientists have labeled this phenomenon) serve as connective conduits for a person's vibrating thought-forms. That is, the person's thoughts and emotions and those of others set off particular vibrations in the so-called implicate order, the ocean of living, pure energy as Bohm, a noted physicist, calls it.

The person then may experience the vibrations as what can be called telepathic messages in the so-called explicate order, the three-dimensional world that the outer self knows. Organizing and directing the emergence of the structure and the flow of the electromagnetic waves, the vibrations, from the implicate order into the explicate order is what Bohm calls the superimplicate order (or what I would call the person's multidimensional consciousness-energy), the infinitely layered superinformation field that surrounds, interpenetrates, and underlies the implicate order. In this context, as Bohm and Naparstek describe it, the world, as the outer self understands it, and everything in it, flows interdependently together as a holistic holomovement, a vast, seamless, whole ocean of energy pulsing with life and intelligence.

In concert with the soul-centered model, what these scientists do not explicitly say but do imply, however, is that the pulsating life and intelligence, that is, this consciousness-energy, interpenetrates and is source energy/spirit or All-That-Is. Further implied is that source energy/spirit's multidimensional nature is expressed multidimensionally within and through each person. A person's evolving nature, therefore, will allow the person telepathically to more efficiently tap into the multidimensional aspects of their self and others.

In turn, the person's evolving nature will allow the person to more clearly understand why they chose their *current racial form* and why others chose theirs. The responsibility that goes along with this gift, therefore, is that in its use it is important that: (1) people use *discernment*, (2) people recognize and honor their own and others' *free will*, meaning their own and others' right to say yes and no, (3) people create *harmonious boundaries* and relationships, and (4) people foster constructive creative or co-creative enterprises for the whole.

THE GIFT OF "VISIBLE AURAS" FOR HUMANITY

The aura, as it is understood and as it relates to the soul-centered model, is the physical manifestation or reflection of a person's personal energy system. In a manner of speaking, then, the opportunity to more *consciously* view one's own aura and the auras of others creates a nurturing context and an opportunity for assisting one another in various paths of growth.

A person's aura, for example, *mirrors* how the person may have programmed various energy-related tendencies and challenges for their life. The person's aura may also show the person and others where particular energies in the person's personal energy system may have become stuck or stagnate, thus allowing the person and others to engage in co-creative, corrective actions for purposes of healing and growth.

In terms of race relations, the gift of visible auras can assist the person and others in more clearly understanding their own and others' racially-linked energy blocks, or the potential for racially-linked energy blocks. There are those known as psychics, mystics, or clairvoyants who have exhibited this gift from the beginning of time, as it is understood. However, a person does not need to be psychic to see or sense an aura.

Some curious observers know, for example, that there currently are technological means to produce pictures of people's auras. Actually, the technology has existed for some time (Note: Kirlian photography was developed in Russia in the 1930s; Guy Coggins' first Aura Camera was invented in 1970; see C. E. Lindgren, D, Litt & J. Baltz's *Aura Awareness*, 2007).

Also, there are methods that a person can learn for enhancing their natural capabilities, if they so choose (e.g., W. Lambert's *Aura Glasses: You Can See Auras!*, 1996; T. Andrew's *How To See & Read The Aura*, 2006). It has been reported that these methods actually allow a person to alter and evolve the biochemistry of their brain (Note: see research of Prof. Konstantin Korotkov and his colleagues, based in St. Petersburg, Russia, in his books, *Effekt Kirlian*, date unknown, *Light After Life: A Scientific Journey into the Spiritual World*, 1998, *Aura and Consciousness: New Stage of Scientific Understanding*, 1999, and *Human Energy Field: Study with GDV Bioelectrography*, 2002; S. G. Shumsky's *Exploring Auras: Cleansing and Strengthening Your Energy Field*, 2005).

The gift of visible auras I am speaking of, therefore, includes both an expansion of people's natural capabilities and an expansion of how people can more creatively modify and utilize the evolving aura technologies. For example, using what some scientists call modern Kirlian technology such as the gas discharge visualization camera, it is now possible to evaluate the degree of conscious control a person has over their energy states and aura.

One of the potential outcomes of the gift of visible auras, therefore, is that people may no longer need to create value-laden meanings in relation to what are now known as race-linked colors. The current race-linked colors now include the colors white, black, red, brown, and yellow, to which some people have attributed various connotative meanings and value judgments and around which some people act out their various projective lower self race games at individual and group levels.

As I have noted earlier, the framework of using value-laden, race-linked colors in relation to what are called racial groups has resulted in a great deal of stereotyping. The race-linked colors themselves are not the issue. Rather, the difficulty emerges in the use of a positive-negative, good-bad value judgment framework in relation to the race-linked colors. The net effect of this circumstance is that it does not allow people to clearly see and appreciate the uniqueness, value, and worth of each person. In consciousness-energy vibrational terms, the person is not consciously resonating with the spiritual energy or soul of those they consider to be the other.

In accord with many spiritual traditions and psychics, I earlier outlined basic colors of the aura as they appear in what is known as the frequency spectrum of the electromagnetic fields, or the range of visible light that currently people can see with their eyes (see Table 2). From lowest to highest vibrations, these colors are known as red, orange, yellow, green, blue, indigo, and violet (ultraviolet).

As I suggested, in terms of consciousness-energy vibrational levels and the chakras, a person's aura and the related colors consist of seven major levels or layers of energy. I have also alluded to the idea that the first three layers of a person's aura are closely aligned with the person's body (the person's physical energy), that the outer three layers of a person's aura are closely aligned with the person's spiritual essence, and that the middle or fourth layer connects a person's spiritual essence and the human body.

As the gift of the visible aura emerges more into humanity's *conscious experience*, people will learn that, beyond skin color, each person's aura has its own unique pattern of colors, size, texture, density, and shape. Also, while there may be a basic pattern, a person's aura also changes with the person's state of mind and life experiences.

Many people already know that colors can have a significant impact on their moods. What people will learn is that their moods can also have significant impact on the colors of their auras, and that their moods are highly connected to whether or not their thoughts or beliefs are helping or hindering the natural flow of the archetypal energies in their aural field and life spaces. This kind of *conscious awareness* can serve as a new framework, then, for allowing people to clearly see and appreciate each person they encounter, including those they consider to be members of other races.

Many people will be tempted to construct various meanings for the colors of the aura. Indeed, there are already various general meanings that currently exist in various spiritual teachings and esoteric writings (see Pamela Oslie's *Life Colors: What the Colors in Your Aura Reveal*, 2000).

What I suggest, therefore, is that if the meanings are used in dogmatic ways or good-bad terms, people may find their outer self recreating the same kind of lower self race games that I have discussed. It is for this reason, therefore, that I recommend that people focus on their higher soul qualities for the meanings of the color in their auras, and that people focus on the extent to which these soul qualities are allowed manifestation and authentic expression in their life spaces. In other words, I am recommending that people focus on their archetypal energies as they are mirrored by the colors in their auras.

The gift of the visible aura, then, will allow a person and others to more efficiently understand their own and others' archetypal energies and more efficiently understand how the person's own outer self and the outer self of others may be allowing or hindering the manifestation and expression of various archetypal energies in their respective life spaces. With such awareness and understanding, a person can more efficiently evolve the *human race game*.

The Maturation of Consciousness Through "Spiritualizing" the Material World and "Soul Linking"

In accord with the soul-centered model, as a person manifests and gives unique form and authentic expression to various archetypal energies, they will also begin to notice their consciousness expanding and maturing. And, a person will begin to understand that these archetypal energies are *underpinnings* for spiritualizing the material world.

The evolutionary idea here is that as a person's consciousness matures, they will experience a greater sense of group consciousness and begin to explore the multidimensional nature of their self, guided and nurtured by their archetypal energies. To some people, however, such an idea may not even seem evolutionary, for they have been experimenting with their sense of vibrational connectedness to source energy/spirit or All-That-Is for some time, as it is understood.

What may feel more evolutionary, then, is the idea that somehow this kind of expansion and maturation of consciousness spiritualizes the material world by raising to a higher frequency the energy vibrations of a person's environment and by enabling the person to more efficiently engage in what has been called soul linking. As this happens, therefore, people will be evolving the human race game.

I earlier discussed how truer self consciousness is emerging into physicality and how the archetypal energies can play an important role in structuring harmonious relationships. What I want to add here is that it is each person's truer self consciousness that will give rise to spiritualizing the material world. That is, as I have implied earlier and in accord with the soul-centered model, consciousness precedes manifestation, so to speak, and not the other way around.

As a person's truer self consciousness then emerges, resonates with, and embodies their archetypal energies (their soul qualities), the person also will be raising to a higher frequency the vibrations of their material form, their physical body, and the physical environment. Further, the person will be radiating these higher vibrations (soul qualities) to others and to their own environment and be open to receiving similar vibrations (soul qualities) from others and the material world. In other words, the person will be spiritualizing their current racial form and their material world and resonating with the authentic spiritual essence of others and the material world.

I understand that some people may have difficulty with this evolutionary idea, and may require a different framework, a more scientific framework, for what I am describing. And so, in accord with what is called the new physics, I will offer a brief reference to what some scientists know as string/M-theory to explain in metaphorical terms, and to some extent literal terms, the maturation of consciousness through spiritualizing the material world, and the implications for evolving the human race game.

However, in order to create a context for this brief reference to string/M-theory, first I will call attention to what some have called pioneering scientific research involving the effect of thought and emotion on matter. This ongoing, groundbreaking research provides some scientific evidence that what people think and feel impacts the molecular structure of the material world. By implication, such research would validate that the vibrational frequency of higher or more spiritually-focused thoughts and emotions can alter the vibrational frequency of the material world or can spiritualize the material world.

More specifically, the pioneering scientific evidence to which I refer involves some thought-emotion impact research in Japan and Russia. In Japan, for example, a scientist known as Dr. Masaru Emoto (see Dr. Emoto's books, *The Hidden Messages in Water* and *Messages from Water and the Universe*; also see the movie, "What the Bleep Do We Know") developed a technique using a very powerful microscope in a very cold room along with high-speed photography to photograph newly formed crystals of frozen water samples.

Dr. Emoto found that crystals formed in frozen water reveal changes when specific, concentrated thoughts are directed toward them. That is, he found that water from clear springs and water that is exposed to loving words show what can be described as brilliant, complex, and colorful snowflake patters. In contrast, polluted water and water exposed to so-called negative thoughts form what can be described as incomplete, asymmetrical patterns with dull colors.

By producing different focused intentions, therefore, through written and spoken words and music and literally presenting it to the same water samples, the water appears to change its form or expression. In his lectures in Japan, Europe, and the United States, Dr. Emoto has conducted live experiments in which he has continued to demonstrate how indeed a person's thoughts, attitudes, and emotions deeply impact their environment.

In Russia, other water-related research by a scientist, Dr. Konstantin Korotko, has provided some additional scientific evidence of the impact of thought and emotions on matter. In one experiment, for example, what he would call two Kirlian Aura images of similar drops of water were used, one of which was "charged" by a famous Russian healer, Allan Chumak, during ten minutes of conscious concentration.

Using modern Kirlian equipment to quantify the effects in terms of the influence of the charge on what is known as the electro-photonic glow or aura, the bio-charged water was found to have a more than thirty times stronger aura vibration. It was also found that the physical and biological properties of the bio-charged water were altered.

As is known, about seventy percent of the environment on Earth is water, and the physical body is also about three-quarters water. If a person's thoughts, then, can impact water, imagine, therefore, how people are currently impacting the material environment and their own physical bodies, and perhaps others', with their current thoughts and emotions. Imagine also how people could spiritualize the material environment and their physical bodies as human beings if they were to allow the free flow of the archetypal energies and give them authentic expression in framing their thoughts, attitudes, and emotions.

In broader terms, to further use a scientific framework, I will expand, at this point, this discussion to briefly refer to what is called string/M-theory. According to string/M-theory, as scientists currently talk about energy and physicality, the elementary ingredients of the universe, as it is understood, are not zero-dimensional point particles, but rather are tiny, one-dimensional filaments somewhat like infinitely thin rubber bands, vibrating to and fro (see Brian Greene's *The Elegant Universe*, 2003).

In string/M-theory, it is the basic interactions between the vibrating strings that build up the physical processes with which people are familiar. In accord with M-theory, therefore, arising from these vibrating strings are what physicists now think are at least eleven "spacetime" dimensions, ten dimensions involving space and one dimension involving time. In this context, spacetime, so-called for the union of space and time that emerges from what Einstein called special relativity (i.e., Einstein's laws of space and time in the absence of gravity), may be viewed as the fabric out of which the universe is fashioned, the dynamic arena within which the events in the manifested universe take place.

In a manner of speaking, then, physicists have, to some extent, scientifically demonstrated and have now come to suspect that all matter and forces (i.e., gravity, electromagnetic, strong, weak) arise from one basic ingredient: oscillating strings. And, physicists, based on string/M-theory, are also now exploring the idea of multidimensionality and have even postulated the possibility of a "multiverse" (e.g., John Gribbin's *In Search of the Multiverse*, 2010).

It is the tiny strings, then, whose vibrational patterns seem to orchestrate the evolution of the cosmos that have often led scientists to use metaphors of music to understand the harmonies of nature. Such metaphors, however, have been used through the ages, as they are understood. Even Pythagoras, for example, spoke of the "music of the spheres." Scientists, therefore, are learning a great deal about the nature of energy as objects and what might be called the vibrating feeling-tones of the universe, as they are physically manifested as objects, time, and space, and as objects in time and space.

I understand that scientists currently have many unanswered questions related to string/M-theory and that indeed the name M-theory has been used to refer to many things—Mystery Theory, Mother of All Theory, and Membrane Theory, for example. The brief reference here, therefore, is not intended to provide full answers, but rather is intended to give guidance for understanding the relationship between spirit and matter.

I am suggesting that both spirit and matter are aspects of the same source energy vibrations. In a manner of speaking, spirit may be viewed as consciousness-energy whose strings vibrate at a higher frequency level, currently beyond the range of the visible light spectrum with which people are currently familiar. Matter, on the other hand, may be viewed as consciousness-energy whose strings vibrate at a lower frequency level well within the range of the visible light spectrum with which people are currently familiar. Also, as I have noted earlier, I am suggesting that consciousness is the inside of energy and energy is the outside of consciousness, both sharing each other's properties but not reducible to each other (see T. J. Chalko's "Is Chance or Choice the essence of Nature?", *NU Journal of Discovery*, 2001. An insight into the Physics of Consciousness in light of recent advances in quantum computing and GDV research).

Scientists, therefore, will continue to find elusive a "Theory of Everything" as long as the phenomenon of consciousness is viewed as a derivative of matter, and not the other way around. While it is laudable that consciousness studies have become a legitimate focus for scientific inquiry as it relates to physicality (e.g., Istvan Czigler & Istvan Winkler's *Unconscious Memory Representations in Perception: Processes and Mechanisms in the Brain*, 2010; Greg Janzen's *The Reflexive Nature of Consciousness*, 2008; Rita Carter's *Exploring Consciousness*, 2004), the current focus of most studies has been on the mind as a derivative of the functions of the chemical processes of the brain, the material mechanism. However, by what physicists know as the law of symmetry in the universe, I am suggesting that consciousness is the invisible or inside ingredient in symmetry with physicality.

Some biological glimpses into this perspective are beginning to be explored. In biological terms, for example, some scientists are exploring the pre-causal role of consciousness in relation to matter, molecular biology, and quantum physics. The exploration relates to how all the cells in a person's body are affected by the person's thoughts and emotions, and how the person's thoughts and beliefs affect their health (e.g., Bruce Lipton's *The Biology of Belief: Understanding the Power of Consciousness, Matter, and Miracles*, 2008.)

It might be helpful, then, to think of consciousness metaphorically, and to some extent literally, as a "blinking unit of awareness," an awareness unit of source energy/spirit or All-That-Is that can take many spiritual and material forms. That is, consciousness as an *awareness unit* of source energy does not blink off and on, but rather blinks in and out of the spacetime continuum that scientists have been exploring.

Each awareness unit, or what I earlier called a CU (consciousness unit), also has its own unique aspects and qualities as it exists in the inner world and the outer world. Each awareness unit thus uniquely contributes to the whole at both the tiniest levels and the largest levels of existence, inside and outside the spacetime continuum. In other terms, I suggest that a person's unique consciousness blinks in and out of the spacetime continuum each night as the person moves into their dream realities and then reawakes in the morning to the physical world with which the person is familiar.

In accord with string/M-theory, consider the possibility that the specific archetypal energies of which I have spoken exist as universal vibrational feeling-tones in a spaceless and timeless inner world, or more precisely in an ever-emerging state of "now." Consider also that as the vibrations of these archetypal energies slow to the frequency of the light spectrum, as it is understood, they naturally and will increasingly blink into the outer world of physicality, time, and space as universal strings. In turn, in accord with the soul-centered model, they will begin to raise the vibrations of the material form. Consciousness or awareness units would direct this process, thus allowing the person's truer self consciousness to emerge into physicality.

A person's truer self consciousness, their spiritually integrated self, therefore, brings together their inner and outer worlds. Indeed, what is called enlightenment implies that the blinking of a person's physically-focused consciousness has quickened to the highest frequency of the light spectrum such that the authentic energy essence of the outside and the inside come together to create the experience of oneness.

It is this process, then, that can spiritualize the material world and allow a person to more efficiently and authentically resonate with the soul qualities of others. It is this process that will allow a person to more efficiently and authentically soul link with others on inner and outer levels in a naturally interdependent manner.

It is fair to say that many techniques have emerged that may assist people in establishing a more efficient and authentic connection to their inner world and to soul link with others in the inner and outer worlds (e.g., guided imagery; time warp visualization; various forms of meditation; Journaling; past life therapy; color therapy; out-of-body or OBE techniques; intuitive techniques; dream work; work with psychics and channelers; ChiGong energizing techniques; aura imaging photography; and the like).

If, for example, a person photographed their aura before and after doing a ChiGong session, they will notice that the colors of their aura change, as the focus of their consciousness energizes the aura. In accord with the soul-centered model, it is the focus of a person's consciousness, therefore, that can alter the biochemistry of that person's brain and the quality of the person's brainwaves that get emitted. It is the focus of a person's consciousness that can alter the nature and color of the energy waves in the person's aura. And, it is the focus of a person's consciousness that can energize the strings of the person's material world and allow the person's outer self to be more open to soul linking with others as auras authentically touch in physicality.

What then are the implications of the above framework for evolving the human race game? One implication is that a person and those they consider members of other races, as well as the physical environment, are all made from the same string stuff.

The Human Genome Project has provided humanity with a much-needed perspective in this regard. When people truly understand that they, others, and everything around them are made of the same string stuff, people will also truly understand the old saying which states that "What you do to others, you are doing to yourself."

If a person does not want to entertain self-destructive thoughts or to engage in self-destructive behaviors, then first the person would love their self. Next, the person would treat those they consider members of other races the way they would treat the self that they love. The person would additionally know that when they do harm to their self, they also are doing harm to others.

While the latter statement may sound strange, I again am simply referencing each person's interdependence with others as made of the same stuff, while still being uniquely one's self. Therefore, I suggest that each person be kind to their self and to those they consider to be members of other races.

Another implication of the above framework for evolving the human race game is that, as scientists continue to probe physicality at micro and macro levels, they will begin to further theorize about the multidimensional nature of the universe. By implication and in accord with the soul-centered model, they will also begin to theorize about the multidimensional nature of consciousness and the multidimensional nature of the self. It will be in this context that "time" will be more fully understood as a circular event, which allows consciousness as an awareness unit to create and to blink in and out of various forms as it gives rise to and resonates with various qualities of string vibrations.

It will be in this context that a person will be able to understand that their current racial form is only one form, albeit an important and highly valued form, of their multidimensional self. Indeed, as implied in the soul-centered model, a person's multidimensional self has had other racial forms in accord with the linear concept that is currently called reincarnation.

It is in this context that the veil between the inner and outer worlds will thin. In accord with the soul-centered model, a person will become more open to other aspects of their self or past lives, which also continue to evolve in so-called alternate times and spaces.

This latter perspective, however, is beyond the current purpose and focus of this book (see Steve Rother and the Group's *Re-Member: A Handbook for Human Evolution*, 2000, & *Welcome Home: The New Planet Earth*, 2002). I reference it here only to introduce the possibility for a more expanded notion of a person's sense of self.

A grander implication of the above framework for evolving the *human race game* is that, with this kind of framework, a person's consciousness and the material world will resonate with and *mirror* events, acts, behaviors, attitudes, programs, policies, laws, personal dramas, societal dramas, cultural dramas, and global dramas in accord with the archetypal energies.

Imagine, then, how the human race game would look, be acted out, and be experienced by each person's outer self in various life spaces, if it was played in alignment with the universal strings of trust, enthusiasm, humor, beauty, hope, flexibility, courage, love, acceptance, inclusion, harmony, understanding, truth, wisdom, patience, inspiration, abundance, compassion, peace, joy, clarity, vision, oneness, unity, and serenity. When each person's truer self consciousness energizes and spiritualizes the material world with such qualities, each person will be evolving the human race game.

EMERGING PATTERNS OF INTERDEPENDENCE RELATED TO HUMANITY'S NEXT EVOLUTIONARY STEP: IMPLICATIONS FOR EVOLVING THE HUMAN RACE GAME

The discussion now moves to a brief look at various emerging patterns that people may notice which signal humanity's next evolutionary step and which have implications for evolving the human race game. While there are a number of patterns that could be identified which have implications for evolving the human race game, I will briefly focus on only three of these patterns.

The three patterns contain and reflect authentic energy essences for impacting the global experience of the human race game. The three patterns relate to what are called the global economy, the Internet, and the reemergence of an interest in the soul and reincarnation or the mind-body-spirit connection.

Each of the three emerging patterns create a focus on the nature of the interdependence of human beings and, hence, a focus on the importance of evolving a mature group consciousness as human beings. In accord with the soul-centered model, beyond what a person may think of as various races, is human being-ness. Human being-ness is a group consciousness-energy that connects all human beings on the planet.

Carl Jung, a noted psychologist, alludes to humanity's collective *inner state* of being-ness, which he called the Collective Unconscious. I am suggesting, however, that humanity also has an *outer state* of collective being-ness, and that the evolving patterns are intended to help people understand the Collective Consciousness in the outer, vibrational world.

INTERDEPENDENCE THROUGH A "GLOBAL ECONOMY"

What is now called the global economy is a *mirror effect* for how people individually and collectively resonate with particular archetypal energies that flow through their personal and collective energy systems. As each person has a personal energy system which processes the flow or regulates the economy of archetypal energies, people also have collective energy systems at various expanding levels of collective human existence that function in a similar fashion.

The collective energy systems emerge in as small a unit as two people and in as large a unit as the collective entity of humanity. At a societal level, a person experiences the collective energy systems in accord with the entities known as families, friendships, networks, organizations, neighborhoods, communities, towns, cities, and nations.

More specifically, then, the global economy, as can be understood, is a mirror effect for how each person resonates with and acts out particular archetypal energies. The relevant archetypal energies are those processed through the head center (abundance, compassion, peace, joy, clarity, vision) and the naval center (enthusiasm, humor, beauty, hope) in connection with the heart center (love, acceptance, inclusion, harmony) at individual and collective levels in various personal, societal, and global life spaces. In a manner of speaking, therefore, the extent to which a person helps or hinders the flow of these particular archetypal energies through their personal and collective energy systems impacts the interdependent state of the global economy.

What is important to understand here, as I have suggested earlier, is that a person's beliefs affect how open or closed the person is to their archetypal energies. The person's beliefs help or hinder the flow of the archetypal energies through their personal and collective energy systems. To change the nature of various lack-of-abundance dramas in people's individual and collective life spaces, then, all persons directly and indirectly connected to the dramas need to examine and alter those beliefs that are limiting.

What are your beliefs about money, for example? Do you believe that there is a scarcity of money in the world, that is, not enough money in the world for everyone? Do you believe that money is the root of all evil? Do you believe that you can only be happy if you have lots of money? Do you believe it is not possible to be happy *and* have lots of money at the same time? Do you believe that only the rich get richer and the poor get poorer? Do you believe that you are primarily a victim of the state of the economy—local, national, and/or global? Do you believe that the so-called poor are in this position because of a lack of character or a lack of will to work? Do you believe that money has nothing to do with energy?

If a person answers "yes" to any of the above questions, then they are using a self-limiting belief in an interdependent manner as they relate to money and abundance in their three life spaces. Each of the above questions is related to two general self-limiting core beliefs that people, individually and collectively, are currently using to structure their economic worlds: the belief in scarcity and the belief in lack (or more specifically, a belief in the lack of energy).

Therefore, if answering yes to any of the above questions, it is important to be aware that the people are contributing at both individual and collective levels to the creation of energy blocks as they relate to the reflection of abundance in the global economy. The people are hindering the natural flow of particular archetypal energies that can transform their lack-of-abundance dramas, dramas that are acted out and mirrored as an imbalanced reflection in the global economy.

As people open individually and collectively to the particular archetypal energies that I have identified, they will then co-create a global economy that *mirrors abundance*, not lack. Indeed, people's interdependence and the immediate impact of their economic beliefs and the focus of their consciousness are *mirrored* daily by what happens in the various stock markets.

Individually and collectively, people's economic beliefs and the focus of their consciousness generate vibrational fields of emotional energy that move in an interdependent manner to influence their abundance dramas. A recommendation, therefore, is to seek to create abundance dramas that are generated from and are carried out in the context of, with a focus on, and with the spirit of mutual empowerment.

It is important, however, to seek to create one's own abundance first so that one will be empowered as she or he assists others interdependently in co-creating their abundance. Indeed, with practice, people may discover that the real challenge will not be how to create abundance, but rather what to do with it once they have created it at individual and collective levels.

Money as a Reflection of Energy and a Recommendation to Use the Archetypal Energies to Enhance the Global Economy

In accord with the soul-centered model, it is important to realize that what is called money is nothing more than a reflection of energy. Indeed, for the most part, humanity has reduced what is called money to individual and collective agreements, values, and meanings that have been given to electrical currents, pieces of paper, and various kinds and shapes of metals. These agreements, values, and meanings, however, are not static, but are in motion as they accurately reflect the natural flow of energy.

It is important to recognize then that human beings, individually and collectively, are the co-creators of the games for how they attract, repel, and play with money, and for how they co-create its reflection in various life spaces. Individually and collectively, these co-creations flow from beliefs about money and abundance in accord with the universal energy laws. The state of the global economy, therefore, will always show a reflection, a mirror effect, of the interdependent flow of money in the world and where that flow is and is not being blocked by the nature of humanity's beliefs, individually and collectively.

I, therefore, recommend the following interdependent framework to enhance and enrich the state of the global economy. First, it is important for people to allow the self to thoughtfully frame individual and collective economic dramas by believing in the archetypal energies abundance, compassion, peace, joy, clarity and vision.

Second, as people act out their economic dramas, it is important that they do so with a sense of enthusiasm, humor, and hope and with a focus on creating beauty in their individual and collective life spaces. It is important that people dare to passionately engage their economic dramas with this kind of sense and focus.

And third, as people's economic dramas unfold, flow, and move, it is important to allow them to do so while maintaining an inner and outer focus, in the heart, on a spirit of love, acceptance, inclusion, and harmony. As people frame their individual and collective economic dramas in this manner, they will, therefore, co-create win-win economic dramas. They will enhance and enrich the global economy. And, they will be evolving the human race game.

INTERDEPENDENCE THROUGH THE INTERNET MIRRORING AN "INNER-NET"

One of the most significant technological advances that mirror interdependence and collective group consciousness as human beings is the Internet. The Internet and the world wide web, as it is understood, are also mirror effects for how people at individual and collective levels resonate with and act out other archetypal energies.

The relevant archetypal energies are processed through the power center (flexibility, courage) and the throat center (understanding, truth, wisdom, patience, inspiration) in connection with the heart center (love, acceptance, inclusion, harmony). And, since people have free will, the Internet dramas have reflected how people have both facilitated and misdirected (blocked) these particular archetypal energies.

Every second, therefore, people create countless dramas in cyberspace and cybertime, individually and collectively. People also give immeasurable expression to and communicate countless beliefs, attitudes, thoughts, and emotions to each other in countless forms and images on the Internet. In a manner of speaking, then, people's experience of a collective consciousness on the Internet is one reflection of the nature and quality of interdependence in the outer, vibrational world.

A METAPHORICAL COMPARISON OF THE INTERNET AND THE INNER-NET: A SPIRITUAL AND SOUL-CENTERED PERSPECTIVE

Metaphorically, in a person's outer world, the Internet mirrors what happens in the person's inner world through what I will call the *Inner-net.* That is, while all is available to everyone and there is instantaneous communication, it is the focus of the person's consciousness and their thoughts and intentions that frame the person's inner and outer realities.

In accord with the soul-centered model, what I am calling the inner-net refers to one way of characterizing the vibrational nature of communication in the inner world. The communication is instantaneous, as one might understand it. That is, a person's higher self instantaneously connects the person with the inner realms of source energy/spirit or All-That-Is.

In the outer world, however, since the Internet has and will continue to take root in the collective consciousness as a reflection of interdependence, I want to present a metaphorical picture here. People might find this metaphorical picture useful as they seek to constructively use and to creatively explore the potentials of the Internet and the inner-net for evolving the human race game.

In the Table that I have outlined (see Table 7), I have highlighted, in metaphorical terms, a number of ways that the Internet and the inner-net *mirror* one another and the nature of

Table 7. A Metaphorical Comparison of the Internet and the Inner-net: A Spiritual and Soul-centered Perspective

The Internet	The Inner-Net
1. Vibrationally, connections on the Internet are made in "cyberspace"	1. Vibrationally, connections in the Inner-net are made in "inner space," or "synchronistic space" (outside of physical space)
2. The Internet operates in "cyber-time" (past, present, & future can be artificially constructed at the same time)	2. The Inner-net operates in what has been called "simultaneous time" or "Psi Time" (past, present, & future operate simultaneously)
3. The Internet requires programming	3. The Inner-net is "programmed" by beliefs, attitudes, & ideas (your core beliefs)
4. You use "key words" to vibrationally "access" what you want on the Internet	4. You use "affirmations" vibrationally as "key words" to "access" & create ("magnetically draw") what you want throught the Inner-net
5. Your experience on the Internet requires *conscious action*, but it can be impacted by "viruses"	5. Your experience in the Inner-net requires conscious action, though it can "resonate" to Unconscious & Subconscious "viruses" in the form of "false beliefs"
6. As a mechanistic form, the Internet operate in accord with the law of cause and effect	6. As a Spiritual and Soul-centered form, the Inner-net operates in accord with Universal Energy Laws, only one of which is the law of consequences
7. The underlying Energy for "movement" on the Internet is conceived of as electronic	7. The underlying Energy for "movement" in the Inner-net may be conceived of as "thought," which has been said to have electromagnetic properties
8. The Internet requires a mechanism called a computer, smart phone, IPAD, etc., the hardware, and you operate it with your Consciousness	8. In Physical Reality, the Inner-net requires a physical mechanism called your "biocomputer," or the brain as a hologram (your Spiritual and Soul-centered hardware) and you operate it with Consciousness

9.	"Chips," "ICloud," etc. are used in relation to the Internet to process & store information	9. From a Spiritual and Soul-centered perspective, information in the Inter-net can be said to be processed & stored in what some have called the Akashic Record
10.	The Internet requires a tool, "the browser," with the capability to "read" & translate information	10. From a Spiritual and Soul-centered perspective, the Observer Self, the quiet aspect of the Mind, is the agent of Consciousness that allows you to see what is going on in the Inner-Net (as well as out-side) without the distortion of the analytic Mind or the static inter-ference of emotional reaction
11.	The Internet requires you to use a "server" to "search out," "connect to," & "open up" relevant sets of data and "show you" the "appro-priate" information that you requested	11. From a Spiritual and Soul-centered perspective, your Higher Self acts as your "server" in the Inner-net to "search out," "connect to" & "open-up" relevant information from Source Energy/Spirit or All That Is or Universal Mind and to "mirror" the results in symbolic or real terms
12.	You can participate in "chat rooms" on the Internet to create experiences	12. From a Spiritual and Soul-centered perspective, "the dream state" may be viewed as your "chat rooms" in the Inner-net for creat-ing & manifesting experiences
13.	Communication transcends "the physical" in terms of two or more people having to be in the same time &/or space	13. From a Spiritual and Soul-centered perspective, communica-tion transcends "the physical" in terms of two or more people not requiring any time or space
14.	When there is an overload of information or a miscue, the Internet may "crash"	14. There may be what might be called Energy "jams" or "spasms" in the Inner-net that could lead to "dis-ease"
15.	Reality exists in relation to the Internet on a physical monitor & in the Mind of the perceiver; Reality in relation to the Internet thus requires cooperation & is interdependent	15. Reality exists in the Mind in the Inner-net (the Universal Mind); Reality in relation to the Inner-net requires cooperation & is interdependent

16.	"Visual props" are used on the Internet to capture & focus your attention	16.	"Visuallization" is used for the Inner-net to focus your attention & intent & thoughts & propel them from your Inner World, the Inner-net, to your Outer World; the stronger your emotions are, the more rapidly you create what you are thinking about; your intent acts to direct your thoughts & emotions, maintaining a steady focus on what you want until you get it.
17.	You decide what you want on the Internet & "pull it up"	17.	You decide what you want through the Inner-net & pull or draw it toward you" (vibrationally attract it); your thoughts set up the model of what is to be created, & your emotions energize your thoughts
18.	Garbage In, Garbage Out	18.	Fuzzy thoughts, fuzzy results

interdependence. Each of the items that I have identified has implications for evolving the *human race game.*

Applied specifically to race relations, for example, as people demonstrate increased flexibility and courage to engage in various kinds of Internet activities that reflect understanding, truth, wisdom, patience, and inspiration in regard to racial matters, they will be creating an enhanced context for and will be nurturing the evolution of interracial connections and interracial dramas that will mirror love, acceptance, inclusion, and harmony in their life spaces.

For example, some people connect in cyberspace and cyber-time as "interracial cyber-pals" (e.g., Facebook) or for various interracial collaborative enterprises. As people continue to do so, they will be mirroring, to some extent, in the outer world their natural spiritual family connections. In accord with the soul-centered model, these connections exist in the inner world in what can be called synchronistic inner space and simultaneous time.

These connections, therefore, transcend people's current racial forms, as they are understood.

I simply suggest that the items I have provided in the Table be reviewed. As readers do so, I suggest that each reviewer use their imagination to create a clear picture in their mind for the inner-net and how it works.

In each person's personal life space, I suggest that the person use their picture of the inner-net during various encounters with those they consider to be from a different race to remind them of their interdependence. In each person's societal and global life spaces, I suggest that each person use their picture of the inner-net to guide the focus of their consciousness toward viewing and co-creating constructive interdependent enterprises with those they consider others from a different race.

In other words, I suggest that people use their pictures of the inner-net to assist them in more fully comprehending the various ways that they are connected interdependently across so-called racial lines. As they do so, each person will be evolving the human race game.

People will find that the effect of using their pictures of the inner-net to specifically and generally evolve the human race game will be mirrored on the Internet, as well as through other events, activities, and interracial and human relationship dramas. In this regard, there are and will be no accidents.

INTERDEPENDENCE THROUGH THE RE-EMERGENCE OF AN INTEREST IN THE SOUL AND REINCARNATION OR AN "AUTHENTIC" MIND-BODY-SPIRIT CONNECTION

In accord with the soul-centered model, evolving the human race game is part of a larger spiritual and soul-centered interdependence game that the greater entity known as humanity has undertaken. That larger interdependent game, as I have suggested, is about what may be called the evolution of consciousness and its various energy manifestations. It is an interdependent game in which a person participates at an individual level primarily by engaging in an ever-evolving and ever-exploratory self-creation process.

In other terms, the larger interdependent game is about how a person's soul can and will come into the person's current life spaces. It is in this context that there have been and will continue to be for a time, as it is understood, many creative ways of mirroring what I am calling a reemergence of an interest in the soul and reincarnation or an authentic mind-body-spirit connection.

To some extent, then, the stated interest represents the mirror effects for how people are resonating with and acting out the particular archetypal energies that are processed through the root center (trust) and the crown center (oneness, unity, serenity) in connection with the heart center (love, acceptance, inclusion, harmony). The implication here is that a person's greatest feeling of trust and security on the physical plane primarily emerges, in the final analysis, when the person recognizes their interdependence or a sense of oneness and unity with others.

I purposefully have used the term reemergence here for people's current collective interest in consciousness (an authentic mind-body-spirit connection) and reincarnation. Such an interest has been present in the past on numerous occasions in a variety of forms and contexts.

The interest was there, for example, during the early time periods of Mu and Atlantis, as the periods are understood, when humanity's connection with spirit was not as veiled. This interest has been extended and reflected in the language of various myths and symbols (James Churchward's *The Lost Continent of Mu*, 2007; L. S. De Camp's *Lost Continents: The Atlantis Theme in History, Science, and Literature*, 1970). The interest can be found among what might be described as the early races of Africans,

Australians, Pacific Islanders and East Indians, the tribes of the
Americas, and ancient Europeans. In broader East-West terms,
the interest can be found in the religious views among groups
called Hindu, Buddhist, Taoist, Egyptian, Persian, Jewish, early
and later Christian, and the Islamic tradition.

In truth, then, the interest in an authentic mind-body-spirit
connection and reincarnation has always been present at individual and collective levels of humanity. However, it has sometimes
been deemphasized for various reasons in humanity's evolution.
The current reemergence, therefore, is simply a reemphasis and
a reaffirmation of what has been called the Eternal Validity of
the Soul. In various cultures today, then, it is not unusual to hear
people once again legitimizing the soul aspect of the self.

In Western cultures, and the United States in particular, the
use of the term soul is becoming more commonplace. Not too
long ago, the primary group in American society labeled as having soul was African Americans (e.g., soul music; soul food).
While African American culture, out of necessity, managed to
maintain many aspects of the energy nature of the soul, those
aspects are currently being reflected and expanded across many of
the so-called cultural barriers in the present-day society.

The transcendences of cross-cultural barriers mirror what
appears to be a reemergence of an interest in an authentic mind-
body-spirit connection. In conversation, for example, African
American slang phrases like "I feel you" and "vibing" can be
viewed at other levels of the larger culture as mirroring an alternate and more inner sense of connecting vibrationally.

In terms of the idea of reincarnation as reflected in the
Western tradition, one may want to examine how this idea was
dealt with during the Greek and Roman empires, the Middle
Ages, the period of the Renaissance and Reformation, the Age of
Shakespeare, the period of eighteenth-century Enlightenment,
the period of Eastern and Transcendental influences in the nine-
teenth century, the Age of Transition in the twentieth century,

and the Theosophical movement. One will find various philosophers, scientists, psychologists, doctors, and religious figures that actually sought to explore and to legitimize the idea of reincarnation (e.g., Joseph Head & S. L. Cranston's *Reincarnation: The Phoenix Fire Mystery*, 1994).

Indeed, the major religions actually affirm the idea of reincarnation, albeit in different and sometimes subtle ways. In Christianity, for example, the idea of reincarnation is affirmed through its focus on an anticipated drama known as the Second Coming. However, as there is much more to this drama, which is beyond the current focus of this discussion, I recommend that people pursue additional spiritual and soul-centered information on this Christian drama in accord with their interests (e.g., see Jane Roberts' *Seth Speaks*, 1972).

In other terms, the great spiritual shifts in consciousness for humanity through the ages, as they are understood, have been brought forth, in a manner of speaking, by the metamorphosis of various great personalities on the planet. Some of the great personalities include, for example, Lao Tsu, Jesus, and Buddha. Through the metamorphosis of their unique mind-body-spirit connection, each of these great personalities became aware of what I earlier referred to as infinite soul and therefore provided spiritual teachings in regard to their particular level of understanding.

I am suggesting, however, that with the reemergence of humanity's interest in the Soul, another Spiritual shift in Consciousness is at play such that individually each person's own unique and authentic mind-body-spirit connection is undergoing a metamorphosis in order to become more aligned with their greater self, their soul. In turn, each person's metamorphosis in their unique life spaces will result in a metamorphosis of the larger group consciousness of humanity.

People's reinvigorated interest in an authentic mind-body-spirit connection has been mirrored in many ways. Many people, for example, have been and are exploring and enhancing their psychic and intuitive abilities (e.g., Dr. Hans Holzer's *Are You Psychic?-Unlocking The Power Within*, 1997) and have been and are experimenting with altered states of consciousness (e.g., Stanislav Grof's *The Cosmic Game: Explorations of the Frontiers of Human Consciousness*, 1998).

There have been numerous self-help books written which deal with the soul and how to affirm and nurture one's greater self and vice versa (e.g., Thomas Moore's *Care Of The Soul*, 1998; Gary Zukav's *The Seat Of The Soul*, 1990). There also have been many how-to books written that deal with what is called channeling (e.g., Vywamus, Channeled by Barbara Burns' *Channelling: Evolutionary Exercises For Channels*, 1997; Sonaya Roman & Duane Packer's *Opening To Channel: How To Connect With Your Guide*, 1993), and meeting and working with spirit guides and angels (e.g., Ted Andrews' *How To Meet and Work with Spirit Guides*, 2006).

Further, a number of people have reported on what have been called their NDEs or near-death experiences, thus providing their spiritual insights (e.g., Raymond Moody & Elizabeth Kubler-Ross' *Life After Life: The Investigation of a Phenomenon-Survival of Bodily Death*, 2001; Evelyn Valarino's *Lessons from the Light: What We Can Learn from the Near-Death Experience*, 2006). Even though some neuroscientists attribute such NDE descriptions to changes in the biochemistry of the brain and have suggested that they can reproduce such near death-type experiences in the lab, the research focus of these scientists is nevertheless reflecting a reinvigorated interest in the soul (e.g., P.M.H Atwater's *The Big Book of Near Death Experiences: The Ultimate Guide to What Happens When We Die*, 2007; Vince Migliore's *A Measure of Heaven: Near-Death Experience Data Analysis*, 2009; Stephen H. Martin's *The Science of Life After Death: New Research Shows Human Consciousness Lives On*, 2009; Craig D. Murray's *Psychological Scientific Perspectives on Out-of-Body and Near-Death Experiences*, 2009; Janice Miner, Bruce Greyson, & Debbie

James' *The Handbook of Near-Death Experiences: Thirty Years of Investigation, 2009;* Pim van Lommel's *Consciousness Beyond Life: The Science of the Near-Death Experience,* 2011).

In other arenas, many psychologists and psychics have been dealing more with clients who now report having anomalous experiences and spiritual crises or breakthroughs (e.g., Matthew Smith's *Anomalous Experiences: Essays from Parapsychological and Psychological Perspectives,* 2009; Etzel Cardena, Steven Lynn, & Stanley Krippner's *Varieties of Anomalous Experience: Examining the Scientific Evidence,* 2004; Robert Bruce's *Astral Dynamics: The Complete Approach to Out-Of-Body Experiences,* 2012; William Buhlman's *Adventures Beyond the Body: How to Experience Out-Of-Body Travel,* 1996). Further, past-life therapy also has been legitimized as an appropriate form of assistance for people who are seeking to better understand their whole self and their current life purpose(s), to heal old wounds, or to release karmic entanglements (e.g., Dr. Linda Backman's *Bringing Your Soul to Light: Healing Through Past Lives and the Time Between,* 2009; Bryan Jameison's *The Search for Past Lives: Exploring Reincarnation's Mysteries, & The Amazing Power of Past-Life Therapy,* 2002; Rabia Clark's *Past Life Therapy-State of the Art,* 1996).

In terms of United States mainstream culture, in spring of 2008 national attention was given to the subject of past-life regression and past-life therapy by the well-known television personalities Oprah Winfrey and her friend Dr. Mehmet Oz. According to Wikipedia (2012), "in recent decades, many Europeans and North Americans have developed an interest in reincarnation. Contemporary films, books, and popular songs frequently mention reincarnation. In the last decades, academic researchers have begun to explore reincarnation and published reports of children's memories of earlier lives in peer-reviewed journals and books." And, as of 2012, there is a popular show on TV titled "Long Island Medium." Overall, then, the increased interest in an authentic mind-body-spirit connection and reincarnation has given rise to a variety of soul-centered experiences and a variety of approaches for evolving one's consciousness and expanding one's soul-centered sense.

Indeed, in reframing my own personal experience, it would appear that spiritual and soul-centered arrangements were made in 1975 for me to gain some insight into a few of my own relevant past lives. At the time, the ego aspect of myself was open and I allowed my outer self to be guided to a gifted psychic. Some of the relevant past lives revealed included, for example, an experience as spirit on the continent of Mu where I reportedly was in a leadership role; an experience during the second destruction of Atlantis where I reportedly was a visionary priest, eventually guiding some Atlanteans into pre-historic Egypt, carrying knowledge into Egypt and becoming a teacher as Atlanteans and Egyptians mingled together; an experience in Greece in an administrative role in Plato's Academy where I reportedly was gifted in science, math, and philosophy and wrote poetry; an experience in Spain during the Inquisition where I reportedly was a fanatical and dogmatic cardinal with the Catholic Church, persecuting those using scientific knowledge as a result of my misinterpreting a spiritual and mystical vision; a short rebalancing lifetime as a bright and sensitive woman in Scotland or Wales where I reportedly had several children; and an experience as a physician or doctor around the time of the French Revolution, where I reportedly became a revolutionary leader, working to overthrow the aristocracy and later becoming very disillusioned when Napoleon created his dictatorship. In this latter life, I subsequently became a very outspoken critic of Napoleon, my life was threatened, and I eventually went to Italy.

While it was revealed that I have had many, other past lives, both male and female, my predominant energy has been and is that of male. The relevant past lives that were revealed, therefore, provided me with insights into my various gifts for this incarnation and information about possible paths for enhancing my current life spaces.

Six Implications for Looking Anew at the Concept of the Self, One's "Current Racial Form," and the Human Race Game

What then are the implications, individually and collectively, of humanity's increased interest in the soul and reincarnation or the mind-body-spirit connection for evolving the human race game? In accord with the soul-centered model, I offer the following six notions for consideration, although I do not intend them to be exhaustive:

- With a spiritual and soul-centered perspective, the concept of self now expands to include the idea that the self a person knows, their *current racial form*, is only a portion, albeit a unique and highly loved portion, of the person's greater self, the person's soul, which has existed before in many racial forms and may exist again in other racial forms, as they are understood.

- In terms of soul perception, since time is experienced as simultaneous, circular or now, all people have been, are, and/or will be members of other races. Since a person's soul is also multidimensional, the person may discern that other aspects of their greater self and their spiritual family also may exist currently in other racial forms.

- From a spiritual and soul-centered perspective, a person's current thoughts, feelings, and racial contacts are mirrors into their soul or reincarnated aspects of the person's human experience. What a person thinks about so-called other races, then, are their own projections, aspects of the person's self.

- From a spiritual and soul-centered perspective, when a person encounters someone from another race and the person holds negative attitudes and feelings, they are actually holding negative attitudes and feelings about aspects of their own greater experience. When a person discriminates, either *consciously* or *unconsciously*, against someone of another race, they are in effect discriminating against aspects of their own greater experience. Therefore, in the broadest sense, racial prejudice and racial discrimination are misguided forms of greater self-hatred, which must be examined and released.

- When a person's fears are misdirected toward someone of another race, they are in effect, fearing aspects of their own greater experience. From a spiritual and soul-centered perspective, then, when a person alternately thinks and acts in affirming ways toward someone of another race, without fear, they are in effect embracing aspects of their own greater experience. In the broadest sense, therefore, truer self-acceptance means racial acceptance or the acceptance of one's greater self, one's soul, in all of its racial forms.

- From a spiritual and soul-centered perspective, when a person recognizes that their own existence includes membership with other races, they will be less tempted to look down upon an individual from another race.

At this point in the discussion, I simply want to suggest once again that one of the purposes of the human race game on the planet is to give the greater self, one's higher self, one's soul, the opportunity to play, to learn, and to grow by engaging various aspects of the human experience. Such a game, therefore, allows one's soul to see and to experience the physical world from different angles.

However, because people have free will, a great deal of energy for playing the human race game has been misdirected, focused primarily on growth with pain. Therefore, I have been recommending ways to evolve the human race game by focusing now on growth with joy in accord with the original intention. Many tools already have and are continuing to emerge to assist humanity in this regard.

EMERGING TOOLS
AND OPPORTUNITIES
FOR EVOLVING
THE HUMAN RACE GAME

I will briefly refer to several tools that have and are emerging to assist humanity in experiencing an enhanced mind-body-spirit connection. These are tools that can be adapted to assist humanity in evolving the *human race game*. Again, the intent here is not to suggest that people must use any of these tools or that these are the only tools. Rather, the intent is to stimulate people's interest in finding relevant tools to which they, individually and collectively, are drawn or to stimulate a person's thoughts in creating their own tools that work for them.

If the tools that I will reference are perceived to have value, then by all means use them to assist the outer self in evolving the human race game in specific and general terms. If the tools that I will reference do not resonate with one's outer self in terms of opening the outer self to experience the mind-body-spirit connection, then I suggest looking for those tools that do or allowing one's outer self to be guided to various tools that will be useful. More important than the specific tools themselves, therefore, is the person's intention to evolve the human race game in specific and general terms as they use the tools.

EMERGING TOOLS FOR HUMANITY'S NEXT EVOLUTIONARY STEP: IMPLICATIONS FOR EVOLVING THE HUMAN RACE GAME

I will begin by simply listing a number of the tools, in no particular order or preference. Then, I will provide a brief discussion of how a person might adapt these tools to evolve the *human race game.*

Some of the mind-body-spirit tools that may be adapted, therefore, are as follows: humor; the use of colors and light (e.g., bioresonant chakra shirt); guided imagery and creative visualization; biofeedback technologies (e.g., biodots and the life shirt); music and art; neuro-linguistic programming; prayer and focused spiritual healing; various energy-focused techniques (e.g., Chigong; Reiki); sex, dance, and various body and mind-body techniques and energy measuring devices; aura imaging photography, video aura imaging technology, and other imaging technologies; meditation and trances; and the mirror effect.

When a person uses any of these tools with the intention of releasing racially-linked energy blocks, they will be evolving the human race game in specific and general terms. The person will also gain benefits in other ways. Again, I recommend that people use the art of discernment in selecting and applying those tools with which they resonate.

THE TOOL OF HUMOR

One of the important ingredients for evolving the human race game is that people must learn to lighten up in regard to their lower self race games. In one's current racial forms and in various interracial dramas, therefore, it is important to learn how to laugh more with one another.

Also, the health benefits of humor have been well documented as a wonderful stress-reducer, antidote for upsets, nurturer for a person's immune system, and facilitator to allow a person's body to heal itself. It is important for a person to notice, then, how their body feels and how they feel one-on-one, in groups, or during particular activities and events in the presence of others when humor and laughter are involved.

Laughter has the effect of shifting the focus of a person's consciousness and transporting the person beyond their ego fears. To adapt the tool of humor to assist one's outer self in evolving the *human race game*, a person can *intentionally* co-create many such therapeutic dramas, including interracial dramas and other human encounters that involve humor. It is important to learn, therefore, to laugh together across what has been called racial barriers.

In India, for example, humor as a healing tool to influence the quality of life—mentally, emotionally, physically, and spiritually—has emerged in the form of a social movement. Dr. Madan Kataria was the initiator of the laughter movement. It has expanded to the United Kingdom of England, and is emerging more in the West.

In line with the laughter social movement, small groups of people simply gather for a time in what are called Laughing Clubs to engage in various forms of laughter with each other. There are also laughing workshops emerging, with facilitators. Personally, I had the privilege, for example, to be quite involved for a time with a wonderful woman, who was a facilitator of Living Laughter workshops.

In a person's personal life space, then, the person could adapt this laughter notion to initiate or to participate in laughing clubs or workshops that *intentionally* bring together people from various races, or those the person considers different. The smile and laughter are universal human experiences, transcending all so-called racial and cultural barriers. They represent one of the common physical or nonverbal ways that each person as a human being expresses their archetypal energies and makes authentic soul contact in physicality.

THE USE OF COLORS AND LIGHT AS TOOLS (E.G., THE BIORESONANT CHAKRA SHIRT)

The use of colors and light as healing tools is an ancient therapeutic approach, which has enjoyed both prestige and disfavor over the centuries. In the world today, the approach is now reemerging once again as a way to restore and to balance cells of the physical body and to stimulate the healing process.

In Western terms, for example, the approach can be traced back to the mythology of ancient Egypt and Greece and the Hermetic tradition, although reportedly it also was used during the periods of Mu and Atlantis. The Hermedic tradition focused on the use of colored minerals, stones, crystals, salves, dyes, garments, oils, plasters, ointments, and painted sanctuaries to treat disease. In broad terms, bright colors were thought to vitalize living things, while dark colors were thought to calm and rejuvenate living things.

More recently, the use of what is called bioresonant technology to study the effects of bioresonant color stimulation has emerged. It reportedly has led to the creation of a new tool that resonates to and balances the chakra centers. I am suggesting, therefore, that the color and light therapy approach can be adapted to assist in evolving the *human race game.*

In accord with the soul-centered model, most people chose to program their current personality with the gift of physical sight so that they could enjoy the wonderful color and light sensations of the physical world. And yet, it has been the misapplication of a good-bad value-laden color code in regard to skin color that has fueled much misinterpretation and misdirection of energy in regard to lower self race games.

Scientifically, it is known that color is simply a person's interpretation of a tiny shift in the wavelength of visible light. Light reflects off an object as a particular shade of color to the person's retina, forming impulses that travel as coded messages to the person's brain where hormones are released, sometimes altering the person's metabolism, sleeping, feeding, and temperature patterns.

Color and light therapy, then, as it is understood, seeks to utilize the healing properties of the visible light spectrum from infrared to ultraviolet.

One emerging tool that utilizes color and light, which can be adapted to assist in evolving the *human race game*, is what has been called the bioresonant chakra shirt. Based on extensive research by Dr. Tom J. Chalko in Melbourne University, Australia, the bioresonant chakra shirt was first made in January of 1997.

The bioresonant chakra shirt is specifically designed, using sixteen key colors, to match the frequency distribution along the body of a person's bio-energy field or aura. Those who have worn this shirt have reported some of the following as common experiences: unusual hot and cold sensations, shivers and tingles down the spine, often described as wind through the person's body at the chakra centers; a better mood and feelings of relaxation and excitement; more frequent smiles, for no apparent reason, often noticed by friends and family first; a stronger aura (Note: what the inventor calls *stimulated electro-photonic glow*) and ability to see the auras of other people better; improved and deeper meditation; and an enhancement of spiritual and intellectual activity. Young children, often a few months to five years old, tend to look above people's head and smile.

One possible adapted use of the bioresonant chakra shirt, therefore, would be to use it whenever a person anticipates some kind of race-related or other human encounters that may have the potential for conflict. The person may find that the energy fields of the participants may be more resonant than discordant.

In broader terms, however, to adapt the use of colors and light as tools to evolve the human race game, a person can expand their focus to include how color and light as vibrational forms of energy can be sensed multidimensionally. From a spiritual and soul-centered perspective, for example, learning how to interpret the colors in one's own aura for racially-linked energy blocks and learning how to use colors and light to create more balance in one's aural field can be beneficial in helping to evolve the human race game.

Placing colors and light within one's field of experience that balance one's mood, then, can assist a person in controlling the flow of energy through their body. Various colors and light, therefore, can affect racially-linked energy blocks, and allow a person to be open during various so-called interracial exchanges and transactions of energy.

In accord with the soul-centered model, it is important also to understand that how a person currently resonates to particular colors and light is often related to past or future lifetimes, or to emotional themes that are influencing the flavor and course of her/his current life. If, for example, a person tends to resonate with bright colors in this life, they may have had a bland or a somewhat depleting past life that now requires them to vital-ize or energize one's self. Or, if a person tends to resonate with darker colors in this life, they may have had a very stimulating or a somewhat unsettling past life which now requires them to calm and rejuvenate one's self.

Implied, therefore, is that both bright and dark colors can be used to assist in balancing a person's overall energy. This, of course, has nothing to do with skin color.

The descriptions here are very broad generalizations regarding the healing properties of color and light and are not intended to be prescriptive interpretations for all instances. In the final analy-sis, beyond the vibrations of particular colors and light, color and light meanings tend to be an individualized and unique experi-ence. It is recommended, therefore, that people have a playful attitude when dealing with the properties and meanings of vari-ous colors and light.

In the discussion so far, I have recommended one self-healing and self-nurturing scheme for how a person may interpret the base colors of their aura and how to engage their archetypal ener-gies (see Table 2). Other such color schemes, however, have been presented in other contexts, which also may be useful for evolving the human race game.

I will present an alternate scheme, therefore, because I do not want people simply to become wedded to one approach as the only approach to adapting colors as a healing tool. With any approach with which a person resonates, it is recommended that s/he playfully reflects on particular healing and nurturing ideas as s/he focuses on a particular color (e.g., they can use a colored panel, page, or other material object).

Here, then, is another color interpretation scheme:

Color	Healing and Nurturing Ideas to Reflect On
Green	Growth, Abundance, Vitality
Red	Energy, Determination, Passion
Purple	Spiritual, Passionate, Visionary
Turquoise	Refreshing, Cool, Imaginative
Gold	Illumination, Wisdom
Lavender	Romantic, Imaginative, Fantasy
Magenta	Outrageous, Imaginative, Innovative
Light Blue	Peaceful, Sincere, Affectionate
Orange	Happy, Courageous, Successful
Indigo	Knowledge, Power, Integrity
Pink	Friendly, Compassionate, Faithful
Yellow	Enthusiastic, Playful, Optimistic
Aqua	Motivated, Active, Dynamic
Brown	Stability, Earthly, Reliable
Blue	Tranquil, Intuitive, Trustworthy

THE TOOLS OF GUIDED IMAGERY AND CREATIVE VISUALIZATION

As I have suggested throughout this discussion, the tool of *creative imagination* is one of the most powerful tools for transformation and evolving the *human race game*. As human beings, people have always used guided imagery and creative visualization, in one form or another, to create their realities, although they may have used different labels for the process and techniques.

Indeed, for quite awhile now, the use of guided imagery and creative visualization has enjoyed much visibility and has resulted in much success for practitioners in both popular and older cultures of the world in both the East and the West (e.g., Shakti Gawain's *Creative Visualization: Use the Power of Imagination to Create What You Want in Your Life*, 2002). The approach involves the use of mental imagery and what is now called affirmations.

The various techniques include relaxing, setting one's goal, clearing blocked energy, creating a clear idea or picture, focusing often on the idea or picture, and giving positive energy for manifestation of what one desires. The strategy of using guided imagery and creative visualization, then, to access the subconscious and the spiritual realms, to change various unsatisfactory life circumstances, and to enhance the quality of life, underlies much of the past and current inner and outer work in regard to the mind-body-spirit connection.

There have been and are many suggestions and recommendations for how best to use guided imagery and how to create effective affirmations. So, I again recommend that people use those approaches and techniques with which they resonate. For example, when a person is feeling unsettled, one approach for grounding the energy of one's emotional body is to visualize a cord running from one's root center or chakra with the person inserting this cord into the Earth.

The focus here is on ways to adapt guided imagery and creative visualization to evolve the *human race game*. I recommend, as do other authors, that in addition to grounding one's emotional body, people use their *journal* to write race-related affirmations. It is important that a person's affirmations expand their consciousness, appeal to their self positively and magnetically, are clear, specific, and declarative, and includes their self and is about their self.

I further recommend that people create other simple race-related mental images that positively evoke their passion. It is important that the person is clearly included in the mental image and it is important to allow one's self to engage in some doable action in accord with the mental image.

For example, after a person grounds their self, they might write the following race-related affirmation: *Every person I meet from another race provides me with an opportunity to learn more about myself.* Then, the person might create a race-related mental image of actually having a creative conversation about a particular passion with a person from another race in their personal life space.

It is suggested that the person chooses someone that they have seen, but with whom they have not had any substantive contact, for whatever reason. When the person next sees this other person, therefore, they would remind their self of her/his affirmation and then they would bother to make contact. It is important to pay attention at this point to how one feels as they make the contact.

It is through inner work of this nature and through such outer creative encounters in their personal life spaces that people will contribute to evolving the *human race game* in specific and general terms. Conscious transformative actions thus flow from such inner work.

THE TOOLS OF BIOFEEDBACK TECHNOLOGIES (E.G., BIODOTS; LIFE SHIRT OR "SMART CLOTHES")

In this discussion, I have suggested that, metaphorically and to a large extent literally, a person's body or her/his *current physical form* is the person's soul in chemical clothes. As such, a person's body will never lie to her/him. A person's outer self and their soul are in constant dialogue through the messages or feedback the person receives in and through their body.

On the one hand, a person's body largely responds to what is in the person's conscious mind and what the person chooses to focus on in their mind. That is, when a person believes something to be true, their body will react as if what they are telling it is true, providing feedback in the form of warning signals, harmonious signals, and rebalancing signals.

On the other hand, when there appears to be some major misdirection of a person's focus and energy, which may not lead to the person's higher good or is not yet in alignment with the vibrations of what the person says they desire, the person's soul also tries to signal the outer self with bodily sensations. In a manner of speaking, then, the body's bioenergetic signals represent the most intimate physical context where a person's inner and outer realities collaborate.

What is now called biofeedback, therefore, is one of the ways that a person's soul works with the person's conscious mind and its materialization as one's body. Biofeedback, then, provides a person's outer self with inner information about how the person is experiencing, perceiving and interpreting their outer or conscious self and their life spaces.

There are numerous biofeedback technologies. So I will only mention two of many which may be adapted to assist humanity in evolving the human race game. One of these technologies is called the biodot. It is literally a small dot-like material that a person can stick to the underside of their wrist, which will change colors in accord with the person's stress or fear level.

The biodot is actually like a miniature thermometer, which can measure the change in temperature at the surface of a person's skin. The biodot, then, will provide a person with quick feedback about changes in their skin temperature, which may be a mirror of the person's stress or fear level. (Note: The biodot color-temperature scheme tends to be: Black- 89.6, Amber-90.6, Yellow-91.6, Green-92.6, Turquoise-93.6, Blue-94.6, and Violet-95.6).

The changes in a person's skin temperature often happen outside of the person's awareness, signaling, however, that the person needs to rebalance their body through breathing and other relaxation techniques. In other terms, I suggest that the biodot is reflecting when a person has and is creating energy blocks.

Because stress or fear is often the precursor or precipitant for a person to engage in one of the lower self race game, the biodot can be adapted as an important biofeedback tool to use when either anticipating or actually having so-called interracial encounters or interracial dramas. The use of biodots, therefore, can be a useful tool to allow a person to monitor their self as they experiment with evolving the *human race game* in specific and general terms.

In a similar fashion, the so-called *life shirt* or *smart clothes* also can provide a person with vital information about the functioning of their body during stress or fear-related circumstances. The impetus would be to return one's body to a state of balance, harmony, and peace.

One current version of the life shirt or smart clothes is a vest that monitors a number of vital bodily functions such as blood pressure, heart rate, and breathing patterns. Sensors are woven into the linen and fabric of the vest, which can provide warning signals for when a person's body is in a disharmonious state or to predict disharmony before it happens.

Like the biodot, then, when the use of the life shirt or smart clothes is adapted to provide a person with biofeedback for the numerous interracial encounters and interracial dramas, the person again can have another tool to assist the outer self in monitoring how they are using their energy. That is, a life shirt or smart clothes can let a person know whether or not they are open or closed before, during, and after various interracial experiences and how this is impacting the state of their body.

People will soon discover that their body will do much better and feel much healthier when they are in an open state during various interracial experiences, as well as during any other-oriented experiences. In this respect, the life shirt or smart clothes may assist a person in reprogramming their outer self in regard to the person's openness to interracial encounters and human relation dramas.

THE TOOLS OF MUSIC AND ART

In a manner of speaking, and in accord with the soul-centered model, a person's entire physical reality and life dramas are a grand musical and artistic game. That is, each person's outer self and those in the person's varied life spaces resonate to, and give expression to, various material and Earth vibrations in accord with the person's physical senses. A person's physical senses thus provide one with the gifts of hearing (or resonances to sound vibrations), seeing (or resonances to light vibrations), touching (or resonances to density and depth vibrations), tasting (or resonances to flavor and texture vibrations), and smelling (or resonances to odor vibrations). Music, sound, the spoken word, and various artistic expressions, then, are principle frameworks each person uses to enrich their life, expand their mind, and enhance their thirst for knowledge.

In other terms, music and art, more specifically, have been used to work therapeutically with a variety of people, particularly those who have unique challenges with their senses (e.g., physically challenged; abused; elderly; Alzheimer and dementia; terminally ill; mentally challenged and developmentally delayed; traumatically brain injured; learning disabled; clinically diagnosed). On the other hand, music and art in general are methods for celebrating life and energy in all of their cultural forms.

Music and art, as people typically think of them, involve singing, listening, playing instruments, composition, moving to music, music and imagery exercises, drawing and painting, sculpting, poetry, acting and the performing arts, and the like. Music and art interventions are often used, then, to restore, maintain, and improve a person's emotional, physical, physiological, and spiritual health and well-being. However, when a person's intention is to create interracial healing and expansive experiences by using music and various artistic expressions, then these approaches also can be adapted to assist in evolving the human race game in specific and general terms.

Like the smile, music and art are other universal human experiences. They are common to all human beings, which mirror humanity's interdependence, albeit through what humanity would call various cultural, rhythmic, and artistic expressions. In accord with the soul-centered model, all of these varied musical and artistic expressions, however, flow from the original creative and vibrational sound and light spark that is known as Om. The many cultural expressions of music and art represent the numerous and creative ways that have emerged through the centuries, as can be understood, for celebrating the wondrous and varied flow of spirit in life.

As a person opens their heart, then, to experience varied musical and artistic expressions, they also are expanding their consciousness. In turn, the person positions their self to make authentic soul contact with others. It is important for people to notice then how they feel when they sing together, chant together, listen and move together to various forms of music, play instruments or drum together, and playfully share various artistic expressions and performances together.

Beyond the acts themselves, therefore, the musical and artistic forms, in a manner of speaking, are methods for making spiritual connections. It is in this context, then, that music and art can be adapted intentionally as tools to assist in evolving the human race game.

THE TOOL OF NEURO-LINGUISTIC PROGRAMMING AND ITS RELATION TO CELLULAR MEMORIES

I have identified neuro-linguistic programming as one of the tools that can be adapted to assist in evolving the *human race game* in specific and general terms. I do so not because of the specific techniques that are employed by its practitioners, but rather because of the *intent* that this approach *represents* in regard to what other authors and I call the mind-body-spirit connection.

From the vantage point of what I have called a soul-centered perspective, the creation of many aspects of lower self race games flow, in part, from neurally programmed cellular memories. In accord with the soul-centered model, these cellular memories are brought forward in this lifetime, as it would be understood, to allow a person an opportunity to release and to work through various energy blocks. Many of these energy blocks have been held in place by what the person has been telling their self, perhaps for numerous life times, about *who* they are and *why* they are. This has been the person's neuro-linguistic programming, in a manner of speaking.

In other words, many energy blocks have been created by various ego and personality orientations and fears, resulting in what might be called the person's *karmic entanglements.* This occurred as the person sought to engage various life challenges for fully embracing their power as a *creator* on the physical plane who mirrors the qualities of various archetypal energies.

From a soul-centered and neuro-linguistic perspective, therefore, each person, individually and collectively, has played out an infinite number of human dramas, including interracial dramas over the centuries, as it would be understood. So far, however, many people's interracial dramas have primarily served to continue an *outer neuro-linguistic program* of *growth with pain.* That is, when it comes to the matter of the phenomenon of race, many people have been so *hypnotized* by the neuro-linguistic programming of the illusion of polarity that the only way they could conceive of growing was to create race-related opposites or race-related enemies. This also applies to the phenomenon of ethnicity and any other-oriented phenomenon.

Many people, therefore, created race-related or other-oriented imbalances of energy or race-related karma, self-oriented karma, and other-oriented karma. In accord with the soul-centered model, this meant that a person would have to play out during the same lifetime or in other lifetimes what they set up as the other side of the race-related, self-oriented, or other-oriented polarity. Further, even between lifetimes the person would construct possibilities for engaging in what they considered the opposite side of the race-related, self-oriented, or other-oriented polarity.

However, people forgot who they are and people forgot to play their race games, self-oriented games, or other-oriented games with a light heart. The result, of course, has been the lower self race games and some of the ethnicity-related dramas, self-limiting cross-cultural dramas, and dogmatic religious dramas that I have noted elsewhere.

I have been suggesting, therefore, that people give the self, individually and collectively, a new neuro-linguistic directive, that is, a neuro-linguistic directive to be open to their archetypal energies. In using this new neuro-linguistic directive, I am suggesting that it will alter the neural patterns that underlie a person's perceptions and experience and will allow the person to *grow with joy*.

In part, the process involves reprogramming a person's self by using their linguistic abilities to create a celebratory self-directed inner dialogue and to engage in a celebratory outer dialogue with others about race-related and other-oriented matters. Therefore, as a moment-to-moment unfolding process, the celebratory neuro-linguistic reprogramming, or celebratory inner and outer dialogues, would seek to nurture the emergence of the person's truer self with their archetypal energies.

The inner and outer dialogues would seek to foster the emergence of a social atmosphere or a social climate with a collective consciousness that has as its focus growth with joy. It is in this manner, then, that the tool of neuro-linguistic programming can be adapted to assist in evolving the human race game in specific and general terms.

THE TOOLS OF PRAYER
AND FOCUSED SPIRITUAL HEALING

I am aware that people may be tempted to view the emphasis on the tools of prayer and focused spiritual healing through religious or dogmatic eyes. That, however, is not the purpose or intent here, nor do I wish to reinforce or affirm any particular religion, dogma, or specific practice with which people are familiar or with which people resonate. The intent here is simply to call attention to the underlying spiritual and soul-centered principles that underlie both of these tools.

In accord with the soul-centered model, I want people to recognize that when they do pray or engage in focused spiritual healing, using whatever faith-based orientation they may have adopted, they are, in effect, calling upon their higher self and soul-source's connection with source energy/spirit or All-That-Is. They are also using the universal energy laws, of which I have spoken, in a co-creative process. As people pray or use focused spiritual healing, therefore, with the intent of healing race-related and other-oriented wounds in their individual and collective psyches, they will be assisting in evolving the human race game in specific and general terms.

To illustrate the point above, and in accord with the soul-centered model, I suggest that arrangements were made at a soul level for me to receive a visit at my office in late August 2010 from a former student and friend, Ernest Best. I love the sound of that name as it resonates with multiple meanings. In our current racial forms, both Ernest and I are considered African American. Ernest proceeded to tell me about his recent experience with cancer, and how through prayer and focused spiritual healing, he had two experiences of *spontaneous remissions* of cancer. Each experience involved a number of medical tests, with diagnoses of cancer in different locations in Ernest's body. That is, the doctors definitely and definitively detected cancer.

More specifically, Ernest spoke of how on both occasions he contacted his family in another state, who then organized family and church-connected prayer vigils on his behalf before and at the specific times of scheduled surgeries. In addition to Ernest's own self-healing prayers and what he described as maintaining positive thoughts and continuing to be himself, everyone doing the vigils, who directly and indirectly knew Ernest, sent forth what they would call "prayerful energy."

On both occasions, Ernest said he "gave it over to God" each time. When the surgeons performed their operations on these separate occasions, both times no cancer cells were found. Although baffled, Ernest said that his medical doctors then proclaimed him cured.

Both Ernest and I agreed that Ernest has a message, and, as I stated at the end of my talk with Ernest, "Ernest, you are the message." Ernest remarked: "If it had happened once, you might write it off as a coincidence. But it happened twice."

Ernest also has his own radio program for delivering his message to various listeners—human beings from all racial groups and all walks of life. Through being the message and sharing his message, letting his soul light shine, so to speak, Ernest is and will be assisting in evolving the human race game in specific and general terms.

During the talk with Ernest, I found myself translating Ernest's statements into ideas that I have shared here and with him. I began to relate what Ernest was saying to the *universal energy laws* and how they function in relation to source energy/spirit or All-That-Is. Ultimately, however, I surmised that even though both Ernest and I may have been provided with and may use different language and lens to understand what had transpired, it did not really matter. The miracles occurred, not once but twice.

I am also aware that people may be tempted here to interpret the emphasis on prayer and focused spiritual healing as a justification to rely *solely* on these methods for all kinds of physical and self-healing. Or, people may be tempted to interpret the emphasis here as a way to avoid having real experiences with real people or to avoid taking any kind of action. Again, that is not the purpose or intent here.

Perhaps it would be more helpful, then, simply to view prayer and focused spiritual healing as complementary tools to the traditional healing methods or affirming actions with which a person is familiar. And, perhaps it would be more helpful for people to consider them as two kinds of potential preparatory tools they may use to assist them in having positive outcomes for their desires and positive outcomes for energy interchanges with others.

Again, in accord with the soul-centered mode, what I want people to realize is that underlying all of these methods and tools, traditional and otherwise, and underlying the co-creation of various contexts for various interracial and other-oriented interactions are the universal energy laws. It is, therefore, how a person uses these various tools rather than the tools themselves that matter. Such strategies, in a manner of speaking, involve a person's use of discernment. Discernment is a way of making choices and decisions and finding one's path to one's truth without judgment.

In the case of prayer and focused spiritual healing and their connection to race-related and other-oriented matters, it is important for each person to realize that they can alter their race-related and other-oriented experiences in positive ways by using these tools and the universal energy laws to co-create the conditions for positive interchanges and healing at all levels. When a person realizes that they are the source of their own creations in regard to their human experiences, including her/his race-related experiences and other-oriented experiences, they will be evolving the human race game in specific and general terms.

Some people, for example, may unwittingly misuse the tools of prayer and focused spiritual healing to misdirect energy in regard to race-related and ethnic-related matters and perceived differences. For example, they, individually or collectively as a part of a group, a community, or a nation, often call upon their versions of

God to help them to defeat their so-called enemies or the villain-ous other. They do this when they focus their consciousness on their fears as they relate to perceived race- or ethnic-related secu-rity, sensation, and power dynamics and perceived differences.

The mirrored effect, however, is that they misuse the universal energy laws by misdirecting their energy toward their polarity beliefs. This misuse of the universal energy laws results in the cre-ation of individual and/or collective karmic entanglements. They create a game whereby they get to view one's self as "heroic" and to view one's projections onto others as "villainous." They may, then, act out against their villainous projections, or the villainous other often in subtle, but sometimes in violent ways with self-perceived, righteous indignations. By the universal energy law of consequences, therefore, the outcomes are race-related and eth-nic-related, individual and/or collective karmic entanglements.

Indeed, my empirical research revealed some of the polarity beliefs or polarity thoughts that may emerge in terms of the value judgments (e.g., good—bad; bright or light—dark; sacred—pro-fane; civilized—primitive; clean—dirty), the fears (e.g., strong—weak; frightening—nonfrightening; tense—relaxed; active—passive), and the understandability (e.g., organized—chaotic; understandable—mysterious; familiar—strange) of people and race-linked phenomena in their worlds (see Ferguson's *A New Perspective on Race and Color: Research on an Outer Vs Inner Orientation to Anti-Black Dispositons*, 1997).

Such polarity thoughts may emerge in connection with a per-son's notions of God and Satan, the nature of Life and Death, the nature of Day and Night, and the nature of Consciousness and the Unconscious and may get projected out onto a person's per-ceived race- or ethnic-related enemies. To a large extent, however, a person's race-related polarity thoughts appear to stem from the primal fear, which is known as the fear of death. In this regard, and in accord with the soul-centered model, a person's ego, whose purpose has been to help the person to survive, has not been able to fully comprehend the idea that their consciousness both precedes and survives what they call the death experience. The outer self, or rather the person's ego, therefore, misperceives their own race-related projections as a threat to their own survival.

In other words, when a person misuses the tools of prayer and focused spiritual healing and directs their focus toward a perceived enemy or villainous other, they simply create more of the perceived conflict that they say they don't want. The person does this by projecting out, onto the so-called enemy, qualities within one's self that they do not like and then they rail against them. The person, in effect, vibrationally sends out enemy-oriented energy toward their own creation (their own feared inner enemy), or the person vibrationally attracts such energy, thus perpetuating their illusion.

In this sense, the person is using a judgmental framework (i.e., an emphasis on good/bad, right/wrong, either/or) to focus their consciousness, and not the emerging gift of discernment. The person is not wisely using the universal energy laws.

It is important, therefore, to seek to use prayer and focused spiritual healing in affirming ways in order to lift one's own spirit and the spirit of others. I am suggesting, therefore, that people *consciously* use the tools of prayer and focused spiritual healing in discerning ways to co-create a friendly world and to affirm that it is so. As people do so, they will be directing their energy toward evolving the *human race game.*

THE TOOLS OF VARIOUS ENERGY-FOCUSED TECHNIQUES (E.G., CHIGONG; REIKI; ENERGY MEDICINE; THE SCIENCE OF RECONNECTIVE HEALING FREQUENCIES)

Throughout the centuries, as can be understood, humanity has developed numerous approaches to remind the self that one's physical body is supported by the subtle energies that interpenetrate one's existence. These approaches simply remind each person's outer self of their connection to universal energy and to source energy/spirit or All-That-Is. They also remind the person's outer self of the extent to which they are open or closed to the interpenetrating-etheric and quantum energy fields for purposes of healing, nurturance, and growth.

I will refer to two approaches, which some people may know as Chigong and Reiki, and a third approach, which some people may know as the emerging field of Energy Medicine. I will also refer to an emerging new science that looks at energy, light, and information for healing purposes or what is called Reconnective Healing frequencies. I am simply referencing these approaches as representative tools of various energy-focused techniques for working with, directing the flow of, and releasing Energy blocks for purposes of health and healing. The intent here is to indicate how these kinds of approaches may be adapted to assist in evolving the human race game, not to glorify these approaches per se. With the appropriate focus, however, these approaches can be quite effective.

THE PRACTICE OF CHIGONG

For those who are unfamiliar with the practice of Chigong, it is in its current form what observers would call a Chinese practice that focuses attention on the many different styles of breathing to maintain and to prolong life. In the practice, universal energy would be called genuine chi (healthy energy). In the practice, ill chi would be referred to as negative chi, or a misdirection, or a block of the flow of universal energy.

More specifically, the practice uses what are often called the body breathing and sleeping arts, the walking art, body universe circulation, and the balancing arts to remind a person of their connection to universal energy. Body breathing refers to breathing through one's largest organ, one's skin, with its pores and capillaries. The sleeping arts involve using various body-breathing techniques while lying or reclining. The walking art involves the practice of learning how to progressively slow down one's breath until one can finally take twenty-four steps as one breathes in genuine chi and twenty-four steps as one breathes out negative chi. Body universe circulation involves deep relaxation and concentrating on what are known as various acupuncture points, alone or with others. The balancing arts involve body breathing while in the proximity of various types of trees.

The general technique of body breathing involves a person simply imagining, as they breathe in, the genuine chi in the universe entering their body through their pores over the entire surface of her/his body. As the person breathes out, s/he imagines the body's negative chi leaving out through their pores and away from their body to a very far distance.

In the practice, therefore, what I have been calling racially-linked energy blocks would be considered negative chi. One way, then, to adapt the practice of Chigong to assist in evolving the *human race game* is to engage in the various Chigong techniques with the *intent* of releasing racially-linked negative chi. For example, as a person becomes aware of any limiting security, sensation, or power feelings emerging during interracial and other-oriented interactions or interracial and other-oriented dramas, the person could use the technique of body breathing to release the race-related or other-oriented energy block at play.

THE PRACTICE OF REIKI

Similarly, Reiki is viewed as a Japanese healing practice that was developed to allow so-called Reiki Energy or life-force energy to flow toward particular hot spots in the body that may need healing. The practice uses focused thought and intention to direct the flow of this Reiki Energy.

Dr. Mikao Usui, who uncovered the healing practice, was in search of the healing principles used by the teacher people know as Jesus (Stein's *Essential Reiki*; Rand's *Reiki The Healing Touch: First and Second Degree Manual*). Dr. Usui, like Jesus or anyone else interested in such a search, uncovered the importance of the law of intention and the law of consequences for healing purposes.

In the practice, then, through the placement of a practitioner's hands in certain positions on or over the body, the practitioner uses intentional thought to assist in the movement and interchange of Reiki Energy between the practitioner and the other person. In the practice, Reiki is a Japanese word meaning "universal life-force energy" and "ki" is simply another name for chi or universal energy. In the practice, therefore, what I have been calling racially-linked energy blocks would be experienced as hot spots in the body. For purposes here, it would be these race-linked hot spots that would be the focus for healing.

In the Reiki practice, there is recognition that there is no time and space to limit spirit, and there is recognition that all is made up of energy. The practice, therefore, includes the use of Reiki for what is called remote healings (Brennan's *Hands of Light* and *Light Emerging*) and Reiki for non-human recipients (e.g., food before eating). Often, objectifying the recipient is part of this aspect of the practice (e.g., imagining one's own body parts as the same as the intended recipient; use of a drawing; use of a teddy bear, pillow or some other physical object as a stand in). In this manner, it is possible to use Reiki on relationships between people.

Theoretically, then, it is possible to adapt this aspect of the Reiki practice to objectify problematic interracial and other-oriented relationships and to apply energy to the object for remote healing. It is in this way, therefore, that the Reiki practice can be adapted to assist in healing racially-linked energy blocks and thereby to assist in evolving the *human race game*.

THE FIELD AND PRACTICE OF
ENERGY MEDICINE

The emerging field of what is called Energy Medicine also holds great promise for healing race-linked energy blocks and other energy blocks. Some have called Donna Eden and David Feinstein the pioneers for this emerging practice in the West (e.g. see Eden's *Energy Medicine* & Feinstein's *The Promise of Energy Psychology*). Knowingly and unknowingly, and in accord with the soul-centered model, Eden and Feinstein have been working with and nurtured by the archetypal energy *harmony*. Through my role and my own work with an organization called the Association for Humanistic Psychology, I have had an opportunity to meet and interact with both Eden and Feinstein.

The practice of Energy Medicine involves assessing where one's energy systems need attention and correcting the energy disturbances. The practice identifies nine primary energy systems and uses techniques such as tapping, massaging, pinching, twisting, or connecting specific energy points on the skin, tracing or swirling the hand over the skin along specific energy pathways, exercises or postures designed for specific energetic effects, focused use of the mind to move specific energies, and surrounding an area with healing energies. Applying or adapting these techniques, therefore, to help release and heal racially-linked energy blocks will assist in evolving the human race game.

THE SCIENCE OF RECONNECTIVE
HEALING FREQUENCIES

In resonance with Energy Medicine, a new science is emerging to change traditional understanding of health and healing. The scientific research relates to what is called Reconnective Healing frequencies, first discovered by Eric Pearl, DC. The research focuses on quantifying the effects of energy, light, and information on human beings. The results of this research, carried out by an international team of well renowned scientists, William Tiller, PhD, Gary Schwartz, PhD, and Konstantin Kortokov, PhD, are powerful and profound.

Dr. Tiller, for example, conducting research on the physical properties of a room or space change as a result of energy healing frequencies entering that room, found that these intelligent frequencies begin changing the quantum field effects of the room, or "conditioning the space," easily thirty-six hours or more before a seminar on Reconnective Healing even begins, dramatically increasing the excess free thermodynamic energy in the room. That is, if this were simply energy typically found in energy healing, the temperature of the room would have increased by 300 centigrades. However, with Reconnective Healing, the actual room temperature does not change, but the amount of energy, light, and information charging the room does change dramatically. And, the effect continues even two days later. Dr. Tiller remarked, "This shift of energy is what allows normal human beings to enter a room and later to walk out with an ability to heal others and themselves, regardless of their background or education."

Dr. Schwwartz and his colleagues at the Laboratory for Advances in Consciousness and Health at the University of Arizona measured people's abilities to work with, feel, transmit, and receive light and other electromagnetic frequencies before and after they attended a Reconnective Healing seminar. Dr. Schwartz and his colleagues found that, following the Reconnective Healing seminar, people walked out with permanently expanded and new electromagnetic abilities, regardless of whether or not they had studied healing or whether or not they were masters/teachers of various old or new energy healing techniques.

Dr. Korotokov's research, using cutting edge imaging and measuring devices, corroborated the findings of Tiller and Schwartz and demonstrated what he calls coherence effects of those participating in Reconnective Healing seminars, that is, he found dramatic spikes in both the intensity and size of the quantum field in the room whenever a new concept or exercise was taught during the seminars. Dr. Korotokov also found that most of those who simply sit in the seminar itself receive positive health effects, sometimes having physical and other healings just from sitting in the seminar during the class.

The emerging science of Reconnective Healing frequencies, therefore, holds great promise for healing in general, and for intentionally healing racially-linked energy blocks in particular. More importantly, however, this emerging science contributes to advancing Humanity to the next stage of evolving the human race game in specific and general terms.

THE TOOLS OF SEX, DANCE, AND VARIOUS BODY AND MIND-BODY TECHNIQUES AND ENERGY MEASURING DEVICES

Earlier, I discussed how what is called *biofeedback* provides a person with important information about the stress on and the energy blocks in one's body. I now want to add to that discussion. Indeed, there are both natural tools and various body and mind-body techniques for relieving stress, releasing energy blocks, and reacquainting a person's outer self with the spiritual aspect of their greater self. Two of those natural tools include sex and dance. Examples of various body and mind-body techniques include approaches such as yoga, Tai Chi, various forms of massage (e.g., shiatsu acupressure), acupuncture, and various physical exercises for the body.

Again, I am referring to these kinds of tools not because of the particular methods themselves, but rather because of what these tools represent. In a manner of speaking, they all have the effect of allowing universal energy and spirit to flow more freely through a person's personal energy system. They also all have the effect of opening the person's outer self to specific archetypal energies such as joy, love, unity, oneness, and serenity.

They all represent, therefore, ways that universal energy and spirit can joyously flow through a person's personal energy system. Without much conscious awareness, many people already have been engaging these tools to assist in evolving the human race game.

Sex as an Evolutionary Tool

A person's sexual energy is often called Kundilini Energy, and it is one of the most powerful energies that a person carries in their body. Through honest acts of sex between consenting adults, a person's senses are aroused, and their chakra centers open to allow the flow of this energy through the body. A person's joy and authentic passion, then, can lead the person to natural spiritual awakening.

Please note that I am making a distinction here between what I am calling a person's authentic passion and the addictive passion that is fueled more by the lower self's addictive sensations that may get misdirected into sex-related power games. I am also referring to adult encounters that are entered into freely and mutually.

One of the traditions that emerged over time to illustrate the effects of authentic passion and joy flowing from honest acts of sex is what is called the practice of tantra. The process starts, of course, with self-love as the person allows their self to accept their joy and authentic passion as they arise. The play then involves seeking and achieving balance with another as each person embraces their joy, love, unity, oneness, and serenity. It is in this manner that aural energies blend, seeking balance as each person makes authentic soul contact.

There are implications here of this balancing process for evolving the human race game. And so it is that many people are currently exploring what is called the connection between sex and spirituality (e.g., see books by David Deida; in Fall 2012, Amazon.com had 3,697 search results related to Tantra).

When Kundilini Energy flows through a person's being as a physical entity, the person may become temporarily frightened at the height of their power, and so the person often has attributed this energy to their partner instead of accepting it as their own. This misunderstanding has been at the core of many of humanity's fears associated with race-related sexual myths and race-related sexual projections.

Historically, for example, some people, who feared and were unable to accept their own sex-related power, projected it out onto another race, fearing and railing against it and seeking to contain it. And yet, it is this very energy that pulls the various races on Earth toward one another in the spirit of joy, love, unity, oneness, and serenity as a person, individually and collectively, seeks balance.

The constant search for balance mirrors the natural flow of energy throughout the universe. In this regard, the search for balance is mirrored by what appears to be the increasing numbers of people engaging in and experimenting with what is called intimate interracial encounters. However, this is not new. Throughout history, as it is understood, intimate interracial encounters have been part of the evolutionary process. Indeed, at a spiritual and soul-centered level, and in accord with the soul-centered model, the blending of the so-called races on Earth is considered a most honored biological step in the evolutionary process.

DANCE AS AN EVOLUTIONARY TOOL

Symbolically, then, sex involves the passionate dance of people's bodies, as they intimately express their joy and authentic passion. However, beyond honest acts of sex, there are numerous other natural expressions of the passionate dance of people's bodies, together or alone. Throughout history and in all cultures, as can be understood, numerous forms of dance have continuously and naturally emerged to represent the infinite passionate and authentic dance of spirit in physical form.

At a cultural level, various forms of dance have come to represent one of the ways that spirit is naturally experienced, expressed, and evolved by the races on Earth. Some forms of these dances, for example, include what are called folk dances, tap dance, show dance, street dance, disco dance, jazz dance, ballet dance, couple dance, circle or group dance, modern dance, free form dance, ethnic/cultural dances and the like.

Such dance activities increase people's curiosity and play with one another. They also often reflect the moods and emotions of a group during various historical times. At the same time, they maintain and advance a sense of tradition and evolution of group life. Therefore, as people increase their passionate and authentic play together through experiencing and sharing dance, they will be evolving the human race game.

Indeed, at an international level, dance can and has been used as a way to have the races of Earth play together and appreciate one another. One example is that of a group calling itself the International Network of Dances of Universal Peace. The group uses many arenas to bring the races together and to participate in simple, meditative, multicultural circles involving chants, music, movements, and phrases from many cultural traditions of the Earth that mirror and reflect spirit. The nature of this kind of dance activity is based on the 1960s work of Samuel L. Lewis. I recommend that people celebrate such efforts and I encourage everyone to allow their outer self to look for ways to dance together, symbolically and literally.

VARIOUS BODY AND MIND-BODY TECHNIQUES AND ENERGY MEASURING DEVICES AS EVOLUTIONARY TOOLS

I want now to call attention to various body and mind-body techniques and energy measuring devices. I reference them here because I want people to understand that they, like the natural tools, may help to facilitate the flow of universal energy through one's body. As there are many such techniques and devices, I will not discuss the merits of any particular technique or device, but I simply suggest that people pursue various body and mind-body techniques and devices in accord with their particular interest.

In that light, I will use a portion of my current awareness of such techniques and devices to present a brief illustrative list. It is not intended to be an exhaustive list. It is meant only to be a list to provide preliminary guidance for those who wish to pursue this topic and approach further.

Such techniques and devices might include, for example:

- What are called *Alpha Level Mind Techniques* to program and re-program one's self for purposes of healing, developing what is called focused intuition, and creating what may be called positive coincidences (Example: Silva Mind Body Methods)

- What are called *Energy Psychology Techniques* (Examples: Thought Field Therapy; Emotional Freedom Techniques; Be Set Free Fast Technique; Tapas Acupressure Technique; Rapid Integrated Transformation Technique)

- What are called *Natural Health Techniques and Relaxation Techniques* (Examples: Electromagnetic Field Balancing Technique; Universal Calibration Lattice Technique; Interactive Guided Imagery; Spiritual Responses Therapy; Theta Healing Autogentic Training, which uses both visual imagery and body awareness to move into deep relaxation; Progressive Muscle Relaxation Technique, i.e., slowly tensing and releasing each muscle group individually, moving from the feet to the head)

- What is called a *Resonant Field Imaging Technique*, an experimental process or technique that allows a person to monitor the auras of humans, animals, and even plants

- What are called *Energy Measurement Devices* that measure subtle electromagnetic fields, and scan the entire frequency range with which people have current awareness (Example: RFI Digital Frequency Counter, which measures Subtle Electromagnetic Fields in the range of 1 MHz to 3 GHz and low-strength fields; RF Field Strength Analyzer device, which scans the entire frequency range from 100 kHz to 2060 MHz)

- What are called *Mind-Matter Interaction Devices* (Examples: The Mind Lamp, apparently the world's first mind-matter interaction lamp, which converts quantum-level phenomena into a digital output that changes the color of the lamp in accord with the focus of a person's mind; the random event generator enables a user to conduct mind-matter interaction experiments on a home computer; SyncTXT is a device to detect synchronicities using random event generator technology that sends text messages to users mobile phones to digitally detect the timing and content of messages)

- What have been called *Electromagnetic Protective Tools* (Examples: The Bee Electro N'Tech device clears electromagnetic pollution resulting from appliances; the Electrosmog Corrector produces the same resonant pulse of the Earth; EarthSafe can produce the exact frequency that will give maximum benefit to the body, and can be re-adjusted in seconds at any time, for any new circumstance, including the changes taking place in the Earth's natural field; the Oscillator is thought to be useful in recharging and rejuvenating cells)

- What can be called *Personal Heart-Centered Devices* (Example: HearthMath's emWave Personal Stress Reliever is a scientifically validated handheld device which uses colorful displays, audio feedback, and a powerful stress relief technique, all designed to significantly reduce a person's stress, balance emotions and increase a person's feelings of well being).

The purpose here is simply to suggest that if a person engages these techniques and devices with the intent of releasing racially-linked energy blocks and with the intent of allowing one's outer self to be open to the archetypal energies joy, love, unity, oneness, and serenity, the person will be adding to the conscious co-creative process and collective atmosphere for evolving the human race game.

THE TOOLS OF AURA IMAGING OR SUBTLE ENERGY PHOTOGRAPHY AND OTHER IMAGING TECHNOLOGIES (VIRTUAL OR 3-D REALITIES)

I have previously mentioned modern Kirlian Aura equipment, such as the Gas Discharge Visualization camera, and aura imaging photography. However, at this point, I am briefly highlighting aura imaging photography and video aura imaging technology as representative of a number of new and emerging imaging technologies that can be adapted to assist humanity in evolving the human race game in specific and general terms.

The inventor of aura photography is Guy Coggins. He and others (e.g., see Johannes P. Fisslinger's books, *Aura Imaging Photography* and *Aura Mastery*; Goggle "Aura Video Station") have extended the technology to include viewing the motion of an aura through interaction with personal computers (e.g., Harry Oldfied's Polycontrast Interference Photography, a scanner that can provide a real time, moving image of the Energy field and can see imbalances in the Energy field).

One emerging aura technology involves the use of sensors on a flat plate or in a glove that measure a person's electromagnetic field in accord with the meridians, or energy pathways, in the person's hands. These measurements are then fed to a small computer, which changes them into colors, based on accepted basic colors of the chakras as correlated with what psychics reportedly see in extensive research with them.

With a still photo, the camera actually takes two separate shots, one shot of the person and one shot superimposing the colors. In a moving image, the information is projected directly onto the computer monitor where it appears either over the person's image transmitted by a video camera or over a silhouette provided by the software, depending on which program the person is using.

The monitor will also display various graphs representing, for example, a person's state of relaxation and the fluctuation of the person's emotions. The moving image can be stopped at any time and a printout made. The moving image, therefore, can also show the effects of anything to which the person might react, such as crystals, remedies, healing, meditation, music, colors, people, or thoughts and emotions about people. The possibility, therefore, for adapting this technology to assist with race-related and other-oriented encounters is evident.

In accord with the soul-centered model, I suggest that the desire and intent underlying this tool was to invent a technology that would remind people (humanity) that everything originates from within. Such a technology would allow people (humanity) to physically see the subtle aspects of universal energy. In accord with the soul-centered model, I further suggest that the hoped for outcome is for people (humanity) to become open to the archetypal energy *truth*, which in turn would motivate people (humanity) to tell the truth to another from their unique perspective.

Once people are authentically visible to one another, there is no need for secrets and people can minimize the temptation to create unknown enemies upon whom they project their fears. It is in this context, then, that the tool of aura imaging photography and video aura imaging technology may be adapted to assist in evolving the human race game in specific and general terms.

For the sake of contrast, I will also briefly refer to another representative imaging technology, which also can be adapted to assist in evolving the human race game. This other imaging technology is known as virtual reality and 3-D imaging. As an interactive technology that transports a person's conscious mind into a virtual reality, such a technology holds vast potential for creating virtual human experiences, including interracial and other-oriented experiences.

With various creative virtual or 3-D programming, then, virtual or 3-D interactive arenas involving interracial and other-oriented experiences can be created to assist in loosening rigid racial and other-oriented ideas and stereotypes. Such virtual or 3-D arenas could further assist in confronting interracial and other-oriented fears and reprogramming the personality to be open to more harmonious interracial and other-oriented beliefs.

As free will is paramount, however, individuals who would engage in this reprogramming process must choose to do so freely as a potential method to assist in their personal and spiritual growth. The potential outcome of such virtual interracial and other-oriented experiences, then, would be that these virtual experiences could assist a person in becoming more open during real interracial and other-oriented experiences. In this regard, the adaptation of the technology of virtual and 3-D reality may be used as a therapeutic tool to assist in evolving the human race game.

THE TOOLS OF MEDITATION AND TRANCES

In this general discussion on existing and emerging tools that can assist in evolving the *human race game*, readers may have discerned by now that there are many approaches for awakening and expanding a person's perceptive abilities in this regard. Some of these approaches include working with biofeedback, dreams, hypnosis, meditation, and any artistic or creative activity. Among the many approaches, however, meditation can be considered one of the most effective means of awakening and expanding a person's perceptive abilities.

What is called meditation gently allows a person to alter their consciousness and to shift their focus into a relaxed inner state or into what is called trance states. A trance state simply means that the person has allowed their self to relax the focus of their consciousness on the outer world in order to tap into the subtler, inner energies.

Meditation can be either active or passive, both forms allowing the person to perceive the inner world or the spiritual realm. The active form of meditation involves using a symbol, image, mantra, thought, idea, and the like and focusing on it to the exclusion of all other thoughts. In this kind of trance state, the person then taps into everything that may be associated with the idea or symbol. The passive form of meditation involves simply allowing images and perceptions to emerge in or rise to the mind as they will, forming themselves around a specific mantra, idea, symbol, and the like.

Using either an active or passive meditative approach, a person can connect with any of the twenty-five archetypal energies that I have discussed, actively or passively receiving various visions, impressions, feelings, and intuitive insights. It is in this manner, then, using the tool of meditation, that a person can draw to their outer self, inner or spiritual guidance to assist in evolving the human race game.

THE TOOL OF THE "MIRROR EFFECT"

If one understands the mirror effect, as I have framed it (see Chapter 4), it should be understood that all of the tools that I have discussed (and many that I have not) represent tools that a person already has or may attract into their experience to assist their outer self in evolving the human race game. That is, once a person has decided to embrace the idea of evolving the human race game, or simply decided to gently shift their consciousness to entertain such a possibility, the person activates the universal energy laws to co-create this reality. In doing so, the person vibrationally attracts or allows their outer self to be exposed to various tools in their life spaces that may assist them in their growth in this area.

All of the tools that I have discussed can be adapted to facilitate a person releasing racially-linked and other-oriented energy blocks and can be used to help create a mirror effect of growth with joy as each person evolves the human race game. It is important, therefore, to acknowledge one's intent to evolve the human race game and then use one's discernment to engage those tools with which one joyfully resonates.

The purpose in referring to the mirror effect at this point is simply to serve as a reminder that, as a tool, it allows a person to discern what is working and what is not, without using the framework of good-bad value judgments. The mirror effect allows a person also to gracefully let go of situations without blame. Further, the mirrored effects allow a person to understand that learning is contained in all experiences, even those experiences that they may have interpreted as negative.

In this discussion on evolving the human race game, therefore, I have been encouraging the use of the mirror effect to assist each person in uncovering those areas of their life spaces where racially-linked and other-oriented energy blocks require release and/or transformation. I have been affirming a person's power of choice as s/he uncovers racially-linked and other-oriented energy blocks. Once uncovered, it is important to affirm for one's outer self that the point of one's power is in the present. A person can then choose to refocus consciousness toward constructing mutually beneficial race relations and human relations.

EMERGING OPPORTUNITIES FOR HUMANITY TO EVOLVE: IMPLICATIONS FOR EVOLVING THE HUMAN RACE GAME

There are many opportunities emerging to assist humanity, individually and collectively, to evolve to a new state of consciousness. As this process unfolds, it also holds vast opportunities to evolve the *human race game*. It is important, however, for each person to practice the art of *discernment* as they seek to find resonance with particular opportunities.

I recommend, therefore, that people seek to align with individuals and groups that uplift their own spirit and those of others. I suggest that people ask whether or not the ideas of the individuals or groups resonate with inclusive and harmonious boundaries rather than with rigid and dogmatic boundaries. It is important to determine whether or not the ideas of the individuals or groups foster recognition that there are many paths to spiritual and consciousness growth.

Any group, for example, with a message which teaches a person that its way is the only way, or teaches a person that they must look down upon or put down another individual or group in order to have value is, to a large extent mirroring self-limiting concepts or a self-limiting ideology. I recommend, therefore, that people use discernment, not a judgmental framework, here and do not give these concepts or ideologies their attention and energy. Simply send the individuals or groups love and remain open to the possibilities of change and transformation for one's outer self and others and growth with joy.

When I use the term "emerging opportunities," I am specifically referring to those mirrored opportunities that emerge in a person's life spaces that have resonance with the twenty-five archetypal energies of which I have spoken. I am also referring to those challenges that may arise in a person's life spaces that provide the person's outer self with opportunities to access and to express their unique versions of the archetypal energies.

As there are numerous such opportunities, which can, will, and/or have already emerged in various arenas and contexts, I will primarily call attention to some general patterns of these opportunities. The intent here is for readers to view these patterns as representative of the kinds of relevant human and race-related opportunities that they may witness, encounter, or co-create in their life spaces.

EMERGING HUMAN AND RACE-RELATED OPPORTUNITIES IN PEOPLE'S PERSONAL LIFE SPACE

In each person's personal life space, for example, *one emerging pattern* of opportunities is that increasingly everyone may find people from a variety of so-called other races and/or relevant human events or circumstances coming into their life in one form or another. As this occurs, it is important to be open to an exploration of the gift of a diverse, yet interconnected world.

As a person begins to shift their consciousness to evolve the human race game, the universe will provide the person with a variety of mirror effects in accord with their focus. That is, people in various physical forms will show up in a variety of arenas and contexts. The arenas and contexts may be formal or informal, work-related or play-related, or may involve personal, societal, or global issues and challenges with which the person identifies. All of these possibilities will allow the person to choose to grow with pain or choose to grow with joy. I recommend the latter.

More specifically, in a person's personal life space, for example, they may find their outer self, without much conscious thought, being attracted to particular people with current racial forms different than their own. They will seem to be on a similar path of growth as the person's self or they may serve as a catalyst for the person's growth.

A person may also find their outer self being attracted to particular consciousness-expanding events, conferences, books, speakers, organizations, groups, television programs, Internet web sites and information, private or public events and figures, spiritual guides and teachers, and the like. They will seem to call to the person and their sense of a diverse, yet interconnected world.

A person may begin to have human and race-related synchronicity events emerging into their day-to-day experiences. These human and race-related synchronicity events will excite the person's imagination about the beauty contained in diversity.

It is important to view these personal experiences, then, as opportunities for learning more about one's self, as opportunities for sharing one's unique perspective on the world with others. It is important to view these personal experiences as opportunities to interactively mirror expressions of one's unique archetypal energies to evolve the human race game.

EMERGING SOCIAL MOVEMENT OPPORTUNITIES IN PEOPLE'S COLLECTIVE LIFE SPACES

At a collective level, a second emerging pattern of opportunities involves experiences that celebrate or call attention to humanity as the "many in one" and the "one in the many." This pattern has and will continue to show up through a variety of what are called social movements.

Examples of some social movements that have called and continue to call attention to people's interconnectedness include the Civil Rights/Civic Engagement movement, the Women's movement, the Human Rights movement, the Ecological movement, the Laughter movement, and what I now call the Synchronistic

Human Potential movement (or sometimes the Synergistic Human Potential movement), and the like.

At deeper levels, these social movements resonate with and are fueled by the archetypal energies of which I have spoken. However, the emerging patterns of social movements, which I will describe shortly, will take place more in people's minds and hearts as people interact with others in their personal life space and interface with the energies in their societal and global life spaces.

To evolve the human race game, therefore, I suggest that people can now co-create social movements which more explicitly allow and mirror the archetypal energies in their various life spaces. Therefore, imagine a world with social movements that: (1) foster and mirror trust, unity, oneness, and serenity; (2) foster and mirror beauty, enthusiasm, humor, hope, abundance, compassion, peace, joy, clarity, and vision; and (3) foster and mirror flexibility, courage, understanding, truth, wisdom, inspiration and patience. Imagine a world where all of the above social movements are linked to an overarching social movement that fosters and mirrors love, acceptance, inclusion, and harmony.

With social movements of this nature, people may learn to view various social movements as aspects of one multidimensional planetary social movement. Therefore, when various archetypal energies are mirrored through various social movements, are linked as aspects of an overarching social movement, and are fostered and mirrored in various life spaces, people will quicken the process of evolving the human race game.

To assist people in linking various social movements to archetypal energies, I will call the overarching social movement the *human planetary synergy and synchronistic movement*. This label will provide a common and general focus on the consciousness-energy, the interconnectedness and interdependence of those social movements that are synergistic aspects of one multidimensional planetary social movement.

When challenges, such as war or threats of war, arise on the world stage to distract people from a focus on their interconnectedness and interdependence, social movements, of the nature that I have presented, serve as reminders in this regard. That is, they serve as reminders to keep each person's focus on "who they are" and "what they want" (what the person is *for*), not on "who they are not" and "what they do not want" (what the person is *against*).

One example of a social movement where there is a vast amount of energy that can be harnessed to mirror interconnectedness and interdependence in a person's world is in regard to what is called the Peace movement. Theoretically, the emphasis of this social movement is on the archetypal energy peace, and not the emotional and thought energies associated with wars. However, currently some in this social movement tend to find purpose only by hating wars. I have noted elsewhere that hating wars will not change such conditions. Instead, it is important to love peace.

Archetypal energies, as aspects of universal energy, are not dualistic and do not comprehend negatives. They transcend the polarities with which people are familiar. So, it is important, therefore, for a person to maintain the focus of their consciousness on, and to send energy only toward "what they want" (what they are *for*) in co-creating their reality.

Another example of a social movement that is currently in its infancy, but one, which holds great potential to assist in evolving a new consciousness, is represented by what is now being called a politics of trust (See Vasconcellos' "Politics of Trust," *AHP Perspective*, December 2002/January 2003; Ferguson's "Fear and Projection as Root Causes of War, and the Archetypal Energies 'Trust' and 'Peace' as Antidotes," *AHP Perspective*, October/November, 2009). At the core of this social movement is the foundational archetypal energy trust.

At the level of a person's personality, the person typically experiences trust as it relates to a feeling of security. However, it is when the person realizes and recognizes their interconnectedness and interdependence that they will truly feel secure. The politics of trust social movement, therefore, is an emerging opportunity that has the potential to assist humanity with this kind of recognition.

Again, social movements that remind people of their interconnectedness and interdependence are fueled by the archetypal energies of which I have spoken. They represent another pattern of emerging opportunities to assist in evolving the human race game.

EMERGING OPPORTUNITIES FOR REUNIONS WITH ORIGINAL SPIRITUAL FAMILIES

A third emerging pattern of opportunities is represented by what might be called the reunion and blending of spiritual families. In accord with the soul-centered model, each person is a member of one of the seven or nine original spiritual families, depending on one's point of view, plus what can be called the original source family.

As the nature of this pattern of opportunities calls a person toward reunion and blending, the person will begin to understand that members of their spiritual family exist in various racial forms. The person will know they are in the presence of someone from their original spiritual family by how they feel. Their energy will feel familiar and will feel like home. The person may find their inner and outer self feeling more balanced and perhaps rejuvenated.

Such reunions need not be long encounters. Indeed, some of these encounters will be experienced as short encounters. Here, a person's higher self guides or urges the person toward such encounters to help the person remember who they really are.

I am emphasizing the point about potential short encounters only because I do not want people to think or feel that they must hang on to their spiritual family members in order to grow with joy. In accord with the soul-centered model, much joy can and will be experienced through acts of blending with family members from any of the original spiritual families, as indeed that is the nature of the pattern I am describing.

This does not mean, however, that so-called long term encounters with one's original family members, or what a person may come to think of as a companion or partner from their original spiritual family, will not be or cannot be part of one's path for *growth with joy*. In accord with the soul-centered model, the reminder here is that people are already whole beings and that a person's reunions and blending encounters are intended to remind the person of how, as a whole being, they are also part of their original spiritual family, and are a part of source energy/ spirit or All-That-Is.

EMERGING TRANSFORMATIONAL EVENTS AND INTER-GROUP AND INTER-FAITH OPPORTUNITIES

A fourth emerging pattern of opportunities is related to the transformations of and establishment of more harmonious boundaries surrounding various religions, race-linked, and/or other human intergroup experiences. One example has been called Operation Compassion, a coalition of religions, formed in Houston, Texas, in the wake of the transformative national event called Hurricane Katrina.

The hurricane significantly impacted New Orleans and Mississippi, with ripples in other Gulf States and throughout the rest of the United States. Many extraordinary and courageous souls were participants in this event, a significant number with *current racial forms* that were people of color or African Americans. The effect of economic disparities as it relates to the phenomenon of race was once again mirrored for the nation. And

Operation Compassion was given birth. Similar dynamics were echoed in the wake of the January 12, 2010, earthquake in Haiti and the February 27, 2010, earthquake in Chile.

Then, in late October 2012, Hurricane Sandy made history as the largest Atlantic hurricane and second costliest on record. Hurricane Sandy again transcended a number of socially constructed national boundaries, impacting the United States (Southeast, Mid-Atlantic, New England, Appalachia, and the Midwest), Jamaica, Haiti, Cuba, Bahamas, Bermuda, and Canada. In the United States, the devastating impact of Hurricane Sandy and the most visible human care responses were mirrored in New Jersey and New York.

I am not suggesting that it requires a transformative hurricane or other transformative Earth-related event like a tsunami or an earthquake to call attention to opportunities to express harmonious boundaries. Many people already recognize the importance of establishing more harmonious boundaries surrounding various religions and/or intergroup experiences, race-linked and otherwise.

Rather, in terms of the *human race game*, I am simply using the Katrina, Haiti, Chili, and Sandy examples to suggest that bridging efforts of this nature can, must, and will take place more in regard to religions, race-linked, and other intergroup experiences as the various archetypal energies are allowed to emerge into various life spaces. Indeed, "interfaith" activities, organized or informal, already exist and will continue to expand (e.g., The Interfaith Alliance; The Interfaith Foundation).

Throughout history, for example, humanity has often misdirected its energy to co-create somewhat rigid, dogmatic boundaries in relation to various religions. As I have noted elsewhere, numerous wars and conflicts, which focus on the phenomena of race and ethnicity and the use of religion as a justification, characterize the nature of many struggles to maintain what people think of as the correct views and practices for relating to source energy/spirit or All-That-Is.

To illustrate, in 2010, many in the United States were provided with opportunities to examine and debate the nature of misdirected energy as it related to the phenomena of religion, ethnicity, and race. The opportunity presented itself in the form of whether or not a so-called Islamic Cultural Center, connected to the Islam religion, should be built near the site of where a highly charged emotional event occurred ten years earlier. Many simply call the event 9/11.

Those who participated in the debate, directly or indirectly, thus had the opportunity, if they chose to take advantage of it, to examine particular beliefs and actions. There was the opportunity, for example, to look at how some beliefs and actions, carried out in the name of a particular religion, can open or close consciousness. There was the opportunity also to look at how energy can be constructively directed or misdirected in relation to the co-creation of harmonious boundaries.

As the transformation and establishment of harmonious boundaries take place, there are those who, out of fear, will seek to maintain the old ways. Out of fear, they will idealize the past, and seek to conserve what was never so. This will eventually give way, however, as what some visionaries call Second Wave Energy and Fifth Dimensional experiences (i.e., new experiments that not only involve height, weight, and depth, but also involve time and space) take root. In accord with the soul-centered model, the archetypal energies, of which I have spoken, are part of the Second Wave Energy and Fifth Dimensional experiences.

The emerging patterns of the new energy, therefore, will urge and support the efforts of those religions that engage increasingly in collaborative and cooperative spiritual enterprises. Such spiritual enterprises are meant to remind humanity that all people are creators and co-creators, and that people do not need to project out their power onto an external source. Indeed, in accord with the soul-centered model, each person is part of the source. And, each person is the source, in a manner of speaking.

At the level of a person's personality, however, these emerging, collaborative religious opportunities are intended to assist the person's outer self in identifying more with their soul qualities, the archetypal energies, which do not involve judgments about current racial forms. They are intended to assist each person in moving beyond the limitations of dogma per se.

They are also intended to help humanity recognize that all religions are simply forms of fellowship, whose purpose is to remind each person that they and their fellow human beings on planet Earth are portions of the same human entity and parts of source energy/spirit or All-That-Is. They are intended to remind each person that they are a conscious creator or co-creator of the world that they know.

THE CHOICE TO EVOLVE THE HUMAN RACE GAME WITH JOY THROUGH "BEING" A CONSCIOUS CREATOR OF NEW SCRIPTS

From a developmental perspective, as can be understood, humanity is now at a point of being conscious co-creators, or more precisely, conscious creators. I will use the two terms to mirror the same idea—that people create their own reality according to the nature of their beliefs. In accord with the soul-centered model, people have always been creators, although prior to this point most people were content to play their games largely being unaware of how they created their games. In terms of the soul-centered model, all of this was necessary in order to allow humanity's consciousness to evolve to the point of being able to handle higher vibratory energies on the physical plane.

In other words, human beings are now at a point to be able to embrace their creative power, fully and consciously, with understanding, passion, and compassion. As a conscious creator or co-creator, a person will now know that they can create more constructively by first consciously focusing their consciousness on love, acceptance, inclusion, and harmony.

In the alternative model of human nature (the soul-centered model), therefore, a person's ever-expanding awareness of their creative power underlies the essence of what I have called the person's ever-emerging truer self, or their spiritually integrated self. Using the creative power of their truer self, then, a person, as a conscious co-creator in their current racial form, can consciously evolve the human race game by writing, or more precisely visioning, personal and collective new scripts that mirror the archetypal energies in the person's various life spaces.

CREATING NEW SCRIPTS: A PRIMARY HUMAN CHALLENGE

One may ask why, at both the individual and collective levels, it has seemed so difficult for humanity to choose to evolve their games with joy, particularly the human race game. There is no one answer for such a question, for each person has the gift of free will.

I can, however, suggest that built into a person's specific race-linked games, and for that matter, all of a person's human games, is what I call a *primary human challenge*. That primary human challenge is a dynamic tension, flowing from a person's creative urge for the freedom to be who they really are in a physical form, and simultaneously to embrace their responsibility for their being-ness.

Freedom and responsibility are flip sides of the same coin. However, when a person embraces their responsibility as a creator or co-creator with free will, there is no one to blame (see Figure 8).

Figure 8. A Human Challenge: The Dynamic Tension Between "Freedom" And "Responsibility"

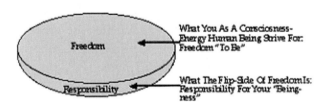

Throughout linear history, as can be understood, there has been reluctance to acknowledge that people are the creators or co-creators of all the horrific conditions, circumstances, and atrocities that they have perpetrated upon one another, for whatever reasons. At the personality level, this has been a most difficult idea to comprehend.

Most people, therefore, adopted numerous self-limiting beliefs, fueled by fear, to structure their reality. It became much easier to play the *blame game* and to attribute one's motives, actions, and reactions to an "evil other" or to some great evil force outside and apart from one's self.

As I have previously suggested, the primary human challenge also has more often than not led many people to believe that anything worth having involved struggle or pain. And so it is that human beings adopted an approach to evolution that involved growth with pain. Up to this point, most people have used this approach, or underlying, limiting belief, subconsciously to write and structure the scripts for their games, including the human race game.

However, as I also have repeatedly suggested, at this point in time, as can be understood, human beings have outgrown such a limiting belief. Now is the time, therefore, to choose to *grow with joy*, for human beings already know how to *grow with pain*. It is time to create or write new scripts to evolve the *human race game*. The universal energy supports are already in place, awaiting the new scripts that only each person can create. It is time to be free and to be responsible for one's creations.

To assist people in their next adventure with script writing, I first want to briefly present a reminder of how a person (humanity) currently co-creates or creates their scripts, that is, how a person currently co-creates or creates their present racial reality (their present human reality) with their mind. Next, I want to briefly discuss how a person (humanity) can co-create or create new scripts, that is, how a person can co-create or create a new racial reality (new human reality) with their mind.

Thirdly, I want to re-emphasize once again the choice that is available to each person—that is, the choice to evolve the human race game with joy. Finally, I want to offer a few suggestions, in the form of reminders, for creating one's most optimal scripts, that is, suggestions for creating a new, optimal racial reality.

HOW HUMANITY CURRENTLY CREATES AND CO-CREATES THE "PRESENT RACIAL REALITY" (THE PRESENT HUMAN REALITY) WITH THE MIND: THE "OLD REALITY CREATION PROCESS" FOR CREATING SCRIPTS

As a reminder of what I will call humanity's "Old Reality Creation Process," I have outlined a six-stage circular process for how a person (people) has been using their mind to co-create or create the present racial reality (the present human reality) with their mind (see Figure 9). The process is circular, as that is the nature of the flow of universal energy.

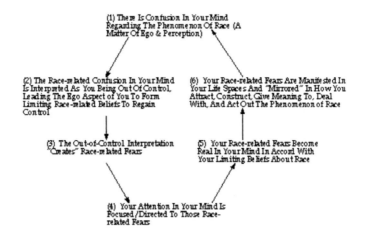

Figure 9. How You Currently Co-Create The Present Racial Reality With Your Mind

(1) There Is Confusion In Your Mind Regarding The Phenomenon Of Race (A Matter Of Ego & Perception)

(2) The Race-related Confusion In Your Mind Is Interpreted As You Being Out Of Control, Leading The Ego Aspect Of You To Form Limiting Race-related Beliefs To Regain Control

(3) The Out-of-Control Interpretation "Creates" Race-related Fears

(4) Your Attention In Your Mind Is Focused/Directed To Those Race-related Fears

(5) Your Race-related Fears Become Real In Your Mind In Accord With Your Limiting Beliefs About Race

(6) Your Race-related Fears Are Manifested In Your Life Spaces And "Mirrored" In How You Attract, Construct, Give Meaning To, Deal With, And Act Out The Phenomenon of Race

First, throughout history, as it can be understood, there has been confusion in the mind regarding the phenomenon of race. In accord with the soul-centered model, when human beings developed an ego as a species, they did so because they felt it was necessary to have a conscious aspect of the self to protect the outer self from perceived dangers and to organize their numerous outer experiences. This was also when human beings gave birth to free will and choice, again feeling that they needed a way to maneuver comfortably in the outer world.

However, the ego aspect of personality has struggled to figure out what to do with its perception of physical differences and the diversity of *racial forms*. Much of this is related to a person's experience with the illusion of duality to structure the games in their world.

In accord with the soul-centered model, dualism was created as an illusion to provide a person with a context for choosing. That is, individually and collectively, the inner self created the illusion of a subjective inner state of being and an objective outer state of being. So, from this dualistic state of mind, there emerged race-related confusion in individual and collective minds about the objective outer forms, and a *second aspect* of the old co-creative process took place.

In this second stage, the ego aspect of personality, in historical terms, erroneously interpreted the confusion in the mind about humanity's objective outer forms—that is, the confusion itself was interpreted as a person (people) being out of control.

As a result, human beings then created race-related, self-limiting beliefs as a method to try to contain or to regain control over those objective aspects of the self that appeared to be out of control. However, as they did so, a *third aspect* of the old co-creative process emerged. Many people found that the effect of their misinterpretation regarding the confusion about humanity's objective outer forms and the race-related, self-limiting beliefs was to generate race-related ego fears.

In the mind, then, humanity's race-related ego fears subsequently captured the attention of many people's consciousness. That is, the attention in the mind got directed and focused on the race-related ego fears about the objective outer forms. This was the *fourth aspect* of the old co-creative process.

As people's attention became more intensified or energized, the result was that these race-related ego fears felt real in the mind, individually and collectively, reinforcing and fueling the race-related, self-limiting beliefs. This was the *fifth aspect* of the old co-creative process.

Many people then used race-related, self-limiting beliefs, in reference to perceived security, sensory, and power issues, to structure their racial (human) reality. Here, many people gave direction to universal energy for how to structure the current racial (human) reality. That is, many people gave energy to their race-related fears to be manifested or mirrored in their life spaces in one form or another.

A person's (people's) creations were/are mirrored, therefore, in how they vibrationally attract, construct, give meaning to, deal with, and act out toward the phenomenon of race. Such mirrored effects, the *sixth aspect*, reflect a person's (people's) race-related scripts, which only serve to reinforce the confusion they carry in their mind about the phenomenon of race.

It is in this manner, then, that human beings have co-created or created the present racial reality (the present human reality) with the mind. However, it is important at this point in time, as can be understood, to know that many human beings have outgrown their old scripts.

How Human Beings Can Create and Co-Create a "New Racial Reality" (A New Human Reality) with the Mind: A "New Reality Creation Process" for Creating Scripts

To assist each person in becoming more *conscious* about a "new reality creation process" for creating scripts, I again have outlined a six-stage circular process for how a person (people) can use their mind to co-create or create a new racial reality (a new human reality) with their mind (see Figure 10).

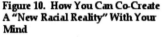

Figure 10. How You Can Co-Create A "New Racial Reality" With Your Mind

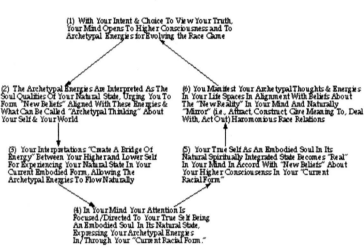

(1) With Your Intent & Choice To View Your Truth, Your Mind Opens To Higher Consciousness and To Archetypal Energies for Evolving the Race Game

(2) The Archetypal Energies Are Interpreted As The Soul Qualities Of Your Natural State, Urging You To Form "New Beliefs" Aligned With These Energies & What Can Be Called "Archetypal Thinking" About Your Self & Your World

(3) Your Interpretations "Create A Bridge Of Energy" Between Your Higher and Lower Self For Experiencing Your Natural State In Your Current Embodied Form, Allowing The Archetypal Energies To Flow Naturally

(4) In Your Mind Your Attention Is Focused/Directed To Your True Self Being An Embodied Soul In Its Natural State, Expressing Your Archetypal Energies In/Through Your "Current Racial Form."

(5) Your True Self As An Embodied Soul In Its Natural Spiritually Integrated State Becomes "Real" In Your Mind In Accord With "New Beliefs" About Your Higher Consciousness In Your "Current Racial Form"

(6) You Manifest Your Archetypal Thoughts & Energies In Your Life Spaces In Alignment With Beliefs About The "New Reality" In Your Mind And Naturally "Mirror" (i.e., Attract, Construct, Give Meaning To, Deal With, Act Out) Harmonious Race Relations

As I have noted elsewhere, all new creations begin with a creative intention. From an energy vibrational point of view, a person's *intention* serves as the initial *law of attraction* message that goes out to universal energy that the person wants to create a new shape, form, or circumstance (a new script) for their experience. In essence, the person is saying to the universe that they prefer this new shape, form, or circumstance (a new script), for they think it is more useful for their growth and development.

The person is also saying to the universe that they think this new shape, form, or circumstance (a new script) has value to help them better understand and learn more about their ever-emerging truer self. The person is saying to the universe that this new script is more aligned with or will allow them to more efficiently view their higher truth and move toward their higher good.

With this creative intention in mind, therefore, a person chooses to move toward, to attract, and to view their own higher truth. In accord with this decision, the person's ego or personality expands and opens to allow them to access and integrate with their higher consciousness and the archetypal energies.

The *first stage* in creating a new racial reality (a new human reality), then, is to initiate a new script with one's intent to do so. A person then decides to allow their outer self to work with their higher consciousness and the archetypal energies. As this work begins, the person begins to call forth various opportunities to experience a greater sense of who they are at a core level of their self and the energies that support the outer self.

As a person begins to open their outer self to genuinely and authentically encounter and experience the archetypal energies, they begin to interpret these energies as aspects of their natural state of being. As such, the person naturally experiences them as their soul qualities.

And so it is that a person can then begin to embrace the Archetypal Energies or their soul qualities, as they urge the person to form new beliefs to structure how to think about their self and the nature of new scripts for their world. This interpretation, then, is the *second stage* in creating a new racial reality (a new human reality). It allows the person to engage in what I call "archetypal thinking" about their self and their world.

Archetypal thinking, therefore, simply means that a person allows the archetypal energies to fuel their thoughts about their self and their world. In other words, archetypal thinking sets the stage for allowing the archetypal energies to flow naturally through the person's personal energy system. The person's interpretation, therefore, creates a soul-centered bridge between their higher and lower self, and their personality is positioned to open to the archetypal energies.

In the person's current racial form, then, the archetypal energies are allowed to flow naturally through their personal energy system, and the person experiences them as their natural state of being. This act of allowance then is the *third stage* for creating a new racial reality (a new human reality). In effect, the person is allowing their truer self to emerge into physicality so they can more consciously generate and act out new scripts in accord with the transformational race game that I earlier discussed.

In the person's mind, as this transformation takes place and their truer self begins to emerge, the person's attention is focused or directed to knowing their truer self as an embodied soul in its natural state in physicality, authentically expressing their archetypal energies in and through their current racial form.

The *fourth stage* in creating a new racial reality (a new human reality), then, has to do with what a person gives or pays attention to in their mind. When a person decides to give attention to the idea that their ever-emerging truer self becomes an embodied soul in their current racial form, the person begins to shift how they view their outer self and the outer self of others in the world.

The more a person focuses on the idea of their truer self as an embodied soul, the focus intensifies and energizes the idea and the more real it becomes in the person's mind. And so it is that a person transcends the dualistic confusion in their mind as they begin to experience their self as a spiritually-integrated self in physicality. In one's current racial form, then, the realness that a person experiences in their mind is in accord with the person's new beliefs about their higher consciousness.

Just as a person valued and used their old beliefs to structure their reality, in a similar manner the person now holds value for and begins to use their new beliefs to structure their reality. This realness represents the *fifth stage* of creating a new racial reality (a new human reality) with one's mind.

Many people used their self-limiting beliefs and gave direction to universal energy to structure their old race-related scripts and the present racial reality (the present human reality) in accord with their lower self race games. Now people can use their new beliefs to give direction to universal energy for how to structure new race-related scripts and a new racial reality (a new human reality) in accord with the higher self race games that I have discussed.

That is, people now can manifest (attract, construct, give meaning to, deal with, and act out) their archetypal thoughts and energies in their personal, societal, and global life spaces in alignment with their beliefs about the new reality in their mind. In doing so, one uses the universal energy laws and, thereby, naturally creates and mirrors harmonious relationships in creating a new racial reality.

This manifestation stage, then, is the *sixth stage* in creating a new racial reality. A person's more spiritually integrated experience, then, reinforces their original intention to view their higher truth. And so it is that in creating a new racial reality, each person, individually and collectively, also creates a new human reality.

THE CHOICE TO EVOLVE THE HUMAN RACE GAME WITH JOY

So, what is the role of the archetypal energy j*oy* in creating new scripts and a new racial and human reality, and how does this relate to a person's free will? As I have discussed, most people's old race-related scripts have been largely structured by the self-limiting belief that the only worthwhile way to grow is to grow with pain.

Again, I have been and am suggesting that it is time to learn how to grow with joy. That is, at this point in each person's individual and collective experiences, it is important for the person to embrace their free will and to use it wisely (not forcefully) to create and allow more joyful experiences to emerge into rheir personal, societal, and global life spaces.

It is important for each person to understand that they always choose in the present. And, it is important for each person to freely choose to embrace the archetypal energy joy as their primary motivation in valuing their process of growth. No one, however, can make that choice for another person.

It is important to affirm within one's self, then, that the point of their power is in the present, and that they can choose moment-to-moment to write new scripts that mirror joy. A person's choice to evolve the human race game with joy in specific and general terms, therefore, takes place instantaneously and in the present.

In resonance with the ideas of Sanaya Roman and Orin on the topic of free will (see *Spiritual Growth: Being Your Higher Self*), I have adapted a presentation here of some of their ideas to assist in creating a new, optimal human and racial reality with joy (see Table 8). I offer these ideas as reminders of what some people may already know at some level. They are suggestions for what to keep in mind, understandings for maintaining a perspective, and explanations for how and why the new energy framework can work.

Table 8.   Reminders/Suggestions/Understandings For How Best To Use "*Free will*" Wisely To Create New Human and Race-Related Scripts With Joy And A New, Optimal Racial Reality

Reminders/Suggestions/Understandings	Explanations For Creating New Human And Race-Related Scripts
1. Start by assuming the Universe is working for you and with you to assist you in creating your Higher Good.	If you use your will as if there is an opposing force, you actually create opposing forces where there are none. Your wise will, therefore, positions you to view Others, including those perceived to be from a different racial group, as people who can assist you in creating your Higher Good.
2. Use the strength of your will to develop a wise and magnetic will and have things come to you more easily.	The strength of your will was perhaps developed at earlier ages to believe in yourself when others didn't support your ideas.
3. Don't make your Self wrong if you had to use a lot of force and will to get things done in the past.	You were doing the best you knew how at the time.
4. It is important to have a well-developed will, for this is necessary to carry out your part in the work of transformation.	You are a creative partner with the Higher forces of the Universe.

5. A wise will is one that does things with thought, planning, and intention.

It thinks of better ways than force to do things.

6. Your wise will surveys all circumstances surrounding the issues, finds effective ways to do things with a minimum of effort, waits until the time is right to make a move, is patient, will persistently and consistently contribute the Energy needed to create your goals, and takes the time and steps needed to do a good job.

Your wise will knows that if the time isn't right, things will take a lot more Energy to accomplish; it knows that some things take time to accomplish; it knows that you don't have to do things all at once.

7. Your wise will is confident, tries out new solutions and takes the initiative.

Your wise will looks for new and better ways to do things; it makes decisions not solely based on impulsive feelings but by blending them with logic and common sense.

8. When the actions you take are aligned with your Higher Self, you will not need force to carry them out.

When you are working toward your Higher goals, you may need to work steadily and persistently, but you will not be pushing against resistant, unmoving forces.

9. You can use your forceful will on your Self, forcing your Self to do things, but not for long. The more you use your forceful will to make your Self do something, the more you push your Self into an opposite reaction.

Your intellect often sets goals for you and wants your forceful will to carry them out; your forceful will may try to do what your intellect tells it to, but if your goal or the way you are pursuing it isn't for your Higher Good, your wise will, will stop you.

10. Your wise will is connected to the Higher Will and your Higher Self.

Your wise will follows the guidance of your Higher Self.

11. Your wise will won't let itself be used against you.

Your wise will is too powerful a force for your intellect to control.

12. You only stick to those things you love; your forceful will only succeeds temporarily in getting you to do things your Higher Self isn't guiding you to do.

When your Higher Self feels it is better for you not to do something, it goes to your wise will and says, "Create resistance; stop; do not carry through with the action. When it is good for you to do something, you will feel a desire to do it; you will be drawn to it because it is something you love and not something you are forcing your Self to do."

13. When you do what you love, it requires no force. Your wise will guides you to those things you love to do.

The only things you do without resistance are those things you love to do and are drawn to. Through trial and error, your experiences teach you what these things are.

14. Your wise will has your Highest Interests in Mind.

Even though a part of you thinks it might be best to do something, if another part of you is resisting, trust that there is a Higher Reason why you are avoiding this.

Instead; Take time to listen to your feelings; Do things only when they feel right and when you would love to do them; then you are operating from your wise will.

15. If you aren't accomplishing a goal your intellect has set, rather than forcing your Self to do it, talk to your wise will and ask, "Why won't you do what I am telling you to do?"

Keep your goal in Mind and ask your wise will what plan of action it will work with you to accomplish; Before you decide to do some thing, get quiet and notice your feelings about doing it. Ask your Self before you take action, "Do I really want to do this? Does it seem *Joyful*? Is there something else I would rather do

16. You can draw what you want to you by allowing it to come rather than by forcing it to come.

When you push too hard to get things, you actually repel the things you are seeking. There is a difference between reaching out for something versus allowing it to come to you.

17. Receive Energy from other people's hearts and not their centers of will, and when you are with someone, practice sending Energy through your heart. This is the primary understanding for creating new race-related scripts with **Joy**.

"It is important to learn not to let the forceful will of others control you. You can know if other people are using their forceful wills to manipulate you through (a) your mental or emotional resistance to them or (b) an uncomfortable feeling in your body when you think of them, often experienced in the pit of your stomach."

18. To assist others in their growth, and not interfere with their growth, do not use your forceful will with others. When you work with people, use your wise will and do not try to make others change if they are not ready.

Your wise will does things easily and gently, and takes action only when the timing is right. It waits until people are ready to hear what you have to say.

19. If there is a quality you want in relating to your mate or a friend or others (e.g., those you consider racially different), demonstrate that quality . your Self

As your life begins to work better, you inspire others to discover the secrets you have found. Find more *Joy* in your life, laugh more, and allow your Self to be happy.

20. To create a desire to grow in others, share your Enthusiasm about your life. Listen to people, draw them out, and find ways to assist them in loving themselves more. Grow yourself and become an example.

There is no one "right" way to grow. There are many paths to enlightenment. See what is beautiful in every person's path, in every religion, and in every belief system. Honor other people's paths even if they are different from yours. There is no right way; there is only the way that is right for you.

21. Be inclusive and loving, and look beyond the form of people's beliefs to the Essence.

There is something unique, perfect, and beautiful in every culture, in every system of belief. Look for what you have in common with others and accept and love those who are on different paths.

In light of these reminders, suggestions, understandings, and explanations, if a person from their own race or another race, as currently understood, is trying to force the person's outer self to do something not in alignment with joy or their higher good, either subtly or not so subtly, they can work at an energy level to change things between both parties:

1. Start by getting quiet and thinking of the other person. As you think of this person, do you have an uncomfortable feeling anywhere in your body? Uncomfortable areas can indicate places where you have taken on other people's energies and are wearing their energy patterns rather than your own.

2. Send light and *love* to this place, and imagine you are reclaiming your own energy in this area.

3. Close off any area in which you have been receiving another's energy, and then add your own light and *love* to this area.

4. Pay attention to where other people are sending energies from, and only accept energies from their heart or higher centers.

5. You can know if people are sending you energy from their will (power center) by getting quiet, thinking of them, and imagining you can tell if they have a vibrational energy cord coming from their will center (power center) toward you. See yourself refusing this energy or imagine cutting the cord, thus cutting the energy coming toward you from another person's will (power center). Then see energy going back to the person so that they can use it any way they can.

6. When you are with someone, practice sending energy through your heart center.

In an earlier description of the spiritually integrative archetypal energy joy, I described joy as an energy aspect of authentic essence or a soul quality that creates light-heartedness. Joy guides the nature of spiritual blending surrounding relating and connecting such that it is experienced as fun. And so this is just a reminder once again that joy guides the nature of play in the universe.

In accord with the soul-centered model, joy naturally emerges in response to any soul contact and comes from creating order with harmony and beauty. Joy resides beneath the surface of apparent polarities in the core of a person's being and springs forth in response to soul contacts.

Joy is the primary vibrational note of the planet Earth, guiding the evolutionary plan and guiding the process of becoming a conscious creator or co-creator in physicality. It is important for each person, therefore, to seek to soul-link with others and to allow their joy to spring forth as they construct their new, optimal racial and human reality as conscious co-creators.

EVOLVING THE HUMAN RACE GAME AS A CONSCIOUS CREATOR OR CO-CREATOR

So, how does a person know if they are being a conscious creator or co-creator of their reality or if they are continuing to react in robot-like fashion to one's self and to others? I offer some ideas here. As a result of intuitive urging, I also shared these ideas in another context (see my chapter in Shostak's *Viable Utopian Ideas: Shaping A Better World*, 2003). As may be surmised, a method of knowing if one is being a *conscious creator* or *co-creator* is to use the *mirror effect* to assess one's personal life space to see if one's outer self and one's life reflect some or all of the characteristics listed below.

CHARACTERISTICS OF A CONSCIOUS CREATOR OR CO-CREATOR: PRACTICAL IDEALIST AND "CHANNELLER" OF WISDOM (SOUL QUALITIES) IN REGARD TO THE HUMAN RACE GAME

I will share, therefore, twenty-four characteristics that a person might find helpful as they move forward into the 21st century as a *conscious creator* or *co-creators*. *Conscious creators* or *co-creators* might have some or all of these characteristics:

1. They have released old programming and beliefs that no longer serve them.

2. They have drawn into their life supportive, positive people.

3. They empower their self and others in what they do and say.

4. They know who they are, why they are here, and what their higher purpose is.

5. Their lifestyle and environment support their life purpose and greater work in the world.

6. They explore new possibilities and choices and continually expand their vision of what is possible.

7. They have the tools to draw to their self the opportunities, people, and events they need to create their life's work.

8. They operate from their heart, and they trust their inner messages and takes action upon them.

9. They are conscious of the energy around them, deciding when to be transparent to it, harmonize with it, or transmute it to a higher order.

10. They are aware of their energy and the effects other people have upon it.

11. They are present in the moment—alert, aware, and at a high level of observation in their everyday experiences.

12. Their increasing aliveness, enthusiasm, and growth spark growth in those around them.

13. They create with energy before they take physical action.

14. They know they can create whatever they want by working with the higher forces and directing their thoughts, emotions, and intent toward their goals.

15. They create change by working at the highest spiritual level rather than at the personality level.

16. They stop before they take action, go within, and receive guidance from their higher self about what action to take.

17. They know that anything is possible.

18. They know that through their understanding of how energy works, they can consciously create what seems like miracles when they have less understanding of the way energy works.

19. They are able to create what they want at a speed that seemed impossible at earlier levels of growth.

20. They are able to handle easily and joyfully the things that used to challenge them.

21. Their lessons come faster, but they will also have the tools to move through them more quickly and easily.

22. They have a clearer sense of direction, a greater feeling of being in control, and a deeper understanding of why things are happening.

23. There is an increasing calm that comes as they begin to enjoy and understand their life.

24. They can truly live a life that is joyful and loving to their self.

As people, individually and collectively, develop the above characteristics for becoming conscious creators or conscious co-creators, each person also will be consciously using the mirror effect to assess their world and to engage in the art of self-creation and reality-creation. In other terms, working and co-creating with universal energy in this way, a person will be acting as a practical idealist and channeller of wisdom in their world, bringing together and using logic and intuitive guidance.

In other words, the person will be allowing their outer self to use their wise will in the manner that I have outlined elsewhere, and the person will seek to mirror some or all of the characteristics outlined above. In turn, the archetypal energy *wisdom* will be channeled through the person's personal energy system, and the person's ideals for a new, optimal reality, inclusive of an optimal racial reality, will be mirrored in practical ways.

A person's ideals flow from their dreams about how to create or manifest their higher good. But, it is up to the person's outer self to make these ideals practical. From a spiritual and soul-centered perspective, however, it is source energy/spirit or All-That-Is and the person's soul as their higher self that dreams and creates ever-emerging visions to playfully learn more about authentic essence.

At the level of a person's personality, however, because of the current dualistic stance, as it can be understood, the person creates, experiences, and expresses (manifests) their soul's dreams through the use of their creative imagination. What some have called the awakening process simply means that a person awakes or becomes aware that they are the soul who is dreaming about how to create/manifest their higher good.

The person, therefore, awakes to their *greater truth*: (1) that they are a spiritual entity with consciousness in physical form, an embodied soul, (2) that they are a unique part of source energy/spirit or All-That-Is, and (3) that they are a unique, conscious expression of the dream(s) of source energy/spirit or All-That-Is. In practical terms, what this means is that the person awakes to their truth about their connection to those in their life spaces.

In terms of the conscious creation or co-creation process and the mind-body-spirit connection, it is difficult to fully represent the dreaming and awakening process in two- or three- or multidimensional visual terms. However, I wanted to provide some visual glimpse of what is involved (see Figure 11)—that is, where and how the "action for awakening and manifestation" takes place, so to speak.

Figure 11. The Conscious Co-Creation Process: The Mind-Body-Soul Connection As Your Emerging True Self Becomes A Conscious Co-Creator and Your Personality Mirrors Your Creations

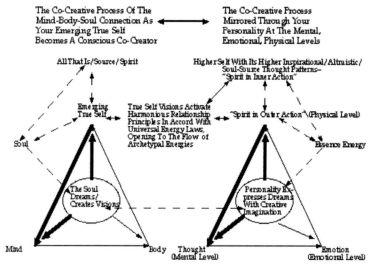

So, I suggest that observers simply allow their outer self to reflect on the visual representation that is provided. The left side of the visual representation is an attempt to show the inner or higher spiritual aspects of the co-creation process of a person's mind-body-soul connection, as the person's emerging truer self becomes a conscious creator or co-creator.

The right side of the visual representation is an attempt to show the more surface aspects of the creation or co-creation process as a person may experience them being mirrored through their personality at the mental, emotional, and physical levels (the more surfaced mirrored effects).

The arrows in the representation are intended to show the spiritual and soul-centered pathways and the direction of the vibrational flow of emerging energies, forms, and visions. The dotted arrows are intended to reflect the person's truer self-soul-source energy/spirit/All-That-Is connection at higher dimensional levels and the person's soul-personality connection in the co-creation process.

At a more surface level in spiritual terms, these vibrational connections may be characterized as the spirit in outer action-authentic essence energy-spirit in inner action connection. That is, at a more surface level in spiritual terms, the person's emerging truer self is mirrored as their "spirit in outer action."

A person's soul is mirrored as their authentic essence energy. And, source energy/spirit or All-That-Is is mirrored as "spirit in inner action" in the form of the person's higher self.

As can be seen, if one visualizes the representation in three-dimensional or multidimensional terms, a person's emerging truer self allows access to the dreams of the person's soul and source energy/spirit or All-That-Is and simultaneous access to the person's conscious mind and body. This experience of access is part of the awakening process.

At a spiritual and soul-centered level, then, it can be said that in larger terms it is actually source energy/spirit or All-That-Is that dreams and gives rise to a person's soul as a unique part of her/his/itself. In turn, the person's soul mirrors the characteristics and qualities of source energy/spirit or All-That-Is.

Likewise, it then can be said that it is a person's soul that dreams and gives rise to the person's ever-emerging truer self, their spiritually-integrated self. In turn, the person's truer self mirrors the characteristics and qualities of their soul. In these terms, a person's truer self reflects the integration of the person's higher and lower selves as I have discussed elsewhere. In a manner of speaking, a person's emerging truer self also is a reflection or manifestation of the person's soul coming into physicality in their *current racial form* to authentically express their soul qualities as an embodied soul.

Again, as a person experiences their truer self emerging at the level of their personality, the person will gain greater knowledge about how they can consciously create, experience, and authentically express (manifest) their soul's dreams with their creative imagination. The person will be using the intuitive urges they get for creating their higher good. The person becomes a conscious creator or co-creator.

I have been calling attention, therefore, to one of the soul dreams of humanity. That is, at a spiritual and soul-centered level, one of the soul dreams of humanity is to evolve the human race game with joy in specific and general terms. I have been inviting each person to take meaningful and courageous first steps to evolve the human race game through evolving their own consciousness.

I have suggested that evolving one's own consciousness includes becoming a conscious creator or co-creator. Rather than continuing to play one's ego-driven human race games (e.g. lower self race games), then, as conscious creators or co-creators people can play more essence-oriented race games (higher self race games) in the physically embodied soul forms.

Essence-oriented human race games, as I have noted, are fueled and supported by the archetypal energies. They are played optimally when people allow the archetypal energy joy to flow naturally. Stimulus events for global transformation that provide glimpses into the experience of joy will continue to emerge for humanity, individually and collectively, in a variety of forms. Of course, how each person responds to and interprets these stimulus events, as well as how each person directs and/or misdirects their energy in regard to these stimulus events, will be in accord with the person's free will.

ARCHETYPAL ENERGIES, THE EMERGENCE OF OBAMA AS A PRACTICAL IDEALIST, AND GLOBAL TRANSFORMATION

In accord with the soul-centered model, for example, a stimulus for global transformation was visibly triggered and was energized through events in the United States that outwardly captured the attention of humanity's individual and collective consciousness. That is, outwardly the whole world in energy terms, as it would be understood, participated in and watched the human drama involving the presidential election of Barack Obama on November 4, 2008, and his inauguration as President of the United States on January 20, 2009.

For many, one initial net effect of this human drama, particularly on Inauguration Day, was to provide a glimpse into how the world, individually and collectively, might feel if human beings on the planet in their three-dimensional world were to globally and simultaneously experience the archetypal energy joy. Symbolically and psychically, the human drama represented a step toward healing a deep wound in humanity's psyche involving the races on the planet.

In broader psyche terms, the drama also represented the emergence of newer possibilities for alternate scripts that involve the *human race game*. Therefore, the drama and the emergence of Barack Obama onto the world stage was not an ending, but rather represented for many people the beginning of a possible alternate psychic journey.

Inwardly, many archetypal energies, primarily trust, inspiration, wisdom, compassion, vision, and hope, were involved in stimulating and nurturing the outward emergence of this human drama. In terms of "psychic politics," as it can be understood, this human drama also represented an aspect of a first phase global consciousness-energy shift or movement toward global transformation.

Inwardly, therefore, at the soul levels, the collective unconscious and collective consciousness of humanity blended and called forth a transformational figure who would also evoke a visceral reaction to align with the deeper archetypal energies. More specifically, to trigger and support the call, the transformational archetypal energies love, acceptance, inclusion, and harmony were stimulated and nurtured by the foundation and spiritually integrative archetypal energies trust, inspiration, wisdom, compassion, vision, and hope. A simple phrase like "Yes We Can," therefore, was used by Obama to evoke a vibrational energy resonance with the authentic essence of *all* who participated directly and indirectly in this phase of the human drama.

In terms of consciousness-energy and specific and general aspects of the human race game, the theme of this human drama was and is authentic change and global transformation. At the individual and collective levels, the choice was and is whether the world (personal, societal and global), as it is understood, will move forward fueled by the foundation and spiritually integrative archetypal energies trust, inspiration, wisdom, compassion, vision, hope, and the transformational archetypal energies, or continue to use fear to fuel the trajectory of many of the larger individual and collective human dramas. As a practical idealist, Barack Obama described this human drama as a choice of "hope over fear" and "unity of purpose over conflict and discord."

I have noted that the world will transform as each person changes their focus and preferences of their consciousness at the individual and collective levels, and wisely use the universal energy laws to co-create a new reality. That transformation involves the metamorphosis of each person's belief structures and each person's personalities to uniquely align and give unique expression to the deeper archetypal energies.

From the vantage point of the soul-centered model, the emergence of Barack Obama may also be viewed as a human drama that mirrors for the world, as it is understood, the process of subtle metamorphosis. As the subtle metamorphosis of Obama's personality is an ongoing, creative process of practical idealism, so too will be the subtle process of global transformation. As Barack Obama seeks to expand his own consciousness as a practical idealist, he will continue for some time to mirror transformation, knowingly and unknowingly.

So it is that as the subtle metamorphosis of Obama's personality continues, he will, knowingly and unknowingly, call upon, be inspired by, and mirror in his expressions many of the archetypal energies. He will increasingly be calling for unity, clarity, patience, peace, abundance, truth, beauty, courage, serenity, understanding, humor, flexibility, enthusiasm, and oneness.

There will be those, however, who, because of ego-related fears, will have difficulty embracing this kind of global transformation, and may, for a time, present arguments against it. Yet, Barack Obama's personality is particularly suited to mirror this practical, idealistic subtle metamorphosis process, as his personal energy system at the personality level naturally gravitates toward organizing, blending, and harmonizing what appear to be disparate or discordant energies. In his current racial form, his personal background, as it is understood, cuts across various so-called racial, cultural, and ethnic lines and belief systems.

To be sure, however, as this is the planet of free will, each person must freely choose to grow in consciousness, aligned with the archetypal energies, or not. In this context, the human race game is simply a matter of how each person chooses to grow.

"Psychic Politics," Obama's Practical Idealism, External Debates in the United States (e.g., Health Care, Economy) and Aftermath Events: The Inner Call to Well-being

As each person engages in the process of evolving the human race game and human consciousness and exploring choices for how to grow, I suggest that a general understanding of the nature of what I call psychic politics is important. Psychic politics involves what may be characterized as creative tensions that may emerge as higher vibrational value fulfillment questions arise for one's individual and collective psyches to consider.

Psychic politics engages a person in an inner and outer dialogue about what kind and quality of reality they want to create or co-create and what the person wants to value individually and collectively. As the dialogue unfolds, there are at least three important psyche-related questions that tend to emerge during transformational periods at individual and collective levels. They are:

1. What is it that you really want to value, give attention to, and nurture in your consciousness individually and collectively;

2. Where do you initially want to point your evolving consciousness individually and collectively to create what you value; and

3. What outer form(s) do you initially want what you value to take.

Behind psyche-related questions are archetypal energies, creatively urging people to move toward their optimal selves and optimal realities, individually and collectively. To illustrate, I will refer to the 2010 Health Care Debate in the United States, which can be viewed as an external mirror, reflecting an inner dialogue about these important psyche-related questions. One initial outcome of the external dialogue, after much ego-related debating, was that President Obama signed into law on March 23, 2010, what can be called historic legislation, or Affordable Health Care Law. It has come to be called Obamacare. Interestingly and ironically, some folks have missed the underlying symbolic meaning of that latter term, which implies that "Obama cares" about their well being.

So, in terms of psychic politics, what does this so-called historic legislation mean? I suggest that it primarily represents a "marker in time," as it can be understood, related to an inner call to consciously attend to well being. In that sense, the legislation can be viewed as an external symbolic message. As such, the message is encouraging people to start lifting the illusion surrounding the ego-related debate about health care so that they may begin to give form to the transformative potential of the archetypal energies that can move them toward well being and optimal realities.

In other words, through the drama of a health care debate, people were and are called to entertain the transformative potential of shifting their consciousness, individually and collectively, toward a focus on well being in their life spaces (personal, societal, and global). In this respect, there was and is a bigger picture at play related to the psychic politics surrounding the health care debate.

What, then, were some of the creative tensions related to the 2010 Health Care Debate in the United States and the *inner call* to *consciously* attend to well being? One creative tension was that the debate itself may have caused some people to lose sight of, or to have difficulty seeing, the bigger picture of an *inner call* to *consciously* attend to well being. Why and how might this happen?

As conscious beings, with free will, a person creates their own realities, according to the nature of their beliefs (beliefs are thoughts, reinforced by emotion and imagination), and what I have called universal energy laws, particularly the law of attraction (energy of any form magnetically attracts similar energy, the intensity of emotions, causing a more intense attraction in both speed and quantity). Beliefs, particularly core beliefs, thus structure a person's realities, and the universal energy laws make more conscious what it is that the person believes to be true and value, knowingly and unknowingly.

Individually and collectively, people's surface selves (ego) use beliefs to create, invite, or allow for possibilities or not, to point their consciousness toward particular foci, and to direct or misdirect energy in their personal, societal, and global life spaces. However, fear-based beliefs can be and are self-limiting, as I have noted elsewhere. They tend to narrow the focus of a person's consciousness. With a narrow focus in relation to an external health care debate, the person may then lose sight of, or have difficulty seeing, the bigger picture.

As psychic politics unfolds, a second creative tension relates to how people may direct or misdirect energy, individually and collectively. As I have mentioned, one's surface self (ego) likes to be in control. If fear-based beliefs, then, were operative for a person in relation to the health care debate, the person's surface self (ego) may have misread or misunderstood the psychic politics at play and the transformative potential related to the inner call to consciously attend to well being.

Out of fear—fear of the future, fear of the unknown, fear of loss, fear of economics, fear of the other—energy, as I have previously noted, can get jammed as the psychic politics, the inner and outer dialogue, unfolds. As a result, the jammed energy may get expressed, acted out, or projected out in distorted ways, individually and/or collectively (e.g., we-they thinking and acting; angry or volatile outbursts; stereotyping; threats of violence; scapegoating). During the health care debate in the United States, for example, the nation witnessed some of these expressions.

As to how this relates to the archetypal energies, fear-based, self-limiting beliefs jam or block the authentic expression of archetypal energies. As a result, conscious attention is shifted away from the inner creative urges of the archetypal energies. And, in turn, the transformative potential of moving people toward a higher good and optimal realities may then get short-circuited. That was the case for some people who engaged the 2010 Health Care Debate in the United States. For others, the short-circuiting continued, even into the 2012 Presidential election, and perhaps beyond.

In the above context, a third creative tension can be discerned in regard to the Health Care Debate. More specifically, those who appeared to have different or opposing points of view tended to perceive the other as "an enemy." The ego reasoned that the other's point of view was to be feared. As a result, energy got misdirected, framed, and expressed as fear-based distortions.

For example, points of views were labeled as conservative, progressive, or liberal and accordingly, energy got misdirected. There is nothing inherently wrong per se with so-called conservative or progressive ideas. By definition, according to Webster's New Collegiate Dictionary, conservative means "tending or disposed to maintain existing views, conditions, or institutions" and progressive means "moving forward, onward, making use of or interested in new ideas, findings, or opportunities." Such ideas can be complementary. Ultimately, however, what really matters is what is being conserved and what is being progressed.

To illustrate, I grew up in what was called the segregated South. In my current racial form as an African American, I personally experienced and can give witness to the unfolding race-related events during that historical period, (e.g., having to sit on the back of the bus; not being allowed to go in the front door of movie theaters; not being allowed to eat in restaurants; seeing signs over water fountains and bathrooms labeled "Colored" and "White Only"). In that context, for those in the majority group, to be conservative during that period meant holding onto what would be considered racist views, practices, conditions, and institutions. So, much energy was indeed misdirected in that regard.

Similarly, there was much misdirected energy during the health care debate and in the aftermath. During the debate, for example, jammed and misdirected energy surfaced in forms such as derogatory name-calling, disrespectful characterizations about President Obama (e.g., a protester's sign had a swastika on it, implying a link to President Obama), fear-based projections related to the phenomena of race and sexual orientation (e.g., epithets were directed at Congressmen John Lewis, who is black, and Barney Frank, who is gay), and threatening letters sent to legislators.

In the aftermath of the debate, jammed and misdirected energy, structured by fear-based, self-limiting beliefs, continued to fuel an unfolding political climate and outward events. For example, in the aftermath, a climate of heated political rhetoric emerged to cloud the inner call to consciously move toward well being and health. One result was the election of politicians in 2010 to the United States Congress whose agenda was to try to repeal the historic legislation. Unwittingly and unknowingly, those enacting such political roles shifted somewhat the focus of some observers from a conscious investment in well being and health toward a focus on the role of a government in such matters.

Also in the aftermath, an extremely violent outward event emerged in the form of what was called the "tragedy in Tucson." While I am not suggesting a direct causal link, I am suggesting an atmospheric energy link in terms of psychic politics. Externally, the state of Arizona had become a visible arena in the United States for conflicting views related to a nation's boundaries, we-they attitudes, and the matter of what is called immigration.

In this external political climate, on January 8, 2011, Jared Loughner, whose energy was/is quite jammed and distorted, acted out violently by shooting twenty people in Tucson, Arizona. His primary focus was on United States Congresswoman Gabrielle Giffords. For Loughner, Congresswoman Giffords had come to represent his personality's unexamined fear-based, self-limiting beliefs, which had led his personality to construct quite distorted perceptions about his inner world and outer world.

The six extraordinarily brave souls, who transitioned during the tragedy in Tucson to the other side through what is called the death experience, included those who had constructed wonderfully caring and giving personalities. Chronologically, these personalities ranged in age from the young to the elderly, and they were already enacting what one would consider noble and caring social roles. In accord with the soul-centered model, all were old Souls.

Three of the six people were already enacting somewhat visible, symbolic social roles that mirrored caring for others. For example, nine-year-old Christine Taylor Green had already mirrored psychic politics and community leadership, symbolized through her birth during another tragic event that is known as 9/11 and through her election to a third-grade leadership role at her school. Sixty-three-year-old John Roll was a respected federal judge who was engaged in administering social justice, particularly as it related to border crimes. Thirty-year-old Gabe Zimmerman was the director of community outreach for Congresswoman Giffords, who saw external politics as a way to carry out his passion for helping others.

In terms of the remaining three people, they were already enacting low-key, yet highly meaningful dramas to mirror the art and gift of caring for others. For example, seventy-nine-year-old Phyllis Schneck was a gifted homemaker and nurturer, who mirrored family love and community care through her volunteer work. Seventy-six-year-old Dorwan Stoddard demonstrated how love for others transcends time as he reconnected with and married his grade-school sweetheart, and carried out numerous construction projects for his community and church. Seventy-six-year-old Dorothy Morris was a retired homemaker and secretary who demonstrated the depth of love as she was married to her high school sweetheart for fifty years.

And so it was that there were some aftermath events that emerged from the 2010 Health Care Debate, unfortunately mirroring the flipside of health. Each in its own way caused a nation to pause. Each in its own way presented an opportunity for each person to do some soul searching about the extent to which they were/are paying attention to the inner call to consciously move toward well being and health, individually and collectively.

For most people, the soul searching took place in the context of the current technologies and their free will. That is, people now have the capability to instantaneously do both inner and outer soul searching, as they explore various points of view on the Internet and Inner-net.

Therefore, some people in the United States did allow the identified aftermath events to serve as a wakeup call for deep soul searching. For other people, the events triggered a brief period of reflection, and they went back to business as usual. Yet, the inner call to consciously move toward well being and health remains an important part of the process of evolving the human race game.

In broad terms, the inner call to consciously move toward well being and health refers to creating and having sociopolitical climates and responsive external systems in place to nurture and to maximize optimal well being and health. These kinds of sociopolitical climates and responsive external systems support the evolution of consciousness, individually and collectively, as they relate to: (1) each person having a healthy body, mind, and spirit; (2) having a healthy state of planetary socioeconomic conditions (e.g., less poverty whereby people have more than enough money to sustain the outer self; less hunger whereby people have enough food to sustain the outer self; less wars whereby people experience more peaceful conditions in their individual and collective lives); and (3) having a healthy planet (e.g., clear air, clean fuel, a healthy climate with regard to global warming and other environmental conditions).

In connection to a highly visible and globally linked aftermath event, the inner call to consciously move toward well-being and health, coupled with the outer debate about the role of government in such an undertaking, became a campaign issue for the 2012 United States presidential race between Barack Obama and Mitt Romney and in various congressional races. After a sometimes bitter, but hard fought and very expensive political process (i.e., the non-partisan Center for Responsive Politics estimated a total spending of a record $5.8 billion), Barack Obama was reelected President of the United States on November 6, 2012; Senate Democrats gained a net of two seats (53 Democrats; 47

Republicans), and House Democrats gained a net of seven seats, while House Republicans maintained a House majority (195 Democrats; 234 Republicans; 6 up for grabs).

With President Obama's reelection, the inner call was positioned externally and globally to keep moving "forward," which was President Obama's campaign slogan. In terms of psychic politics, the reelection of President Obama, in overly simplistic terms, represented externally the value and importance of the inner call. The inner call, however, did not and should not end with President Obama's reelection. The reelection simply marked yet another point in time that externally and globally echoed the subtle metamorphosis process unfolding, and it is poised and should continue to unfold beyond Obama's presidency. I suggest, therefore, that people heed the inner call, individually and collectively, to consciously move toward health and well-being. In doing so, people will contribute significantly to evolving the human race game in specific and general terms and growth with joy.

TOWARD A "NEW MYTHOLOGY" ABOUT THE "BEGINNINGS" OF THE HUMAN RACE GAME: "OVERLEAF UNDERSTANDINGS"

So, I end this discussion by calling upon all of the archetypal energies to assist each person in creating optimal scripts for a new racial and human reality, particularly the archetypal energies hope, understanding, vision, joy, and love. Hopefully, there is now a better understanding of that age-old drama that I have called the human race game. Hopefully, there is also a better understanding of some of the tools available to each person, individually and collectively, to consciously, joyfully, and lovingly evolve this game through evolving and expanding one's own consciousness.

In this light, I offer a concluding "overleaf understanding" as it is intended to vibrationally resonate with each person's heart center and the transformational archetypal energies, particularly the archetypal energy *love*. By definition, according to Webster's New Collegiate Dictionary, the word overleaf literally means "on the other side of the page." In this instance, therefore, I am referring to a possible spiritual and soul-centered perspective "on the other side of the page" of the human experience for understanding the beginnings of the human race game.

The overleaf understanding was actually received intuitively on May 22, 2000, many years prior to actually completing the first draft of this book. I have waited until now (2014) to introduce this book in order to allow various energy circumstances to materialize in the world in accord with particular energy adjustments.

The overleaf understanding was intended to be the closing remarks for this book, addressed to readers, and so it appears essentially as it was received. I include it here to mirror and emphasize the idea that a spiritual and soul-centered perspective transcends linear time, as it is understood.

"Overleaf Understandings" Related to Evolving the Human Race Game (Intuitively Received 5/22/2000 before book was actually written)

All of what you, as human beings, think you know about the phenomenon of race, therefore, has been part of your own process of self-creation throughout linear history, as you understand it, expressed in and through your various lifetimes and life spaces. If you understand the material in this book, however, you also will understand that, in regard to the phenomenon of race, you, as human beings, made it all up. Further, you will understand that there have been consequences in your individual and collective experiences for your various scripts and dramas that you have subconsciously co-created as you have played the human race game in specific and general terms.

The human race game, in specific and general terms, has been part of the illusion of your ever-emerging ego and personality processes as beings on various planes of experience during and between various lifetimes and life spaces. The higher purpose has been to understand your greater self and source energy/spirit or All-That-Is and to uncover or recognize more and more of the truth of who you are as you expand your consciousness.

If you understand the material in this book, you will also understand that we have been suggesting that it is time for you to more fully comprehend how you are the creators or co-creators that you already are. However, you are at a point in the evolution of your consciousness on the physical plane that you now can become conscious creators or co-creators rather than subconscious creators or co-creators, as you align the human race game in specific and general terms to your higher qualities as human beings.

In accord with your core beliefs about your self during and between various lifetimes and life spaces and in accord with the universal energy laws, particularly the law of attraction and the law of consequences, you have often allowed fear and confusion to direct the nature of your outer experiences in regard to the human race game in specific and general terms. You have not wisely used your feedback, the mirror effect, to assist you in your growth and expansion of consciousness.

By consciously aligning how you play the human race game in specific and general terms to your higher qualities, these higher qualities can and will now influence the quality of your experiences, as you play the human race game in specific and general terms. How you then view the phenomenon of race, therefore, and the human race in general, can and will then be reflected back to you through the mirror effect in accord with these higher qualities. That is, your world, your three life spaces (personal, societal, and global), individually and collectively, can and will mirror a transformed view of the human experience and the phenomenon of race, as the world reflects the archetypal energies or your soul qualities and you vibrationally and uniquely resonate with them.

A "New Authentic Essence Mythology" about the Creative Impulse for Evolving the Human Race Game

So, what is the essence of (or creative impulse underlying) the human race game? As many people require a mythology, scientific or otherwise formulated, to focus their inner urges and outer actions, in accord with the soul-centered model, I offer the following focus on this authentic essence mythology about the creative impulse for evolving the human race game. In this light, the human race game is a game of projection and illusion that was born out of the primordial struggle of source being (source energy/spirit or All-That-Is) to resolve the question of how I can be one and be many at the same time.

Time nor space existed as one might surmise, and source energy/spirit or All-That-Is only knew she/he/it existed now in what might be called "timeless space," but felt conscious parts of her/his/its self emerging as she/he/it dreamed. Source energy/ spirit or All-That-Is, therefore, created the illusion of time and space and various planes of existence to serve as platforms of expansion and growth and as opportunities to learn more about their self.

In a burst of inspiration and love (vibrational frequencies of light, color, and sound), source energy/spirit or All-That-Is knew they must lovingly let go and give free will to diverse beingness— that is, to those parts of their self that were conscious within and desired to be free. With free will, the "I-ness" or "It-ness" of source energy/spirit or All-That-Is would be in a process of becoming in each state of being. That process, therefore, gave rise to all forms of diversity of beings of spirit and matter.

There were initially seven primary and twelve overall planes of existence (or multidimensional beingness), including the illusion or hologram of the physical plane. What is commonly called the human being, with its diverse races, existed first as beings of spirit in higher, etheric vibrational forms, with etheric bodies.

The so-called races, then, are spectrums or sparks of the light, color, and sound of inspiration and the vibrational expressions of love. And so the game was for source energy/spirit or All-That-Is to experience a sense of "I-ness" or "It-ness" with free will in many diverse forms in order to grow joyfully and to increase their understanding of their self. The sense of "I-ness" or "It-ness" meant that each being (spirit and matter) had consciousness, unique unto their self, and was free to grow as they willed or naturally allowed their self to grow in accord with its authentic essence.

On the physical plane, therefore, consciousness in regard to being human was to take many forms through an incarnation process called lifetimes so that the entity could create lessons and learn through exploration. The original intention was and still is to expand the spark of love consciously.

The general evolutionary process involves each consciousness uncovering more about their self as their "I-ness" comes to know the many aspects of their self as portions of source energy/spirit or All-That-Is. In rejoining with, or more precisely reawakening as source energy/spirit or All-That-Is, each consciousness would do so naturally, or willingly in the case of the human experience, or through allowance, and would continue to know their self as their self and more.

The physical plane was where light-color-sound energy was most dense. That is, the vibration was slow and thus created what was experienced as solidity. In this regard, it was a fertile arena for a game of diversity, as light could be contained and shaped in many diverse forms. This was a time when there was spirit and matter.

Human beings, therefore, were spirit, vibrating at a higher frequency of light-color-sound than matter. Each human being, therefore, through many incarnations was to search for light and color and in so doing was to come to know their connection to or as source energy/spirit or All-That-Is. Each human being then was to eventually know that their authentic spiritual essence chose their various physical forms (various races), and various mental and emotional states. Each incarnation would be chosen to provide opportunities for challenges and lessons for growth, as each consciousness and human being evolved to consciously know that they, as their greater self or soul, is a unique portion of source energy/spirit or All-That-Is.

Authentic spiritual essence is commonly known as the soul. It is the soul, one's greater self, which is aware of all of its creations of physical forms and personalities throughout many incarnations. It is the soul, one's greater self, which continues with eternal validity beyond the various incarnations and personalities and physical forms, while maintaining also the continuity of the various incarnations on their varied paths of growth. It knows that once something is created, it is never lost or uncreated. There is transformation, however, but with awareness and consciousness.

BRIEF COMMENTARY ON THE NEW ESSENCE MYTHOLOGY

I realize that this essence mythology may only resonate with those who are more spiritually inclined. Some people may also try to use this essence mythology in relation to what are called intelligent design and creationism. That is not the intent here, as the intelligent design and creationism notions as they are currently presented, tend to use externalized projections to separate a person and their consciousness from the material world and All-That-Is. However, I encourage those who are more scientifically inclined to look behind the description of this essence imagery.

One may find that there is resonance with scientific theories as mirrored in the theories related to what is called the new physics and the quantum/string reality that has been proposed and is now being explored.

Indeed, in a limited way, scientists may refer to what I have called the burst of Inspiration as the Big Bang. That is, they would say pure energy converted to matter created the Big Bang. They may also begin to suggest that the light, color, and sound, as I described it, reflects the emergence of visible matter and the "birthing" and formation of galaxies from what is now called dark matter (e.g., Evalyn Gates' *Einstein's Telescope: The Hunt for Dark Matter in the Universe*, 2010; Richard Panek's *The 4-Percent Universe: Dark Matter, Dark Energy, and the Race to Discover the Rest of Reality*, 2011). Further, scientists may find that the flow and structure of what I have called awareness and consciousness is fueled by the discovery and validation of the theorized Higgs boson particle or the so-called God Particle (The conceptual work was first published by British physicist Peter Higgs in 1964; Leon M. Lederman elaborated in his book, *The God Particle: If the Universe is the Answer, What is the Question?*, 1993; Higgs boson was then discovered in July 2012, by scientists working with the Hadron Collider in Switzerland). A boson particle is a type of particle that allows multiple identical particles to exist in the same place in the same quantum state. That is, the Higgs boson is the manifestation of the so-called Higgs field, an invisible energy field filling all space. The Higgs boson gives mass to other subatomic particles such as protons, neutrons, quarks, and leptons.

The essence mythology is intended, therefore, to serve as one of the many metaphors emerging to assist in bridging science and spirit (e.g., Norman Friedman's *Bridging Science and Spirit: Common Elements in David Bohm's Physics, The Perennial Philosophy, and Seth* and *The Hidden Domain: Home of the Quantum Wave Function-Nature's Creative Source*; Fred Alan Wolf's *Mind into Matter: A New Alchemy of Science and Spirit*,

The Spiritual Universe, The Dreaming Universe, Parallel Universes, The Body Quantum, Taking the Quantum Leap, and *Space-Time and Beyond*). I encourage scientists, however, to consider the idea that consciousness precedes manifestation, and not the other way around. Such a consideration, as I have discussed, can and will be helpful in evolving the *human race game* in specific and general terms. The intent in this book, therefore, was to present some essential spiritual and soul-centered perspectives in this regard from different angles.

A Request: Dare to Allow the Outer Self to Become a "New Human Being" by Saying "Hello" to One Another's Higher Self as Each Person Seeks to Evolve the Human Race Game

On a final note, when a person allows their personality to be open to their higher self, they will also be allowing their outer self to say hello to the unconditional love and joy inside of their inner self as they evolve the human race game and become a "new human being." In this context, the person first learns to love their whole self unconditionally. As they do so, they will become aware that with unconditional love, it does not matter whether or not the other person is able to love them back at that moment.

What a person will also learn is that when they allow their self to love someone else unconditionally, inside they also experience their own joy in their awareness of having this capacity inside of their self. That is, as a person loves someone else unconditionally, they, in effect, are mirroring their own unconditional love for their self with joy. And, it is out of that inner state of love and joy that the person authentically resonates with the higher self of others, even when the person's personality may not realize it.

That is the wonder and that is the simplicity of allowing one's personality to learn how to love unconditionally. That is the secret of unconditional love. That is the secret of learning to live in awareness of the love and joy inside of one's self as one plays with another and evolves the human race game. That is the secret of becoming new human beings.

So, I suggest that people evolve the human race game with joy in specific and general terms, and seek to play it as it was originally intended. It is important that each person allows their outer self to be open to their higher self and the archetypal energies. It is important for each person to allow their self to be open to becoming a new human being. It is important, therefore, for each person to be the conscious co-creator or conscious creator that they already are.

I suggest that people use those creative tools with which they resonate to expand their consciousness. I suggest that people work with the universal energy laws to construct a new human and racial reality—one that mirrors, in practical terms, new interracial and human dramas and new scripts in alignment with the archetypal energies. In this light, I suggest that people seek to construct joyful intra-racial, interracial, and general human enterprises in service to one another. In turn, I suggest that people use the mirror effect more wisely.

In essence, I am suggesting that people seek to soul-link with those in their life spaces who are thought to be the other or thought to be from a race other than their own, as well as to soul-link with those thought to be from their own race. In this light, I suggest that people use their free will to make choices in the present that invite joy into their moment-to-moment experiences, including their interracial experiences.

It is important to know that in one's current racial form, one is an embodied soul, as are others in their current racial form. It is important to know also that, in larger terms, all people are aspects of source energy/spirit or All-That-Is, independent and yet interdependent.

I suggest, therefore, that people be playful with their own self and be playful with one another as they expand their consciousness, individually and collectively, become new human beings, and evolve the human race game in specific and general terms. And yes, I suggest that people send *love* to their race-linked fears and human drama fears. As I have stated elsewhere, a person's fears, including their race-linked fears, are the places within that await the person's love.

The human race game, therefore, awaits each person's love. And so I request: dare to allow the outer self to become a "new human being" by saying hello to one another's higher self. Dare to be open to the love inside of one's self and to authentically send love to one another and to receive love from one another as each person consciously evolves the human race game and becomes a new human being.

REFERENCES

Andrews, Ted. 2006. *How to See and Read the Aura*. St. Paul: Llewellyn Worldwide.

Andrews, Ted. 2006. *How to Meet and Work with Spirit Guides*. St. Paul: Llewellyn Worldwide.

Arntz, William, Betsy Chasse, and Mark Vicente. 2007. *What the Bleep Do We Know?: Discovering the Endless Possibilities for Altering Your Everyday Reality*. Dearfield Beach: Health Communications, Inc.

Atwater, P. M. H. 2007. *The Book of Near Death Experiences: The Ultimate Guide to What Happens When We Die*. Charlottesville: Hampton Roads Publishing Company, Inc.

Aurobindo, Sri. 2010. *The Life Divine*. Twin Lakes: Lotus Press.

Backman, Linda. 2009. *Bringing Your Soul to Light: Healing Through Past Lives and the Time Between*. Woodbury: Llewellyn Publications.

Bartlett, Richard. 2009. *Matrix Energetics: The Science and Art of Transformation*. New York: Atria Paperback (A Division of Simon & Schuster, Inc.).

Bennett, Lerone. 1968. "Was Lincoln a White Supremicist?" *Ebony*. February Vol. 23, No. 4.

Bohm, David. 2002. *Wholeness and the Implicate Order.* New York: Routledge Classics.

Brennan, Barbara. 1993. *Light Emerging: The Journey of Personal Healing.* New York: Bantam Books.

Brennan, Barbara. 1988. *Hands of Light: A Guide to Healing Through the Human Energy Field.* New York: Bantam Books.

Browne, Sylvia. 2002. *The Other Side and Back.* New York: New American Library (Division of Penguin Putnam Inc.).

Bruce, Robert. 2012. *Astral Dynamics: The Complete Book of Out-of-Body Experiences.* Charlotteville: Hampton Roads Publishing Company.

Bruce, Robert and C. E. Lindgren. 1999. *Astral Dynamics: A New Approach to Out-of-Body Experience.* Charlotteville: Hampton Roads Publishing Company.

Buhlman, William. 1996. *Adventures Beyond the Body: How to Experience Out-of-Body Travel.* New York: HarperSanFrancisco (An imprint of HarperCollins Publishers).

Byrne, Rhonda. 2006. *The Secret.* New York: Atria Books.

Cardena, Etzel, Steven Lynn, and Stanley Krippner. 2004. *Varieties of Anomalous Experiences: Examining the Scientific Evidence.* Washington: American Psychological Association.

Carter, Rita. 2002. *Exploring Consciousness.* Berkeley: University of California Press.

Chadwick, Gloria. 2009. *Reincarnation and Your Past Lives: You've Been Here Before.* San Antonio: Morpheus Books.

Chalko, Thomas. March, 2001. "Is Chance or Choice the Essence of Nature?" *NU Journey of Discovery Vol. 2.* http://NUjournal.net/choice.html

Christeaan, Aaron, J. P. Van Hulle, M. C. Clark, and Michael Friday. 1988. *Michael: The Basic Teachings.* Napa: Michael Education Foundation.

Churchward, James. 2007. *The Lost Continent of Mu*. Kempton: Adventures Unlimited Press.

Clark, Rabia. 1996. *Past Life Therapy-State of the Art*. Scotts Valley: Rising Star Press.

Czigler, Istvan and Isrvan Winkler. 2010. *Unconscious Memory Representations in Perception: Processes and Mechanisms in the Brain*. Amsterdam: John Benjamins Publishing Company.

Dale, Cyndi. 2009. *The Subtle Body: An Encyclopedia of Your Energetic Anatomy*. Boulder: Sounds True, Inc.

De Camp, L. Sprague. 1970. *The Atlantis Theme in History, Science, and Literature*. New York: Dover Publications, Inc.

Deida, David. 2007. *The Enlightened Sex Manual: Sexual Skills for the Superior Lover*. Boulder: Sounds True, Inc.

Deida, David. 2006. *The Way of the Superior Man: A Spiritual Guide to Mastering the Challenges of Women, Work, and Sexual Desire*. Boulder: Sounds True, Inc.

Deida, David 2006. *Dear Lover: A Woman's Guide to Men, Sex, and Love's Deepest Bliss*. Boulder: Sounds True, Inc.

Deida, David. 2006. *Blue Truth: A Spiritual Guide to Life & Death and Love & Sex*. Boulder: Sounds True, Inc.

Deida, David. 2005. *Finding God Through Sex: Awakening the One of Spirit Through the Two of Flesh*. Boulder: Sounds True, Inc.

Deutsch, David. 2011. *The Beginning of Infinity: Explanations That Transform the World*. New York: Penguin Group, Inc.

Deutsch, David. 1990. *The Fabric of Reality: The Science of Parallel Universes and Its Implications*. London: Penguin Books.

Easwaran, Eknath. 2007. *The Upanistads*. Tomales: Nilgiri Press.

Eden, Donna and David Feinstein, David. 2008. *Energy Medicine: Balancing Your Body's Energies for Optimal Health, Joy, and Vitality*. New York: Jeremy P. Tarcher/Penguin (a member of the Penguin Group Inc.).

Emoto, Masaru. 2010. *Messages from Water and the Universe.* Carlsbad: Hay House, Inc.

Emoto, Masaru (translated by David Thayne). 2005. *The Hidden Messages in Water.* Hillsboro: Beyond Words Publishing, Inc.

Feinstein, David, Donna Eden, and Gary Craig. 2005. *The Promise of Energy Psychology: Revolutionary Tools for Dramatic Personal Change.* New York: Jeremy P. Tarcher/Penguin (a member of the Penguin Group Inc.).

Ferguson, Carroy. 2012. "Beyond Self-Limiting and Addictive Cultural Scripts: The Power of Preference in the Now." *AHP Perspective.* October/September 6-8.

Ferguson, Carroy. 2012. "Beyond Dogma: The Role of 'Evolutionary' Science and the 'Embodiment' of Archetypal Energies." *AHP Perspective.* August/September 6-7.

Ferguson, Carroy. 2009. "Fear and Projection as Root Causes of War, and the Archetypal Energies 'Trust' and 'Peace' as Antidotes." *AHP Perspective.* October/November 6-7.

Ferguson, Carroy. 2004. *Transitions in Consciousness from an African American Perspective: Original Essays in Psycho-Historical Context.* Lanham: University Press of America.

Ferguson, Carroy. 1997. *A New Perspective on Race and Color: Research on an Outer vs Inner Orientation to Anti-Black Dispositions.* Lewiston: The Edwin Mellen Press.

Fisslinger, Johannes. 1998. *Aura Mastery.* Columbia: Interactive Publishers.

Fisslinger, Johannes. 1995. *Aura Imaging Photography: Seeing the Colors of Your Aura.* Fairfield: Sum Press.

Friedman, Norman. 1997. *Bridging Science and Spirit: Common Elements in David Bohm's Physics, The Perennial Philosophy, and Seth.* Needham: Moment Point Press, Inc.

Friedman, Norman. 1997. *The Hidden Domain: Home of the Quantum Wave Function, Nature's Creative Source.* Needham: Moment Point Press, Inc.

Gates, Evalyn. 2010. *Einstein's Telescope: The Hunt for Dark Matter in the Universe.* New York: W. W. Norton & Company.

Gawain, Shakti. 2002. *Creative Visualization: Use the Power of Imagination to Create What You Want in Your Life.* Novato: Nataraj Publishing (a division of New World Library).

Green, Brian. 2003. *The Elegant Universe: Superstrings, Hidden Dimensions, and the Quest for the Ultimate Theory.* New York: W. W. Norton & Company.

Gribbin, John. 2010. *In Search of the Multiverse: Parallel Worlds, Hidden Dimensions, and the Ultimate Quest for the Frontiers of Reality.* Hoboken: John Wiley & Sons, Inc.

Grof, Stanislav. 2012. *Healing Our Deepest Wounds: The Holotropic Paradigm Shift.* Newcastle: Stream of Experience Productions.

Grof, Stanislav. 1998. *The Cosmic Game: Explorations of the Frontiers of Human Consciousness.* Albany: State University of New York Press.

Grof, Stanislav. 1993. *The Holotropic Mind: The Three Levels of Human Consciousness and How They Shape Our Lives.* New York: HarperCollins Publishers.

Head, Joseph and Susan Cranston. 1994. *Reincarnation: The Phoenix Fire Mystery.* San Diego: Point Loma Publications Inc.

Heideman, Carol (Michael). 1994. *Searching for Light: Michael's Information for a Time of Change.* Chandler: Twelve Star Publishing.

Hermes.1884. and John Everard, John (translator). 2010. *The Divine Pymander of Hermes Mercurius.* Whitefish: Kessinger Publishing, LLC.

Hicks, Esther and Jerry. 2006. *The Amazing Power of Deliberate Intent: Living the Art of Allowing*. Carlsbad: Hay House, Inc.

Hicks, Esther and Jerry. 2005. *Ask and It Is Given: Learning to Manifest Your Desires*. Carlsbad: Hay House, Inc.

Holzer, Hans. 1997. *Are You Psychic?: Unlocking the Power Within: A Guide to Developing, Controlling, and Using Your Psychic Abilities*. New York: Avery (a member of Penguin Putnam, Inc.

Hoodwin, Shepherd. 2013. *The Journey of Your Soul: A Channel Explores the Michael Teachings*. Berkeley: North Atlantic Books.

Howe, Linda. 2010. *How to Read the Akashic Records: Accessing the Archive of the Soul and Its Journey*. Boulder: Sounds True, Inc.

Huxley, Aldous. 2009. *Perennial Philosophy: An Interpretation of the Great Mystics, East and West*. New York: Harper Perennial Modern Classics.

Jamieson, Bryan. 2002. *The Search for Past Lives: Exploring Reincarnation's Mysteries, & The Amazing Power of Past-Life Therapy*. San Diego: Driftwood Publications.

James, William. 2012. *The Varieties of Religious Experiences: A Study in Human Nature Being—The Gifford Lectures on Natural Religion Delivered at Edinburgh in 1901-1902*. Charleston: Forgotten Books.

Janzen, Greg. 2008. *The Reflexive Nature of Consciousness: Advances in Consciousness Research*. Amsterdam: John Benjamins Publishing Company.

Jelm, Christopher and Jeannine. 2012. *Transcendent Humans, Transcendent Earth*. Chino Valley: One World Press.

Jelm, Christopher and Jeannine. 2009. *New Humans, New Earth: The Grand Celestial Plan for Personal and Planetary Transformation*. Tucson: Lightarian Institute for Global Human Transformation.

Johari, Harish. 2000. *Chakras: Energy Centers of Transformation.* Rochester: Destiny Books.

Jung, Carl. 1981. *The Archetypes and the Collective Unconscious.* Princeton: Princeton University Press.

Kaehr, Shelley. 2010. *Beyond Reality: Evidence of Parallel Universes.* Lewisville: Out of This World Publishing.

Kaku, Michio. 2006. *Parallel Worlds: A Journey Through Creation, Higher Dimensions, and the Future of the Cosmos.* New York: Anchor Books (A Division of Random House, Inc.).

Kaku, Machio. 2009. *Physics of the Impossible: A Scientific Exploration into the World of Phasers, Force Fields, Teleportation, and Time Travel.* New York: Anchor Books (A Division of Random House, Inc.).

Keyes, Kenneth. 1997. *Handbook to Higher Consciousness.* Buckingham: Eden Grove Editions.

Korotkov, Konstantin, Bernard Williams, Terrence Bugno, and Pamela Parsons. 2002. *Human Energy Field: Study with GDV-Bioelectrography.* Fair Lawn: Backbone Publishing Company.

Korotkov, Konstantin. 1999. *Aura and Consciousness: New Stage of Scientific Understanding.* Fair Lawn: Backbone Publishing Company.

Korotkov, Konstantin. 1998. *Light After Life: A Scientific Journey into the Spiritual World.* Fair Lawn: Backbone Publishing Company.

Korotkov, Konstantin. 1995. *Effekt Kirlian.* Unknown Binding (Russia Edition).

Lambert, Wendy. 1996. *Aura Glasses: You Can See Auras.* Broumana: Earthopia.

Lasio, Ervin. 2009. *The Akashic Experience: Science and the Cosmic Memory Field.* Rochester: Inner Traditions.

Lazaris-Purcel, Jach. 1987. *The Sacred Journey—You and Your Higher Self.* Palm Beach: NPN Publishing.

Lederman, Leon. (1993; 2006). *The God Principle: If the Universe is the Answer, What is the Question?.* New York: Mariner Books.

Lee, Jenny. 2010. *The Universal Life Energy.* Bloomington: Author House.

Li, Jixing, Erica Woods, and Patrick Lugo. 2008. *The Theory of Multi-Dimensional Unified Universal Energy.* Fremont: TC Media International.

Lindegren, C. E., D. Litt, and Jennifer Baltz. 2007. *Aura Awareness: What Your Aura Says About You.* Nevada City: Blue Dolphin Publishing.

Lipton, Bruce. 2008. *The Biology of Belief: Unleashing the Power of Consciousness, Matter, & Miracles.* Carlsbad: Hay House, Inc.

Lommel, Pim van. 2011. *Consciousness Beyond Life: The Science of the Near-Death Experience.* New York: HarperOne.

Mackey, Robert, October 9, 2012 (10:57 am), comment on Malala, "Pakistani Activist, 15, Is Shot by Taliban, *The Lede—Blogging the News with Robert Mackey*, October 9, 2012, http://thelede.blogs.nytimes.com/2012/10/09/pakistani-activist-14-shot-by-taliban/?_r=0

Martin, Stephen. 2009. *The Science of Life After Death: New Research Shows Human Consciousness Lives On.* Richmond: The Oaklea Press.

Migliore, Vince. 2009. *A Measure of Heaven: Near-Death Experience Data Analysis.* Folsom: Blossom Hill Books.

Miner, Janice, Bruce Greyson, and Debbie James. 2009. *The Handbook of Near-Death Experiences: Thirty Years of Investigation.* Santa Barbara: Praeger Publishers.

Mirovalez, Mansur. 2011. "Thousands of Russian nationalists march in Moscow." *The Boston Globe*, November 4. Accessed November 5, 2011. http://www.boston.com/news/world/europe/articles/2011/11/04/thousands_of_russian_nationalists_march_in_moscow/

Moody, Raymond and Elizabeth Kubler-Ross. 2001. *Life After Life: The Investigation of a Phenomenon-Survival of Bodily Death*. New York: HarperOne.

Moore, Thomas. 1999. *Care of the Soul: How to Add Depth and Meaning to Your Everyday Life*. New York: Harper Publishers.

Morton, Samuel. 2012. *Crania Americana*. Charleston: Forgotten Books.

Murray, Craig. 2009. *Psychological Scientific Perspectives on Out-of-Body and Near-Death Experiences*. Hauppauge: Nova Science Publishers, Inc.

Napastek, Belleruth. 2009. *Your Sixth Sense: Unlocking the Power of Your Intuition*. New York: HarperOne.

Nichols, Michelle. 2013. " Pakistan's Malala, Shot by Taliban,, Takes Education Plea to UN, July 12. Accessed July 23, 2013. http://www.reuters.com/article/2013/07/12/us-malala-un-idUSBRE96B0IC20130712

Nicholson, Reynold, trans. 1990. *Mathnawi of Jalaluddin Rumi (3 Volume Set)*. Cambridge: Gibb Memorial Trust.

Oslie, Pamala. 2000. *Life Colors: What the Colors in Your Aura Reveal*. Novato: New World Library.

Panet, Richard. 2011. *The 4-Percent Universe: Dark Matter, Dark Energy, and the Race to Discover the Rest of Reality*. Boston: Houghton Mifflin Harcourt.

Pinckley, Christopher. 2008. *Reality Creation 101: Mastering Manifestation Through Awareness*. Charleston: BookSurge Publishing.

Plato, reprinted 2012. *The Republic*. Hollywood: Simon & Brown.

Rand, William. 2000. *Reiki: The Healing Touch-First and Second Degree Manual*. Southfield: Vision Publications.

Rinpoche, H. E. Kalu. 2004. *Foundations of Tibetan Buddhism*. Ithaca: Snow Lion Publications.

Robbyn and His Merrye Bande. 1993. "Why Have An Ego?." *Spirit Speaks*. 31-33.

Roberts, Jane. 1994. *The Nature of Personal Reality (A Seth Book): Specific, Practical Techniques for Solving Everyday Problems and Enriching the Life You Know*. San Rafael: Amber-Allen Publishing.

Roberts, Jane. 1994. *Seth Speaks*. San Rafaek: Amber-Allen Publishing.

Roman, Sanaya and Duane Packer. 2000. *Newsletter/Catalog (Spring & Summer): Awakening Your Light Body—Orin & DaBen*. Medford: LuminEssence Productions.

Roman, Sanaya and Orin. 2007. *Creating Money: Keys to Abundance*. Tiburon: HJ Kramer, Inc.

Roman, Sanaya and Orin. 1997. *Soul Love: Awakening Your Heart Centers*. Tiburon: HJ Kramer Inc.

Roman, Sanaya and Orin. 1992. *Spiritual Growth: Being Your Higher Self.* Tiburon: HJ Kramer Inc.

Roman, Sanaya and Duane Packer. 1993. *Opening to Channel: How to Connect with Your Guide*. Tiburon: HJ Kramer.

Roman, Sanaya and Orin. 1986. *Personal Power through Awareness: A Guidebook for Sensitive People*. Tiburon: HJ Kramer.

Rother, Steve and the Group. 2002. *A Welcome Home: The New Planet Earth*. Poway: Lightworker.

Rother, Steve and the Group. 2000. *Re-Member: A Handbook for Human Evolution*. Poway: Lightworker.

Saradananda, Swami. 2008. *Chakra Meditation: Discover Energy, Creativity, Focus, Love, Wisdom, and Spirit.* London: Duncan Baird Publishers.

Schucman, Helen. 2011. *A Course in Miracles: The Combined Original Edition.* Guilord: White Crow Books.

Schwartz, Gary. 2003. *The Afterlife Experiment: Breakthrough Scientific Evidence of Life After Death.* New York: Atria Books.

Shostak, Arthur, Ed. 2003. *Viable Utopian Ideas: Shaping A Better World.* Armonk: M E Sharpe, Inc.

Shroder, Tom. 2001. *Old Souls: Compelling Evidence from Children Who Remember Past Lives.* New York: Simon & Schuster (A Fireside Book).

Shumsky, Susan. 2005. *Exploring Auras: Cleansing and Strengthening Your Energy Field.* Franklin Lakes: New Page Books (A division of The Career Press, Inc.).

Small, Jacquelyn. 1994. *Transformers: The Artists of Self-Creation.* Camarillo: Devorss & Co.

Smith, Houston. 1989. *Beyond the Post-Modern Mind.* Wheaton: Quests Books, The Theosophical Publishing House.

Smith, Matthew. 2009. *Anomalous Experiences: Essays from Parapsychological and Psychological Perspectives.* Jefferson: McFarland & Company, Inc.

Smuts, J. C. 2010. *Holism and Evolution.* Whitefish: Kessinger Publihsing, LLC.

Sri S. Satchidananda, 1990. *The Yoga Sutras of Patanjali.* Translated by Edwin Bryant. New York: North Point Press.

Stack, Rick. 1988. *Out-Of-Body Adventures.* Lincolnwood: Contemporary Books.

Stein, Diane. 1995. *Essential Reiki: A Complete Guide to an Ancient Healing Art.* New York: Crossing Press (an imprint of the Crown Publishing Group, a division of Random House).

Stevenson, Ian. 2000. *Children Who Remember Past Lives: A Question of Reincarnation.* Jefferson: McFarland & Company, Inc, Publishers.

Todeschi, Kevin. 1998. *Edgar Cayce on the Akashic Records: The Book of Life.* Virginia Beach: A.R.E. Press.

Tolle, Eckhart. 2008. *A New Earth: Awakening to Your Life's Purpose.* New York: Penguin Group Inc.

Tolle, Eckhart. 2004. *The Power of Now: A Guide to Spiritual Enlightenment.* Novato: New World Library.

Trine, Cheryl. 2010. *The New Akashic Records: Knowing, Healing, and Spiritual Practice.* Portland: Essential Knowing Press.

Tucker, Jim. 2008. *Life Before Life: A Scientific Investigation of Children's Memories of Previous Lives.* New York: St. Martin's Press.

Valarino, Evelyn. 2006. *Lessons from the Light: When We Can Learn from the Near-Death Experience.* Needham: Moment Point Press, Inc.

Vasconcellos, John. 2002/2003. "Politics of Trust." *AHP Perspective.* December/January.

Vywamus and Barbara Burns. 1997. *Channelling: Evolutionary Exercises for Channels.* Flagstaff: Light Technology Publishing.

Wauters, Ambika. 1997. *Chakras and Their Archetypes: Uniting Energy Awareness and Spiritual Growth.* Freedom: The Crossing Press.

White, Ruth. 2009. *Using Your Chakras: A New Approach to Healing Your Life.* York Beach: Samuel Weiser, Inc.

Wilbur, Ken. 2003. *The Spectrum of Consciousness.* Wheaton: Quest Books.

Wilbur, Ken. 2000. *Sex, Ecology, Spirituality: The Spirit of Evolution.* Boston: Shambhala Publications, Inc.

Williamson, Marianne. 2006. *The Gift of Change: Spiritual Guidance for Living Your Best Life*. New York: HarperCollins Publishers, Inc.

Wolf, Fred Alan. 2000. *Mind into Matter: A New Alchemy of Science and Spirit*. Portsmouth: Moment Point Press, Inc.

Wolf, Fred Alan. 1998. *The Spiritual Universe: One Physicist's Vision of Spirit, Soul, Matter, and Self*. Portsmouth: Mount Point Press, Inc.

Wolf, Fred Alan. 1995. *The Dreaming Universe: A Mind-Expanding Journey into the Realm Where Psyche and Physics Meet*. New York: A Touchstone Book (Simon & Schuster).

Wolf, Fred Alan. 1990. *Parallel Universes: The Search for Other Worlds*. New York: A Touchstone Book (Simon & Schuster).

Wolf, Fred Alan. 1989. *Taking the Quantum Leap: The New Physics for Nonscientists*. New York: Harper & Row.

Wolf, Fred Alan. 1986. *The Body Quantum: The New Physics of Body, Mind and Health*. New York: Macmillan Publishing Co.

Wolf, Fred Alan. 1983. *Space-Time and Beyond*. New York: Bantam Books.

Wolf, Fred Allen. 1990. *Parallel Universes*. New York: Touchstone (A Division of Simon & Schuster, Inc.).

Woodhouse, Mark. 1996. *Paradigms Wars: Worldviews for a New Age*. Berkeley: Frog, Ltd. (North Atlantic Books).

Zukav, Gary. 1990. *The Seat of the Soul*. New York: A Fireside Book (Simon & Schuster).

ABOUT THE AUTHOR

Carroy U. Ferguson has a Ph.D. in Psychology from Boston College. He is currently Co-President (and Past President) of the Association for Humanistic Psychology, making history in 2006 as the first African American and first person of color to be President of this national and international Association. He is a tenured Professor and Past Acting Dean, College of Public and Community Service at University of Massachusetts-Boston, is a co-founder of two organizations (Interculture, Inc. and Associates in Human Understanding), has been a clinical practitioner for over thirty-five years, is a human relations, multicultural, and organizational development consultant, and workshop facilitator, is an Associate Editor of the *Journal of Humanistic Psychology*, and is a published author of books, articles, and other writings. (e.g., *A New Perspective on Race and Color; Transitions in Consciousness from an African American Perspective;* and *Innovative Approaches to Education and Community Service*).

INDEX

Old souls 181
Om 285
One-dimensional linear
    experience 23
Oneness 75, 79, 162
One, the 45
Operation Compassion 315
Original Spiritual Families 314
Ornstein, Robert 71
Oslie, Pamela 242, 371
Other, the 2, 17, 34, 54, 113,
    129, 172, 220, 229,
    237, 241, 347, 360
  Bad, alien, foreign, or dif-
    ferent other 34
Other-oriented karma
  Race-related karma 286
Other race 112, 129, 210,
    270, 300, 331
Outer creations 149
Outer-oriented 122
Outer Self 27, 29, 35, 36, 39, 47,
    50, 51, 101, 105, 107, 115,
    117, 121, 143, 146, 150, 152,
    153, 155, 160, 161, 162, 164,
    171, 173, 182, 189, 191, 195,
    196, 197, 201, 206, 207, 208,
    218, 220, 222, 223, 224, 225,
    228, 231, 236, 238, 239, 242,
    243, 250, 252, 268, 273, 275,
    281, 282, 283, 284, 292, 293,
    298, 301, 307, 308, 310, 311,
    318, 323, 326, 327, 331, 335,
    338, 339, 351, 359, 360, 361
Outer Vibrational world or
    experience 45, 55
Overarching Social Movement 312
Over-identification
  Ethnic or tribal over-
    identification 34
Overleaf Understandings 352, 353

P

Pace v Alabama 108
Packer, Duane (DaBen) 266, 372
Panet, Richard 371
Paradigm
  New paradigm 39
  Old paradigm 39, 71, 73, 123
  Paradigm Shift 4, 38, 57, 58, 232
Parent/Child interracial role
    relationships 168
Past lives 252, 269, 270
  Past-life therapy 267
Patanjali 72, 373
Path of the Bridger 9, 27,
    163, 185, 187
Patience 75, 159
Peace 3, 93, 97, 161, 163, 171, 174,
    178, 191, 203, 204, 252, 254,
    257, 283, 312, 313, 344
Peace movement 313
Pearl, Eric 296
Perennialists 72, 115
Personal and Group
    Consciousness 27
Personal Energy System 47, 96,
    97, 98, 101, 107, 121, 145,
    152, 163, 171, 178, 195, 225,
    228, 235, 239, 240, 253,
    298, 299, 326, 338, 344
Personal Heart-Centered
    Devices 303
Personality 11, 12, 13, 14, 21, 22,
    26, 41, 45, 50, 52, 59, 66,
    67, 68, 72, 73, 76, 77, 78,
    82, 88, 93, 97, 98, 103, 106,
    107, 110, 113, 114, 115,
    116, 119, 120, 121, 122, 125,
    128, 137, 144, 151, 153, 167,
    168, 177, 180, 181, 183, 188,
    190, 191, 192, 196, 200, 208,

Transformers- The Artists of
Self Creation 373
Trine, Cheryl 374
True power 120
Truer Self 9, 185, 187, 215, 217
Trust 75, 106, 152, 153, 227,
313, 366, 371, 374
Truth 75, 79, 115, 158, 365
Tucker, Jim 374

U

Ultimate Ground of Being 42
Unconditional Love 111, 190,
199, 200, 359, 360
Unconscious Mind 50, 51
Universal Energy Laws 91
Table of Seven Universal
Energy Laws 92
Universal Governing Energy
Principles 42
Universal laws of relationships 215
Universal Life-Force Energy 295
Universal Love 183
Universal strings 249, 252
Upanishads 72
Usui, Mikao 295

V

Valarino, Evelyn 374
Value judgments 79, 118, 124, 138,
139, 167, 241, 291, 308
Van Hulle, J. P. 52
Vasconcellos, John 16, 374
Vaughan, Frances 16
Vibrational bodies and realities 38
Vibrational Energies 29,
44, 45, 47, 48
Vibrational feeling-tone 48
Vibrational fields 41, 255
Vibrational Harmony

Principle of 205, 218, 235, 237
Vibrational mental tools 51
Vibrational reality (ies)
Of the Higher Self or Higher
Consciousness 44
Vibrational Universe 46
Vibrational World
Of Experience and Wisdom 43
Vicente, Mark 363
Victimization 77
Virtual Reality 306
Visible auras
"Gift" of 233, 240, 241
Vision 36, 71, 89, 93, 97, 98, 154,
162, 171, 177, 191, 192, 203,
205, 214, 219, 232, 233, 234,
238, 252, 254, 257, 268,
312, 336, 342, 343, 352
Visualization 95, 241, 250,
274, 279, 280
Vywamus 266, 374

W

Warmoth, Arthur 16
Watcher, the 45
Wauters, Ambika 374
White race 61, 203
White, Ruth 374
Whole Self 73, 153, 155, 170, 183,
195, 208, 225, 267, 359
Wilbur, Ken 374
Williamson, Marianne 375
Williams, Robert L. 16
Will to act, the 177
Will to cause, the 177
Will to evolve, the 177
Will to express, the 177
Will to harmonize, the 177
Will to initiate, the 177
Will to unify, the 177
Winfrey, Oprah 98, 267